Linguistic Data Science and the English Passive

Language, Data Science and Digital Humanities

Series editors: Mikko Laitinen (University of Eastern Finland, Finland) and Jukka Tyrkkö (Linnaeus University, Sweden)

The growing availability of computer-readable language data, increasing computational power and rapidly evolving statistical methodologies have had a profound effect on how scholars study and analyse human language use. However, the fields of linguistics, computer science and digital humanities have largely developed their own separate approaches and paradigms, often failing to communicate across disciplines in an effective way.

Language, Data Science and Digital Humanities bridges these disciplinary gaps by publishing monographs and edited volumes that explore disciplinary synergies and introduce new theoretical principles. Written in clear and transparent language, these books offer cutting-edge digital methodologies and create new opportunities for understanding how problems and research questions can be approached from different perspectives.

The methodological range of the series covers empirical linguistics, natural language processing, machine learning, data visualization, text mining, mark-up and annotation, statistical tools in analysing language data, and multimodal analysis. The volumes explain methodological solutions in detail using worked examples, and are supported by companion websites, allowing authors to share primary data, scripts, sophisticated data visualizations and other digital content.

Editorial Board

Titles in the series

Linguistics across Disciplinary Borders, edited by Steven Coats and Veronika Laippala
Text Analytics for Corpus Linguistics and Digital Humanities, Gerold Schneider

Linguistic Data Science and the English Passive

Modeling Diachronic Developments and Regional Variation

Axel Bohmann, Julia Müller, Mirka Honkanen, and
Miriam Neuhausen

BLOOMSBURY ACADEMIC
LONDON • NEW YORK • OXFORD • NEW DELHI • SYDNEY

BLOOMSBURY ACADEMIC
Bloomsbury Publishing Plc, 50 Bedford Square, London, WC1B 3DP, UK
Bloomsbury Publishing Inc, 1359 Broadway, New York, NY 10018, USA
Bloomsbury Publishing Ireland, 29 Earlsfort Terrace, Dublin 2, D02 AY28, Ireland

First published in Great Britain 2026

Series design: Elena Durey
Cover image © Reinhard Dirscherl/Getty Images

A catalogue record for this book is available from the British Library.

A catalog record for this book is available from the Library of Congress.

ISBN: HB: 978-1-3503-8654-9
ePDF: 978-1-3503-8655-6
eBook: 978-1-3503-8656-3

Series: Language, Data Science and Digital Humanities

Typeset by Newgen KnowledgeWorks Pvt. Ltd., Chennai, India

For product safety related questions contact productsafety@bloomsbury.com.

To find out more about our authors and books visit www.bloomsbury.com and sign up for our newsletters.

Online resources to accompany this book are available at https://www.bloomsburyonlineresources.com/language-data-science-and-digital-humanities. If you experience any problems, please contact Bloomsbury at: onlineresources@bloomsbury.com

We dedicate this book to our supervisor, teacher, and colleague Christian Mair.

Contents

Figures

Tables

Acknowledgments

This project initially unfolded after a Python basics workshop at the University of Freiburg and over the years grew into a research project that easily filled a book.

As is always the case, numerous colleagues and friends were involved in the development of our thoughts, the theorizing of our arguments, and the application of the theory in the analysis of specific data.

We would like to thank the numerous audiences, peer reviewers, and exchanges that our project has benefited from: the research colloquium at the English Department at the University of Freiburg, organizers and participants at the 2020 IRG Symposium in Fribourg and ICAME 41, the anonymous Bloomsbury reviewers, and, of course, the highly productive exchange with numerous colleagues who gave us extensive input and feedback—Alice Blumenthal-Dramé (who always has amazing ideas), Lotte Sommerer (who translated cognitive linguistics into sociolinguistics for us), Mathias Seyfert (who provided coding support), Richard Zimmermann (who offered detailed and valuable feedback), Florent Perek (who shared insights into distributional modeling at an early stage of our project), Jiří Zámečník (for sharing his code with us), and, last but not least, Axel's and Julia's wizard computers as well as the powerful machines in the Digital Humanities Lab at the University of Freiburg that ran our models on masses of data over the course of days or sometimes even weeks. We would also like to thank Faina Krasnopolska for bearing with us and helping us with a major part of the formatting jobs—despite the fact that their thesis deadline was the same as for our book—and Theresa Heyd for providing research assistant hours.

1

Introduction

When speakers and writers of English produce a verb phrase in the passive voice, they are presented with two options in the auxiliary slot: *be* or *get* can act as the passive auxiliary, as in Examples (1) and (2).

(1) I knew that plane had gotten hit by lightning. (COHA/1975/news)[1]

(2) I knew that plane had been hit by lightning.

This apparently simple binary alternation has garnered significant interest in the linguistic community since the 1930s (Rice 1932), and particularly so over the past fifty years (e.g., Chappell 1980; Collins 1996; Fleisher 2006; Schwarz 2018). Weiner and Labov (1983: 43) even refer to it as "one of the most active grammatical changes taking place in English." Yet, many of the nuances conditioning the selection of *be* or *get* remain elusive. The present book addresses this issue in what is to our knowledge the first large-scale quantitative analysis of the English passive alternation, relying on big corpus data and sophisticated methods from machine learning and natural language processing.

There are a number of reasons why findings on the English passive remain inconclusive to date and why the methods we outline on the pages of this book are necessary. First among these is the fact that two changes are involved, which cannot be considered in isolation from each other. The GET-passive is a recent and rapidly expanding innovation, associated with informal and spoken registers. At the same time, the passive on the whole appears to have been declining in frequency, a development linked to the overall informalization of (written) English (Dixon 2005: 354; Leech et al. 2009: 164). The speed of the change toward *get* and the related register dynamics make any statements about constraints on the alternation highly volatile and render native-speaker intuitions problematic, especially where they come in the form of categorical statements.

The next issue lies in the operationalization of constraints on the passive alternation. The GET-passive was first discussed as a "dynamic counterpart" of the BE-passive, but later scholars have emphasized semantic, pragmatic, and syntactic differences between the two constructions (Toyota 2008: 17, 148). However, many of the conditioning factors supposedly favoring *get*—that it is used when something good happens to the sentence subject or especially when something bad befalls them and when the subject referent potentially carries some responsibility over the situation—are relatively subtle, subjective features that have not been amenable to formal operationalization and thus large-scale hypothesis testing. Much of what has been proposed concerning the strength and direction of these constraints thus remains anecdotal or at least contested. Restrictions have also been suggested in how the GET-passive combines with sentence elements such as adverbials, *by*-phrases expressing an agent, *to*-complements, or certain sentence subjects and verb tenses. Overall, more has been suggested than has been supported by data, and it is not clear which of these restrictions continue to apply as the GET-passive has been becoming more and more frequent over time. A big part of the motivation for the present book is to develop automated operationalizations of these constraints in a way that allows subjecting them to testing based on large datasets.

What makes investigating the passive alternation particularly difficult is the fact that the passive as a whole is not a clearly delimited phenomenon. It is not readily distinguished by surface form alone from other constructions, such as copular verb phrases with adjectival participles as in Example (3) or idiomatic expressions as in Example (4).

(3) She got bored sitting there. (COHA/1977/fiction)

(4) both men wanted to get started as soon as possible (COHA/1996/nonfiction)

The GET-passive in particular needs to be understood in relation to a wider range of constructions. It involves the high-frequency lexeme *get*, such as lexical verb *get* meaning "obtain, fetch," which can be monotransitive, as shown in Example (5) or ditransitive, as illustrated in Example (6). It also covers the meanings "receive" in Example (7) or "reach, arrive" in Example (8). *Get* with inchoative meaning is illustrated in Example (9), while examples of possessive and existential (*have*) *got* are provided in (10)–(11). Last but not least, semi-modal (*have*) *got to* is displayed in (12). *Get* may also co-occur in form of various particle verbs, such as *get at*, *get into*, and so on (Biber, Conrad, & Leech 2003: 171–2). For more details on these different uses, see Bruckmaier (2017).

(5) We all sat down, except Ronni, who got coffee from the room service wagon and began to serve it. (COHA/1983/fiction)

(6) I got my mom her own tv in the guest room with headphones. (GloWbE/Hong Kong/blog)[2]

(7) I got mail. I got a wonderful letter from my old Sunday school teacher. (COHA/1977/TV/movies)

(8) The old woman went home. And when she got home her daughter awoke. (COHA/1887/nonfiction)

(9) Antarctica is getting colder and increasing mass. (GloWbE/Australia/general)

(10) He's got two fantastic sisters, he couldn't possibly need anyone else. (GloWbE/India/general)

(11) Then you've got the eight meter long octopus. (Bruckmaier 2017: 125)

(12) You have got to tell the family; nobody can do it better. (COHA/1865/fiction)

Get is among the lemmas that show the most drastic frequency increase across the time span covered by the Corpus of Historical American English (COHA, Davies 2010). Its normalized frequency increases almost tenfold between the 1820s and the 2010s, from 325.15 to 3,250.21 instances per million words. When testing for the most rapidly rising surface forms in the corpus via the Spearman correlation between frequency and year (as argued for in Grieve, Nini, & Guo 2017), "getting" occupies place 32 out of the 18,000 most frequent types, and "get" place 156. While we do not investigate other nonpassive uses of *get*, the question remains what role the GET-passive plays in this observation and to what extent it contributes to the general frequency increase of *get*.

In addition to prototypical passives and instances that clearly cannot be conceived of as any kind of a passive, there is also a significant gray area where a participle is more verbal or more adjectival, which has inspired several grammarians to posit a "passive scale" (Svartvik 1966: 156) or a "passive gradient" (Quirk et al. 1985: 167). We acknowledge the complexity of the phenomenon and take steps to eliminate clearly nonpassive instances from our analysis (see Chapter 3).

While the above paragraphs highlight the need for a robust empirical and quantitatively based analysis, this difficulty in delineating the feature and defining the relevant envelope of variation has not been conducive to large-scale analyses of the English passive alternation. As a consequence, almost all research to date has restricted itself to relatively low numbers of manually selected and annotated examples. Early papers on the passive tended to rely on invented examples as data and a single researcher's intuitions as grammaticality judgments (e.g., Hatcher

1949; Chappell 1980; Sussex 1982). These studies were important in raising awareness of the passive alternation as a noteworthy subject of investigation, but their results have limited relevance at present. The next wave of studies started quantifying the differences between the two constructions using empirical data and discussing the restrictions in the use of the GET-passive and, in some cases, the potential loss of these restrictions over time. However, many studies relied on small, handcoded datasets and have therefore not produced representative results (e.g., Collins 1996; Hundt 2001a; Fehringer 2022).

Today's large corpora and advances in natural language processing and quantitative methods enable new kinds of investigations that consider the weight of and interactions between different predictor variables conditioning a dependent linguistic variable, such as the choice of the passive auxiliary. In one of the first mixed-model studies, Fehringer (2022) examines the passive alternation in a diachronic corpus of spoken British English from Tyneside. Unlike other studies that have tended to suggest that the increasing frequency of the GET-variant has led to a loosening of semantic and syntactic restrictions in its use, Fehringer (2022: 23–4) concludes that the GET-passive is an "important pragmatic marker" and that an increased use of a construction does not seem to automatically mean that constraints on its use weaken. In a similar vein, Mair and Leech (2020: 268) are convinced that the GET-passive has not "been involved in any direct grammatical changes in the past century," but its growing frequency represents "a discourse phenomenon," essentially a symptom of colloquialization. In this book, we examine these claims and others that have been made about the conditioning of the passive, in terms of the relative frequency of the two constructions and constraints influencing the choice between these, relying on two large datasets reflecting overtime as well as regional variation in Present-Day English.

The first of our two studies aims to map diachronic developments in the English passive alternation. Changes in the passive have been reported to be more noticeable in American than in British English (Leech et al. 2009: 148, 156). We examine change in the passive in American English over the past two hundred years, employing the Corpus of Historical American English (COHA, Davies 2010). COHA is a diachronic corpus representing five genres (fiction, magazines, newspapers, nonfiction books, and TV and movie) and nearly two centuries of American English in approximately 475 million words. In a second study, we investigate synchronic regional variation in the passive, drawing on twenty varieties of English represented in the corpus of Global Web-based English (GloWbE, Davies 2013): United States, Canada, Great Britain, Ireland, Australia, New Zealand, India, Sri Lanka, Pakistan, Bangladesh, Singapore,

Malaysia, Philippines, Hong Kong, South Africa, Nigeria, Ghana, Kenia, Tanzania, and Jamaica. The 1.9 billion words in this corpus were collected from blogs and other websites. In addition to the predictors generally hypothesized to condition the passive alternation, we draw on the status of English and substrate influence in the respective countries as potential explanations for the tendencies we find. In both studies, we test the influence of constraints relating to formality, subject responsibility, adversativity, non-neutrality, and the structure of the sentence as suggested in previous literature.

This book presents not only two studies on the passive alternation but also a collection of methods and resources that can be applied to other cases of linguistics variation. In this sense, the book is situated in the context of the emerging field of computational sociolinguistics (Nguyen et al. 2016). The common denominator in our approach is that it shifts the analytical procedure from a simple statistical study of a given phenomenon to a data-analysis pipeline, where statistical procedures are applied to approximate and delimit the various dependent and independent variables to be analyzed. To circumscribe our outcome variable, we employ a binomial logistic regression model that distinguishes central from less central passives. For testing the hypothesized role of subject agency in the choice of passive auxiliary, we draw on dependency parsing in order to identify the head of the subject noun phrase and assign it a category on an animacy scale. In addition, we approach the purported effects of adversativity or non-neutrality through sentiment analysis, which we apply both at the level of the individual verbal participle and at the level of the entire clause containing the passive verb phrase. For this purpose—to detect the sentiment of the clause—we train our own classifier. We further draw on word embeddings—the representation of words as vectors in high-dimensional space—to investigate particular collocational effects of individual verb classes. Such an approach to probabilistically deriving predictor variables, sometimes referred to as feature engineering, is established in machine learning and data science contexts but remains underutilized in variationist linguistics. Yet, with the size of available corpora ever increasing, attempts to automate and streamline variable coding carry enormous potential, especially where hypothesized constraints are less than clear-cut. We hope the approach introduced here may serve as a model for other variationist studies in the future. To maximize the utility of our approach to other researchers, we make available all code underlying the analyses reported in this book via the companion website.[3]

The book is structured as follows: Chapter 2 delves into the extensive previous literature on the passive alternation, first introducing the passive voice in general and then zooming in on the English GET-passive in particular. We discuss its origin and its suggested characteristics one by one and illustrate the findings of previous sociolinguistic studies regarding the conditioning of the passive alternation, including classic sociodemographic variables and variation across regional varieties of English. Chapter 3 returns to the issue of the passive gradient—the fact that any automatic form-based retrieval method will also collect observations that are superficially reminiscent of the passive but do not semantically correspond to it, fully or at all. We illustrate previous criteria and solutions to distinguishing central passives from noncentral ones and from nonpassives, and present our own automated approach. Chapters 4 to 6 address different alleged semantic features of the GET-passive and describe how we operationalize these in our analysis. Chapter 4 discusses subject responsibility—the idea that the subject of the GET-passive may be held partly accountable for the events that take place. Chapter 5 considers the claim that the GET-passive expresses adverse or beneficial events and describes our approach to it through sentiment analysis. In Chapter 6, we explore the idea that the passive alternation may be sensitive to verb semantics, with certain groups of verbs preferring *be* as passive auxiliary more strongly and others co-occurring with *get*, and how we investigate this with a distributional semantic model. Chapter 7 lays the ground for an investigation of regional variation in the English passive by discussing potential substrate influence from local languages on the different varieties of English considered in our analysis. Chapter 8 outlines the remaining independent variables and describes the entire structure of the two mixed-effects models employed.

The next two chapters, Chapters 9 and 10, are dedicated to presenting and discussing the results of our analyses. We present our two datasets (COHA and GloWbE) and two case studies involving mixed-effects regression models, and visualize and discuss all significant main effects and interactions. While Chapter 9 explores changes in the passive alternation over time based on written American English from several genres and nearly two centuries, Chapter 10 investigates the passive in varieties of English around the world, relying on web-based writing in blogs and on other websites. Finally, in Chapter 11, we compare our findings with previous studies and strive to provide a big picture of what our analyses reveal concerning the conditioning of the passive alternation. Moreover, this concluding chapter outlines where we think the passive construction is heading, discusses possible directions for future research on the passive alternation, as well as evaluates the methods developed in the course of the book and presents ideas for their further application.

2

The English Passive Voice: *Be* and *Get*

In this chapter, we define the passive voice and show that active and passive categories are not always clearly distinct. We subsequently lay out potential origins of the GET-passive and discuss several factors that have been linked to the GET-passive in previous studies, such as subject responsibility, adversativity versus non-neutrality, formality and genre, and syntactic constraints.

2.1 Defining the Passive

Voice is a grammatical category that expresses the relation between an event and its participants, that is, the way that semantic roles map onto syntactic functions (Huddleston & Pullum 2002: 68). The major reference grammars (Huddleston & Pullum 2002: 68; Biber, Conrad, & Leech 1999: 475–6; Quirk et al. 1985: 57–8) treat passive clauses as transformations of active clauses, with the object of the latter assuming the role of subject and the verb phrase being formed with *be* or *get* followed by a past participle. In addition, a middle voice exists in some languages, which shares characteristics of both active and passive constructions. In English, however, the middle forms a minor category and is morphologically indistinct from active constructions. Still, a ternary distinction is often maintained on a combination of morpho-syntactic and semantic grounds: in the active voice, the subject is in control of the action and not impacted by it; in the passive voice, the subject is impacted by the action but not in control of it; and in the middle voice, the subject is both the entity impacted by the action and usually also shares some responsibility for bringing about the action (Croft 1991: 248).[1] Examples (13)–(15) illustrate these categories in the English language.

(13) My company sells books. (active voice; GloWbE/Canada/blog)

(14) These books are sold internationally and many of them have been translated into other languages. (passive voice; GloWbE/Kenya/general)

(15) I hope that your book sells well (middle voice; GloWbE/Great Britain/blog)

In the active sentence (13), the subject "my company" is the agent (the doer) of the act of selling, and the object "books" is the patient (affected entity). In (14), the patient "these books" acts as the grammatical subject, while the agent has been omitted; this is a classic passive. The middle voice in (15) has the target of selling in the subject position, with the implication that the qualities of the book matter in whether it is sold or not. There is no grammatical object but often an adverb of manner, here *well*. In natural speech, the active is the unmarked, canonical voice and the overwhelmingly most frequent one. The active subject can take on semantic roles as well beyond that of the agent. The middle voice is morphologically marked in some languages (Kemmer 1993) but may lack overt marking in many others, including English.

The passive accomplishes discourse-pragmatic and stylistic functions. This includes regulating given and new information, centering or decentering participants in a situation, and contributing to a more impersonal and concise style, such as in academic or news writing (Granger 1983: 8–10; Quirk et al. 1985: 166; Biber, Conrad, & Leech 2003: 168–9; Huddleston & Pullum 2002: chap. 16; Dixon 2005: 354–7). Huddleston and Pullum (2002: 1366) consider the passive an "information-packaging construction": clauses that differ only in voice display the same content but vary in how the content is presented (2002: 46). The use of the passive is said to be conditioned by modality (e.g., speech vs. writing in Biber, Conrad, & Leech 2003: 167) and genre (Quirk et al. 1985: 166; Phoocharoensil 2020). In this book, we focus on the passive voice in the English language.

In English, the passive voice is marked through word order, a supporting verb, and inflection. The passive verb phrase consists prototypically of an auxiliary that is either *be* or *get* and a past participle of the lexical verb. The affected patient is the passive subject, while the agent is syntactically pushed back to a *by*-prepositional phrase (PP) or omitted. Further auxiliaries marking tense and aspect may be included but are rare (Biber, Conrad, & Leech 2003: 169). The auxiliary may be omitted, for example, in some relative and adverbial clauses (Wanner 2009: 83–5) and genres, such as news headlines. Such "bare passives" (Huddleston & Pullum 2002: 1265) may constitute a significant portion of all passives in some genres (Wanner 2009: 170) but are not relevant to the present study, where we investigate the choice between *be* and *get* in the passive sentence.

Some scholars place the GET-passive in-between the middle and passive voices or in both categories (Hundt 2001a; Toyota 2008; Mitkovska & Bužarovska 2012). Downing (1996: 183), for instance, considers the GET-passive a "hybrid" with features of both a passive and "a copula of becoming." Others do not accept the construction *get* + past participle as a passive voice for different reasons. For some, *get* is not a passive auxiliary because its syntactic behavior and semantic profile differ from those of *be* (e.g., Haegeman 1985; Banks 1986; Hundt 2001a; Toyota 2008). Firstly, observing their syntactic properties, *be* is a full auxiliary in the passive sentence, while *get* does not have the "NICE properties" (Huddleston 1976) of an auxiliary but behaves syntactically like a lexical verb (e.g., Haegeman 1985: 54–5; Downing 1996: 183): it requires *do*-support in interrogative and negated sentences and does not occur in tag questions and other ellipsis constructions. Secondly, as the subject of the GET-passive arguably may exert some responsibility or control over the situation, some scholars see a closer semantic connection between the GET-passive and causative *get* than with the BE-passive (Dixon 2005: 358; Cho & Ahn 2017: 299). Arce-Arenales, Axelrod, and Fox (1994: 17) even propose that instances of *get* + past participle should be "treated as active constructions." However, they focus disproportionately on special cases, such as *getting dressed* or *laid*. Similarly, Banks (1986: 125) argues that GET-passives have no semantically equivalent active counterpart and should thus not be classified as such.

By contrast, others argue that even the BE-passive implies some agency. Carter and McCarthy (1999: 43) disagree with the idea of the GET-passive as fundamentally different from the BE-passive in terms of agency, believing that "degrees of focus on agency are evident in all passive clauses."

The English passive is best conceptualized as a fuzzy category, with a cline from central to less central to nonpassive forms. Numerous scholars have pointed out that there is no unambiguous boundary between verbal-dynamic and adjectival-stative meanings of formally identical participles (e.g., Biber, Conrad, & Leech 2003: 167). There are also formally similar constructions with *get* that do not fit the definition of passive fully or at all (see also Chapter 1). Many scholars have posited a continuum ranging from prototypical passives to less prototypical ones (e.g., Carter & McCarthy 1999: 47). We address this cline in more detail in Chapter 3. The rest of this chapter will focus on the GET-passive and its characteristics and alternation with the BE-passive as discussed in previous literature.

On the semantic level, one undisputable difference between *be* and *get* preceding a past participle is that only the latter construction is always dynamic, that is, denotes an action and not its outcome (Huddleston & Pullum 2002: 1422). Replacing *be* with *get* eliminates a potential ambiguity (Quirk et al. 1985: 162; Wanner 2009: 87), theoretically present in sentences such as Example (16), which may depict either a past event (passive) or a past state (nonpassive); by contrast, *get*, as in Example (17), is restricted to a dynamic interpretation.

(16) The house was painted white on the front (COHA/1950/fiction)
(17) the house and outbuildings too got painted (COHA/1959/fiction)

It is not clear how relevant dynamicity is in the passive alternation. Downing (1996: 184) points out that in her dataset ($N = 846$), the overwhelming majority of GET-passives is clearly dynamic—and would be even if we changed the auxiliary to *be*. Disambiguation might not be a major reason for choosing *get* as a passive auxiliary. In fact, some constructions with *get* remain ambiguous: if the participle can be construed as an adjective, the sentence may, instead of a passive past event, express an inchoative meaning: the beginning of a new state (cf. Chapter 3).

Even after acknowledging these complications, we call *get* a passive auxiliary and the construction of interest the GET-passive. This decision is made not only for convenience's sake but also because our approach assumes that the speaker does have a choice between *be* and *get* in many situations. *Get* followed by past participle may express a passive meaning, although depending on the lexical context, it may have additional or alternative semantic nuances, too. That the syntactic behavior of *get* deviates from a prototypical auxiliary is not a problem from the usage-based perspective we are adopting here. Before discussing the sociolinguistic, syntactic, and semantic conditioning of the passive alternation, we briefly address the origin and grammaticalization of the GET-passive.

2.2 Origins of the GET-Passive

The English passive constructions can be traced back to Old and Middle English, which had two main passive auxiliaries: *bēon/wesan* "be" and *weorðan* "become" (Toyota 2008: 152; Fryd 2009: 277). The latter disappeared during the sixteenth century, but another variant appeared in the nineteenth century: *get* (Toyota 2008: 152). Increasingly frequent, *get* developed a range of interrelated meanings and grammatical functions over the course of the nineteenth and twentieth centuries (Hundt 2001a: 77). The lexical verb *get*, in Middle English *geten*, had been borrowed from Scandinavian languages in the thirteenth century (Fryd 2009: 280). Its meaning broadened from a verb of acquisition to a verb of reception or possession (Fryd 2009: 280–1; see Chapter 1 for an overview of different functions of *get* with example sentences). The earliest alleged evidence of the GET-passive dates back to the mid-seventeenth century, but its use remained "sporadic" until the nineteenth century (Fleisher 2006: 227). Since then, *get* has established itself as an alternative to *be* in many passive contexts.

The exact origin of the GET-passive is uncertain, and we will focus on two competing theories in the following. While some scholars maintain that the construction derives from inchoative *get* (e.g., Gronemeyer 1999; Fleisher 2006; Honda 2012), others see a path through reflexive causative sentences as more likely (e.g., Haegeman 1985; Givón & Yang 1994; Hundt 2001a; Dixon 2005; Toyota 2008).

According to the first view, the GET-passive developed from inchoative *get*, that is, a verb marking the beginning of an action or situation. Both inchoative and passive *get* imply the beginning of a new situation, so they have a natural semantic connection (Fleisher 2006: 229). Another necessary piece of the puzzle is the "morpho-syntactic" and "semantic ambiguity" of forms like *married*, *frustrated*, or *involved* in-between adjectives and verbs (Fleisher 2006: 236; Honda 2012: 81). According to this theory, inchoative *get* + adjectival passive participle got "reanalyzed" as passive *get* + verbal participle (Fleisher 2006: 230–2). Arguably, *get* first occurred with adjectival participles but later also with ambiguous and verbal ones (Honda 2012: 72). Some researchers (Fleisher 2006; Honda 2012) analyze the emergence of the GET-passive within the generative framework. While this theory is plausible concerning the development of the main verb, it does not account for the selection of *get* as a passive form and the semantic changes it has undergone (Toyota 2008: 175–6).

The alternative line of thinking suggests that the GET-passive stems from a middle or reflexive usage of *get*, through the following intermediate steps (Toyota 2008: 176):

(a) onset of possession, lexical *get* "fetch"

(18) He gets her a present. (Toyota 2008: 180)

(b) causative *get*

(19) He gets her to say some words (Toyota 2008: 179)

(c) causative reflexive *get oneself*

(20) One of the most costly, splendid, and elaborate structures in the world … got itself built. (Oliphant 1877: 12; cited in Toyota 2008: 181)

(d) causative reflexive *get* + past participle

(21) I am resolv'd to get introduced to Mrs Annabella. (Powell 1693: 10; cited in Toyota 2008: 181)

Note that, while (21) does not include a reflexive pronoun, Toyota (2008: 182) maintains that examples like this "can imply a reflexive reading" and consequently treats them as inherently reflexive. According to this view, possessive *get* could first be used for "causing someone to possess something," which developed into causative "cause someone to do something" (Toyota 2008: 177–9). The details of the process, discussed in Givón and Yang (1994: 124) and in Toyota (2008: 177–9), lie beyond the scope of our treatment. Importantly, the meaning of *get* "changed from possession (or causation of possession) to causation alone" (Toyota 2008: 179). The appearance of a reflexive pronoun created clauses that share characteristics with the middle voice (Toyota 2008: 182). However, sometimes, this reflexive pronoun was not overtly present, and when the subject gradually lost control over the situation, the sentence could be read as passive (Toyota 2008: 184). Arguably, this path of origin accounts for the meaning of "subject responsibility," often associated with the GET-passive (Dixon 2005: 358). Critical voices, such as Fleisher (2006: 240), a proponent of the first view, hold that this theory does not sufficiently explain the change in the status of the subject from the reflexive to the passive sentences on the semantic and syntactic levels. Similarly, Honda (2012: 79–80) argues that a causative reflexive with a participle was very rare during the onset of the emergence of the GET-passive. For the purposes of our study, it is not necessary to take a stand on which of these theories explain the emergence of the GET-passive in a more credible way.

There is also a body of literature focusing on the passive alternation from a second language acquisition perspective (e.g., Pinker, Lebeaux, & Frost 1987; Marchman et al. 1991; Israel, Johnson, & Brooks 2001; Hinkel 2002) and from a generative universal grammar point of view (e.g., Lakoff 1971; Levin & Rappaport 1986; Reed 2011; Alexiadou & Schäfer 2013; McIntyre 2013; Deng 2017). Similarly, the "passive transformation" played a key role in Chomsky's (1957) generative theory. As these approaches are not directly relevant for the sociolinguistic conditioning of the variable, we do not address them here.

Instead, the following sections focus on the literature on the passive alternation as a linguistic variable and the factors conditioning its use. These are the aspects immediately relevant for our study of the competition between *get* and *be* in passive constructions in the past 200 years and across the English-speaking world.

2.3 Variation between *Be* and *Get* in the Recent History of English

This section presents an overview of previous sociolinguistic studies on the English passive alternation. Of the numerous studies devoted to the English passive, some explore diachronic change but relatively few deal with regional and other synchronic variation. The focus has largely been on British and American English, although first studies into the passive in World Englishes have also been carried out. Overall, fairly small datasets have been used. After observing overtime developments and regional differences, we will discuss studies exploring other sociolinguistic variables, including age, gender, and class.

Many diachronic corpus studies report an increased use of the GET-passive relative to the BE-passive over time (e.g., Sneller & Fisher 2015; Schwarz 2017; Fehringer 2022: 13). In the *TIME* magazine corpus (Davies 2007), covering 275,000 articles from the eponymous American news magazine released between 1926 and 2006, Schwarz (2017: 314) finds a significant rise in the use of *get* only in the latter half of the twentieth century, accompanied by a simultaneous, much more dramatic decline in the use of the BE-passive. This decline is of such a magnitude that the increasing popularity of *get* may at most be a minor factor among many feeding this development (Mair & Leech 2020: 268). It seems that, overall, the passive is being used less than before.

Despite these changes, it is important to note that the BE-passive remains overall much more frequent than its younger competitor. For example, for each GET-passive in Brown (Francis & Kučera 1963–4), LOB (Leech, Johansson, & Hofland 1970–8), Frown (Mair 1992–6), and FLOB (Mair 1991–6)—four reference corpora representing published written English from the United States and the UK in 1961 and 1991—there are 400 BE-passives (Leech et al. 2009: 156). It is only for a handful of verbs, such as *caught*, *paid*, *smashed*, and *hit*, that *get* truly competes with *be* (Leech et al. 2009: 158).

The overwhelming preference for *be* has been attested particularly in written data and may not apply to all spoken contexts. In Fehringer's (2022: 5–6) interview data from Northern England in the 1960s to the 2000s, the GET-passive comprises 37.4 percent ($n = 296$) of all passives ($N = 792$).

Moreover, the GET-passive may be socially constrained. For some social groups, particularly African-American speakers in New York City and Philadelphia (Labov et al. 1968: 254; Weiner & Labov 1983: 43), the GET-passive may be the preferred variant, as will be discussed later in this section.

Most studies on the GET-passive have investigated varieties of British and American English, particularly the Brown family of corpora, which allows for comparisons across time, genres, and varieties. This set of four corpora of one million words each covers British English (BrE) and American English (AmE) in the 1960s and the 1990s. Studies report slightly differing frequency counts for the GET-passive in these corpora depending on their retrieval methods and coding criteria, which mirrors the difficulty of judging what a passive sentence is (see also Chapter 3). Table 1 shows the ranges of reported frequencies in different studies (Collins 1996: 54; Hundt 2001a: 87; Mair & Leech 2020: 268; Wanner 2013: 51; Bruckmaier 2017: 100). In both varieties, we observe a slight increase in the use of the GET-passive over time, but it seems steeper in AmE.

Most studies on the GET-passive have involved regional comparisons between BrE and AmE, while research considering other varieties is still relatively rare. Studies have suggested further regional differences in the use of the GET-passive, but these claims are often based on mere comparisons of frequencies across fairly small datasets without relating them to the total number of passive constructions in the same data (e.g., Collins 1996).

In some cases, the frequency of the GET-passive is compared to the frequency of other GET-constructions (Hundt 2001a, 2001b; Bruckmaier 2016, 2017). These studies have no special interest in the passive; Hundt (2001b) justifies this based on her primary interest in the grammaticalization of *get*, and Bruckmaier's (2016, 2017) focus lies on *get* in World Englishes. It is, however, not always clear how the decision to compare the GET-passive to other *get*-constructions only (not including the BE-passive) was made. After all, Hundt (2001b) investigates whether varieties of English may be converging or diverging with regard to several features, with the GET-passive being one of them. Based on absolute frequencies of GET-passives as well as the proportion of all GET-constructions these passive uses comprise in the respective varieties, she suggests a similarity between Australian English (AusE), New Zealand English (NZE), and the varieties represented in the Brown corpora in terms of the use of the GET-passive (Hundt 2001b: 744).

Table 1 Ranges of Raw Frequencies of the GET-Passive in the Brown Corpora[2]

	1960s	1990s
BrE	27–35	47–53
AmE	29–35	57–64

Bruckmaier (2016, 2017) investigates both diachronic and regional variation in the use of constructions involving *get*. In terms of diachronic variation, she considers changes in BrE from the 1960s to the 1990s in LOB and FLOB; see Table 1 for results. Regarding regional variation, she compares the three varieties BrE, Jamaican English (JamE), and Singapore English (SingE) in the respective ICE corpora (Greenbaum & Nelson 1996; Bruckmaier 2017) and in the respective components of the GloWbE corpus (Davies 2013; Bruckmaier 2016). Bruckmaier (2016: 131–2) first hypothesizes that SingE may be more colloquialized than BrE and could thus contain more GET-passives in writing (Bruckmaier 2016: 128), but then reconsiders and says that as a result of "exonormative orientation," comparable frequencies can be expected in the two varieties. She finds that the GET-passive is more frequent in JamE than in BrE and SingE in both absolute terms and relative to other usages of *get* (Bruckmaier 2017: 100–1).[3] She ascribes this to potential substrate influence from Jamaican Creole, which has its own GET-passive (Farquharson 2013: 86; cited in Bruckmaier 2017: 95–6), and to Jamaica's geographic proximity to the United States, where the GET-passive is allegedly used more (Bruckmaier 2017: 95).

Regional variation has also been investigated by Collins (1996: 44). He compares written BrE, AmE, AusE, and Indian English (IndE) in eight corpora containing a total of 5.3 million words and 291 "central" GET-passives (see Chapter 3 on centrality).[4] He finds AusE and IndE to contain more GET-passives than the two older varieties BrE and AmE and ascribes this to "linguistic non-conservatism" in AusE and the "striving for linguistic independence and identity" in IndE (Collins 1996: 53–4), without elaborating much on either. Importantly, Collins (1996: 53) points out that the data he used might not accurately reflect regional differences because they represent different time periods. In a follow-up study, Collins and Yao (2013) compare the GET-passive to the BE-passive in ten varieties of English, which they classify both in terms of Kachru's (1985) distinction between Inner and Outer Circle and according to the developmental phases as per Schneider's (2007) dynamic model. The ratios of *get* to *be* range from 0.035 in AmE to 0.004 in IndE and are ordered as follows: AmE, NZE,

AusE, Canadian English (CanE), SingE, Philippine English (PhE), Hong Kong English (HKE), BrE, Kenyan English (KenE), and IndE (Collins & Yao 2013: 496). In Collins's (1996) first study, AusE and IndE display the most GET-passives, while IndE now features the lowest ratio of *get* among the ten varieties examined. The investigated Inner Circle Englishes use more GET-passive than the Outer Circle ones, with the exception of the more conservative BrE. Within the Outer Circle, the three South East Asian varieties cluster together on the one hand, with slightly higher rates of GET-passives compared to the two non-South East Asian varieties on the other hand (Collins & Yao 2013: 500–1).

Findings suggesting regional differences are challenged by Hundt, Dallas, and Nakanishi (2023), who examine the passive alternation in ten ICE corpora. As one of the first and few studies relying on a multifactorial generalized mixed-effects model, Hundt, Dallas, and Nakanishi (2023) explore the influence of multiple independent variables on the choice of the passive auxiliary at once. Their results suggest that language-internal constraints are more influential in the variation between *get* and *be* than a division into Inner and Outer Circle or any regional grouping. Regional variety is a statistically significant variable, but none of its direct influence or interactions pattern systematically along any expected division line into Inner and Outer Circle, world region, or colonial influence (Hundt, Dallas, & Nakanishi 2023: 17). Therefore, Hundt, Dallas, and Nakanishi (2023: 2) conclude that their data do not suggest that variety-specific restrictions are developing but support the view that World Englishes "share a core grammar." All in all, previous studies into the GET-passive across varieties of English mainly demonstrate that there is a general interest in the topic but also a desperate need for bigger datasets and a more explicit focus on the passive alternation.

Other studies have examined correlations between traditional sociolinguistic, sociodemographic variables and the passive as well as the social meaning of *get*. A common finding is a pattern of age differentiation whereby older participants prefer *be* more strongly than younger ones (Feagin 1979: 97; Weiner & Labov 1983: 43; Sneller & Fisher 2015: 4; Fehringer 2022: 17–18). This difference was present in data from the 1970s and 1980s and still persists in the 2010s and 2020s. This aligns with the fact that the GET-passive has constantly been becoming more and more popular. These findings also allow for making predictions in line with the apparent-time construct (Bailey et al. 1991; Labov 1963): if young speakers use *get* more than older ones, we can expect its frequency to continue to grow in the future (Fehringer 2022: 12).

In an apparent-time study on spoken data from Philadelphia, Sneller and Fisher (2015) observe an increase in the use of *get* (by birthdate) from 1900 till the 1960s, but then this comes to a halt.[5] In a second part, they investigate six commonly passivized verbs—*catch*, *fire*, *shoot*, *chase*, *kill*, and *arrest*—in American fiction from Google Ngrams (Sneller & Fisher 2015). These written data initially show a similar trend as the spoken data: a steady rise from the 1800s and stagnation in the 1950s (Sneller & Fisher 2015: 7). However, in the written data, this is short-lived, and from the 1970s onward, the proportion of GET-passives to all passives is found to be rising again (Sneller & Fisher 2015: 7). The authors interpret this to mean that during the 1950s, the GET-passive became salient and stigmatized and some people started avoiding it (Sneller & Fisher 2015: 4), which caused a temporary disruption in the "S-curve" (Tagliamonte 2011: 44) of language change (Sneller & Fisher 2015: 7–8).

In addition to youth, the GET-passive has been associated in multiple sociolinguistic studies with male biological sex, social status, and Blackness. In Sneller and Fisher's (2015: 5) data, *get* was avoided particularly by women. Feagin (1979: 97) presents similar findings for White Alabama English: teenage males use the GET-passive the most. Assuming that men tend to use non-standardized features more than women (Labov 1990), one can interpret this finding to support the stigmatization hypothesis by Sneller and Fisher (2015: 4), as does the fact that in younger age groups, speakers of a lower social status use *get* more than speakers of a higher social status (Sneller & Fisher 2015: 6). In interviews in Philadelphia and New York (Weiner & Labov 1983: 43), Black male adolescents use the GET-passive the most, with young males using the GET-passive even more than the BE-passive (Weiner & Labov 1983: 43). Overall, the GET-passive is the predominant variant also for Black and Puerto Rican speakers in New York City (Labov et al. 1968: 254).

Givón and Yang combine an analysis of literary works from the fourteenth century onward with Herold's (1986) unpublished findings on social status differences. They suggest that the GET-passive emerged in the speech of less educated people and is still used more by them (Givón & Yang 1994: 138). This corroborates earlier findings: in Macaulay's (1991: 98) interviews with twelve Scottish adults, speakers of a lower social status employ the GET-passive more (20.1 percent of their passives, $n = 284$) than speakers of a higher social status (4.4 percent, $n = 181$). The same is found for working-class speech from both teenagers and adults from Alabama (Feagin 1979: 97).

In summary, previous literature suggests that the passive alternation is conditioned by age, gender, race, and social status, which entails the expectation that the GET-passive is used most by young, Black, male speakers of a lower social status. The corpora that we use do not include systematic information on such sociodemographic factors so that they cannot be included in our analysis. However, further studies may include data from contemporary speakers and larger sample sizes to confirm the veracity and persistence of these suggested patterns.

2.4 Subject Responsibility

In the course of the almost 100 years of scholarship into the passive alternation (e.g., Rice 1932), scholars have suggested semantic differences between the BE- and GET-passives beyond dynamicity. One commonly discussed difference concerns the question of who bears responsibility over the situation (Lakoff 1971: 155; Chappell 1980: 426; Collins 1996: 50; Huddleston & Pullum 2002: 1442; Dixon 2005: 357; Toyota 2007: 148, 2008: 156). It has been argued that in the BE-passive, the agent, whether omitted or relocated to a *by*-PP, retains full responsibility for the described event, while the grammatical subject maintains none. By contrast, in the GET-passive, the grammatical subject shares at least part of this responsibility. Examples (22) and (23) demonstrate this difference in allocating responsibility.

(22) He was robbed in broad daylight ... probably for his watch. (GloWbE/Canada/general)

(23) If you get robbed, you install locks, and learn how to protect yourself. We almost got robbed, even though we had some of the elements I listed above. But clearly, it's not a strong enough system. (GloWbE/USA/blog)

In (22), the grammatical subject "he" is not assumed to have any responsibility for being robbed; the author speculates that the reason the person was robbed was his watch. Adding that this happened "in broad daylight," the speaker underlines the improbability of a robbery, emphasizing that the subject could not have foreseen this turn of events and thus carries no responsibility. By contrast, (23) focuses on actions that the grammatical subject should take to avoid getting robbed. If the situation has a negative outcome, the subject carries responsibility for it due to their "misbehavior, carelessness or negligence or sheer bad luck" (Downing 1996: 198); if the outcome is favorable to the subject, their involvement may mean either "good fortune or ... efforts or contrivance" (Downing 1996: 198). Chappell (1980: 437) suggests that the GET-passive can be used when the speaker or writer wants to cast doubts as to the worthiness and innocence of a subject to whom something good happens.

Collins (1996: 50–1) points out that *get* is also more common than *be* in the following constructions, all of which involve agentive subjects, along with the imperative mood:

try to/and be/get V-ed

go and be/get V-ed

manage to be/get V-ed

Wanner suggests that this feature might have arisen from the causative use of *get* (2009: 106). The degree of supposed agentivity of *get* varies from full causation to a mere hint of involvement. Based on Vanrespaille's (1991: 107) agentivity gradience, Toyota (2008: 157) places subjects on a continuum, with the passive subject showing varying degrees of control over the situation. Toyota (2008: 156–7) advocates for finer distinctions, that is, describing the difference between "subject control" and the "general characteristics of subject" enabling an event. In his example of someone getting promoted, it may also be more general circumstances rather than specific actions on part of the subject that lead to a particular outcome.

The idea of subject responsibility has been broadly advocated. However, Wanner (2009: 104) suggests that "the responsibility factor, if it exists, is not built into the *get*-passive as construction, but may be a reading that becomes available under certain circumstances."

In order to investigate subject responsibility, scholars have taken an interest in the animacy of the grammatical subject of the GET-passive, as only animate entities are compatible with the idea of having any responsibility over the occurred events (e.g., Givón & Yang 1994: 120; see Chapter 4). Studies that have tried to operationalize subject responsibility have connected this concept to the semantic feature animacy, the semantic role agent, and the syntactic function subject (Macaulay 1991). The agent is assumed to exhibit "intentionality, control, responsibility, and consciousness" (Dahl & Fraurud 1996: 58). Following this argumentation, the agent is prototypically animate because only animate beings can embody these characteristics.

Previous studies show that the GET-passive favors human or other animate subjects (Herold 1986; cited in Givón 1993: 69; Macaulay 1991: 98; Toyota 2008: 161; Fehringer 2022: 17–18; Hundt, Dallas, & Nakanishi 2023: 12), while the BE-passive favors inanimate subjects (Toyota 2008: 161; Fehringer 2022: 17–18; Hundt, Dallas, & Nakanishi 2023: 12). Toyota (2008: 161) documents a diachronic change in BE-passives from animate to more inanimate subjects, which may reflect *get* taking the lead with animate subjects. However, *get* is not restricted to animate subjects but also occurs with inanimate ones. When this happens, responsibility may be assigned to a related animate entity that might be, for instance, the possessor (Chappell 1980: 440; Downing 1996: 199) as in (24).

(24) Jane's bike got stolen. (Chappell 1980: 440)

Another factor that has been related to subject responsibility is the presence or absence of a *by*-PP to name the agent. Banks (1986: 127) judges an example like (25) to be "of doubtful acceptability" because it feels like two agents are named for a single action.

(25) Mo got shot by Blake.[6] (Banks 1986: 127)

(26) Mo got shot by the guerilla. (Banks 1986: 128)

Banks (1986: 128) considers this type of sentence more acceptable if the agent is such that it "preserve[s] anonymity," as (26) arguably does.[7] If a *by*-agent is named in the GET-passive, it is more likely to be inanimate (Quirk et al. 1985: 161), "impersonal or nonhuman" (Rühlemann 2007: 118; Carter & McCarthy 1999: 51).

Hence, it does not come as a surprise that a *by*-PP is less likely to occur with the GET-passive than the BE-passive (Hatcher 1949: 435; Leech & Svartvik 2002: 301–2; Quirk et al. 1985: 161; Johansson & Oksefjell 1996: 69; Huddleston & Pullum 2002: 1441; Xiao, McEnery, & Qian 2006: 113). The percentage of GET-passives containing a *by*-PP in previous studies varies from 1.4 to 16.1 percent depending on the dataset (Collins 1996: 46; Downing 1996: 192; Carter & McCarthy 1999: 51; Hundt 2001a: 75; Toyota 2008: 159), but the low overall frequencies make the figures less reliable. Hatcher (1949: 436) interprets this dislike for the *by*-agent in the GET-passive to mean that "the agent does not completely dominate the situation" in this construction; instead, some of the responsibility lies with the grammatical subject. The agent is absent in the majority of BE-passives as well, but still more common than with *get*, occurring 20–30 percent of the time (Svartvik 1966: 141; Leech & Svartvik 2002: 301–2; Quirk et al. 1985: 164). We outline how we treat subject responsibility in our study in detail in Chapter 4.

2.5 Adversativity and Non-Neutrality

Another semantic condition often associated with the GET-passive is the depiction of something undesirable happening to the sentence subject (Hatcher

1949: 441; Chappell 1980; Biber, Conrad, & Leech 1999: 481; Carter & McCarthy 1999: 49; Gronemeyer 1999: 7; Huddleston & Pullum 2002: 1442; Rühlemann 2007: 120; Toyota 2008: 168; Hundt, Dallas, & Nakanishi 2023: 12), as in Example (27). Typologically, this is not unusual; some of the world's languages display such an adversative passive, for instance, Mandarin Chinese and Vietnamese (Chappell 1980: 412–13; Toyota 2008: 164).

(27) Within eight months I got fired, primarily because of differences in approach to doing business. (GloWbE/Tanzania/general)

Aside from adversativity, multiple scholars have argued that the GET-passive can also encode situations that are favorable for the subject (e.g., Hatcher 1949: 441; Chappell 1980: 435; Collins 1996: 51), as in Example (28).

(28) Is it necessary to assimilate to Western culture in the US workplace if you want to get ahead and get promoted? (GloWbE/Bangladesh/blog)

Many studies have investigated the association between the GET-passive and non-neutral meaning. Most, though not all, of them distinguish between adverse, beneficial, and neutral outcomes. An overview of findings is provided in Table 2.

In several corpora, more than 60 percent of GET-passives carry an adversative meaning. Even in Xiao, McEnery, and Qian's (2006: 116) data, where 37.7 percent adversativity may not seem high, when contrasted with only 15 percent of adversative BE-passives, the results still suggest a connection between *get* and adversativity. However, the percentages vary dramatically from one dataset to the next, and so do scholars' interpretations. For example, Phoocharoensil (2020: 132–3) finds adversity in the majority of GET-passives but interprets the fact that one-third of them are non-adversative to indicate that the construction is rather neutralizing and becoming less strongly associated with unfavorable events. Additionally, Coto Villalibre (2015: 21–2) argues that previous research has tended too quickly to pass over GET-passives carrying a neutral meaning, and the construction is, in fact, neutralizing. Some scholars, moreover, have suggested that adversativity could be an epiphenomenon of the informal nature of the GET-passive (Wanner 2009: 99; Coto Villalibre 2015: 24), supposing that there are more colloquial expressions expressing negative than positive outcomes and that *get* is used with them because they are informal rather than because they are adversative. Overall, considering also the low number of observations in most studies, it seems that the relationship between the GET-passive and adversativity remains a matter of debate.

Table 2 Proportion of GET-Passives Displaying an Adversative versus Beneficial versus Neutral Meaning in Various Studies

Adversative	**Beneficial**	**Neutral**	**Total (*N*)**	**Data: modes, variety, period**	**Corpus**	**Source**
statistically significant correlation between *get* and adversativity			296	spoken BrE from Tyneside	DECTE	Fehringer (2022: 17–18)
c. 90%	<5%	*c.* 5%	139	spoken BrE	CANCODE	Carter and McCarthy (1999: 49)
70.9%	12.1%	12.5%	846[8]	spoken and written BrE and other varieties	Bank of English	Downing (1996: 194)
67.4%	23.4%	9.3%	291	spoken BrE and AusE; written BrE, AmE, AusE, and IndE	various	Collins (1996: 52)
66.3%	33.7%		107	written BrE and AmE/1990s	Frown, FLOB	Biber, Conrad, and Leech (1999: 157)
63.8%	29.5%	6.8%	49,530[9]	spoken and written AmE	COCA	Phoocharoensil (2020: 130)
60.3%	39.7%		63	written BrE and AmE/1960s	Brown, LOB	Leech et al. (2009: 157)
44%	16%	40%	50	spoken BrE	ICE	Coto Villalibre (2015: 19)
40.6%	25%	34.4%	64	spoken SingE	ICE	Coto Villalibre (2015: 19)
37.7%	3.4%	58.9%	1,359	spoken and written BrE	FLOB, BNC Demo	Xiao, McEnery, and Qian (2006: 116)
37.1%	25.8%	37.1%	35	spoken HKE	ICE	Coto Villalibre (2015: 19)
26.3%	73.7%		209	spoken and written BrE	London-Lund, LOB	Toyota (2008: 169)
26.2%	9.5%	64.3%	126	spoken IndE	ICE	Coto Villalibre (2015: 19)
21.0%	79.0%		62	eighteenth-century BrE	Helsinki, ARCHER	Toyota (2008: 168)

A further point of criticism and debate is that in many previous studies, the concept of adversativity is not exactly defined. Some scholars draw on Persson's (1990: 52) test for determining adversativity (Coto Villalibre 2015: 18; Schwarz 2015: 150). This test asks for each proposition X whether it is "worse to be X than not to be X"; if the answer is yes, the sentence is adversative; if being X is neither better nor worse than not being X, the sentence is neutral; if being X is better than not being X, the sentence is beneficial. An alternative, stricter method suggested by Fehringer (2022) looks for lexemes such as *unfortunately*, *hope*, *want*, *try*, or *avoid* co-occurring with the GET-passive. Fehringer (2022: 8) argues that such words unambiguously indicate non-neutrality, whereas all other cases, where no such lexemes occur, should be coded as neutral.

Toyota strives to develop a distinction between "lexical adversativity" arising from specific negative lexical verbs and "syntactic adversativity," where the structure of the GET-passive itself is the supposed source of adverse meaning (2008: 168). However, upon closer examination, his examples of syntactic adversativity seem to be cases where the adversativity emerges from the larger sentential context, as in (29).

(29) I mean but they can do something fairly minor and <u>get sent</u> there.
(London-Lund; cited in Toyota 2008: 168)

Finally, Toyota (2008: 170–1) suggests that the affected entity—the "sufferer" or "beneficiary"—may, in fact, be none of the referents encoded in the sentence but the speaker or writer themselves. Lakoff (1971: 154; cited in Collins 1996: 51–2) also suggests that the favorability of a situation may not be assessed from the sentence subject's perspective but the speaker's or writer's.

More generally, the use of the GET-passive has been claimed to involve some evaluation or a subjective viewpoint on part of the speaker or writer (e.g., Toyota 2007: 149). For instance, Downing (1996: 201) suggests that *get* may express an "emotional attitude, whether sympathetic or disapproving" on the part of the speaker or writer, while Toyota (2008: 162) talks about "sentiment [or] sympathy." According to Carter and McCarthy (1999: 54–5), the GET-passive primarily marks the speaker's "stance" toward situations and subjects, often viewing them as "problematic" or at least "noteworthy." Others call it speaker "attitude" (Lakoff 1971: 154; Banks 1986: 126). This can mean many different things: whether the speaker "feels they [the described events] are good or bad, or reflect well or poorly on him [*sic*] or the superficial subject of the sentence" (Lakoff 1971: 154). Banks (1986: 130) claims this attitude can encompass a development seen as "detriment[al]" or strenuous and tries to combine the two in suggesting that the essence of *get* is distance between the speaker and their statement. Fryd (2009: 293–4) argues that using *get* as a passive auxiliary opens a space for looking inside a moment of transition, for instance, suitable for describing "a protracted and difficult process."

However, it can be questioned how linguists are supposed to correctly identify the speakers' inner thoughts and motives (Collins 1996: 52). A close examination of the context might reveal this, but it will not always do that. Cheshire (2005: 100) points out that concepts such as stance are difficult to operationalize for a quantitative analysis and have therefore not gained any official "status within any syntactic theory of language." Some claims about the semantics of the GET-passive are altogether not operationalizable: for instance, Feagin (1979: 96) states that *get* makes the meaning of a passive sentence "stronger, more lively, more intimate or more earthy." Our approach to adversativity, relying on sentiment analysis on the level of the lexical verb but also more broadly for the whole clause, is laid out in Chapter 5.

2.6 Formality and Genre

For the analysis of grammatical change, considering genre, register, and style is vital. These factors can "promote or constrain the spread of an innovation" (Mair & Leech 2020: 267), and syntactic change often spreads at a different pace in different genres (Hundt 2001b: 746). In this section, we review previous literature on how formality and genre affect the passive alternation.

The passive in general has been linked to written language (Biber 1988: 228), where it is said to occur five times as often as in speech (Chafe 1982: 42). The passive is used the most in academic prose and news writing, and the least in conversation (Biber, Conrad, & Leech 2003: 167). Quirk et al. (1985: 166) argue that this is a stylistic matter, and "informative" writing in general favors the passive, while "imaginative" does not.

Interestingly, these tendencies do not seem to hold for the newer GET-passive, which has been widely reported to be more common in informal genres and spoken discourse (e.g., Johansson & Oksefjell 1996: 62; Huddleston & Pullum 2002: 1442; Leech & Svartvik 2002: 301–2; Collins & Yao 2013: 496; Sneller & Fisher 2015: 7; Cho & Ahn 2017: 303; Hundt, Dallas, & Nakanishi 2023: 12). Biber, Conrad, and Leech (1999: 476) claim that the GET-passive is found "only in conversation, except for an occasional example in colloquial fiction." But it is found in written genres as well, albeit less often than in spoken language (e.g., Leech et al. 2009: 156–8).

Leech et al. (2009) investigate developments over time (1960s vs. 1990s) across four written genres (press texts, general prose, academic prose, and fiction) and two varieties of English (British vs. American). In the earlier dataset, fiction contains the highest number of GET-passives, followed by press and only a few instances in the other two genres (Leech et al. 2009: 156). In the 1990s data, counts have risen across the board, but more dramatically in genres other than fiction (Leech et al. 2009: 156). In BrE, press texts even surpass fiction as the text type with the most instances of the GET-passive per-million-words (pmw) (Leech et al. 2009: 156). This might suggest that the GET-passive is neutralizing in terms of genre. This claim is, however, not supported by Cho and Ahn (2017: 303), who show *be* + past participle to be dispersed over a much larger proportion of the different BNC corpus files than *get* + past participle is. They interpret this to mean that *get* is more selective in terms of lexical main verbs as well as genre (Cho & Ahn 2017: 304–5).

Scholars have discussed the role of prescriptivism in the spread of the passive voice and GET-constructions from different perspectives (e.g., Denison 1998: 182). The passive voice has long been disparaged in style manuals (Pullum 2014: 60). Schwarz (2015: 153) speculates that the two passives might be differently influenced by this sort of prescriptivist influence. Namely, Pullum (2014) points out that many writers—including journalists—are actually not able to identify a passive construction but mistake various active constructions for passive (e.g., "The butler was dead" or "you guys are wanting to dissect the past"; in Pullum 2014: 67). However, Schwarz (2015: 153) supposes that people are even less equipped to correctly classify the GET-passive, and therefore the recommendation of style guides to avoid the passive might influence it less than the BE-passive.

On the other hand, *get*, especially when following possessive *have*, was criticized by grammarians and teachers in the nineteenth and early twentieth centuries (Rice 1932). As a result, *get* may have been perceived as overall inappropriate for formal communication (e.g., Smith & Rayson 2007: 140). The GET-passive started growing a century earlier in AmE than in BrE, and Hundt (2001a: 71) proposes that this lag may have been caused by the stronger influence of prescriptivism in Britain.

Yet, the influence of prescriptivism has allegedly been diminishing (Denison 1998: 320; Bruckmaier 2016: 127, 2017: 101), and instead, since the twentieth century, a trend has been detected toward more "colloquialization" (Mair 1997). This term refers to written language adopting patterns from spoken language (Mair & Leech 2020: 268; Leech et al. 2009: 146; Schwarz 2017: 308). The increasing frequency of the GET-passive (e.g., Leech et al. 2009) is sometimes linked to this development. Mair and Leech (2020: 168) suggest colloquialization to be the main reason for the decrease of *be* and the increase of *get* as passive auxiliaries, and Collins and Yao (2013: 480) draw on different attitudes toward colloquialism and informality as explanations for differences in the frequency of the GET-passive across English-speaking countries.

2.7 Syntactic Constraints

The variety of different syntactic contexts in which *get* occurs is an indication of how far it has proceeded on its path from a lexical to grammatical element. As constructions grammaticalize, they "come to serve a larger and larger range of meaningful morphosyntactic purposes" (Hopper & Traugott 2003: 100). In Construction Grammar, the term "constructionalization" is used for essentially the same process of increasing schematicity within a certain construction (Traugott & Trousdale 2013). While some say that the GET-passive has been "fully grammaticalized" (Leech et al. 2009: 154), others name restrictions and investigate which syntactic contexts favor which passive auxiliary.

First of all, it has been suggested that the BE-passive co-occurs with third-person subjects, while the GET-passive is relatively more common with first- and especially second-person subjects (Toyota 2008: 162–3). Fehringer (2022: 12) points out that this could be related to the connection between *get* and animate subjects, which first- and second-person pronouns are. Yet, in fact, the relative dislike of *get* for third person persists when looking at human subjects only (Fehringer 2022: 21–2). Bruckmaier (2016: 135) finds third-person subjects to be the most common type with the GET-passive in three ICE corpora, but her study does not consider the BE-passive at all. Therefore, this finding is likely to represent the overall distribution of grammatical persons in the data rather than reveal anything about the GET-passive.

The co-occurrence of the passive voice with other tense and aspectual forms and modal auxiliaries has been a topic of much speculation and some research. Studies show that the overwhelming majority of BE-passives are nonprogressive and non-perfect (Quirk et al. 1985: 166; Schwarz 2017: 316). In Biber, Conrad, and Leech (2003: 173), the past and particularly present perfect are the only complex verb phrases to occur in the passive with any frequency, while Denison (1998: 183) expects language users to forgo the perfect passive in favor of a plain BE-passive. Combinations of progressive and passive used to be avoided

(Denison 1998: 151; Hundt 2001a: 79; Smith & Rayson 2007: 130); one reason suggested for this was an alleged *horror aequi* effect (Rohdenburg 2003), a dislike for stringing together two forms of the verb *be* (Quirk et al. 1985: 166; Denison 1998: 155). While Smith and Rayson (2007: 136) testify to an increasing frequency of the present progressive passive in the twentieth century in Brown corpora, Schwarz (2017: 316) still finds "very few progressive BE-passives" in the *TIME* magazine during the same time period.

Combinations of complex tense and aspect forms with the GET-passive may be even rarer. Disfavoring the perfect progressive BE-passive because of the "awkward" combination of *be* and *being* (Quirk et al. 1985: 166) could lead to the progressive favoring *get* over *be* (Smith & Rayson 2007: 132; Hundt, Dallas, & Nakanishi 2023: 4). This expectation does not materialize at least in the ICE corpora (Hundt, Dallas, & Nakanishi 2023: 17). In fact, Hundt's (2004: 99) study on the ARCHER corpus suggests that the progressive GET-passive only emerged in the twentieth century. The perfect is also rare. Fehringer (2022: 11) finds no instances of the present perfect passive, and Schwarz (2017: 317) reports the perfect to be "virtually absent" with *get*. She concludes: "Only BE-passives regularly co-occur with perfect aspect" (Schwarz 2017: 324). The DECTE corpus contains some instances of the GET-passive combined with *will*, *would*, past and conditional perfect, as well as the infinitive (Fehringer 2022: 11), and Fehringer's (2022: 16–17) mixed-effects model suggests that the construction prefers present and past tense over "other" tenses.[10] Schwarz (2017: 315) finds no remarkable developments in the use of tense forms (present vs. past vs. other) in the two passives in twentieth-century AmE. Similarly, the proportion of different aspectual forms (simple vs. progressive vs. perfect) remains stable in that diachronic dataset, with simple covering more than 80 percent of observations with each auxiliary (Schwarz 2017: 316–17).

Furthermore, it has been reported that adverbials disfavor the GET-passive. Xiao, McEnery, and Qian (2006: 116) find this to be the case especially in speech. Carter and McCarthy (1999: 53) point out that adverbials direct the attention to the verb, which might be incompatible with the GET-passive's focus on the grammatical subject. In their spoken BrE data, the only adverbials in GET-passive sentences are negating particles, obligatory complements of the verb, and "intensifying or focusing" items *actually*, *nearly*, and *really*, and none of these occurs between *get* and the main verb (Carter & McCarthy 1999: 53).

In a more exploratory approach, Fehringer (2022) includes in her mixed-effects regression model also the syntactic variables of polarity (affirmative vs. negative) and clause type (main vs. subordinate; declarative vs. interrogative), but none of these three prove significant in predicting the choice of passive auxiliary. A final syntactic restriction that has been suggested is that only the BE-passive can be followed by a *to*-complement clause (Xiao, McEnery, & Qian 2006: 112).

2.8 Lexical Aspect

In this section, we discuss various further semantic constraints on the passive alternation suggested in the literature. Scholars describing the GET-passive have looked for semantic and aspectual restrictions in its use, barring it from co-occurring with certain types of main verbs. Downing (1996) examines different verb groups as classified in Halliday's (1994) systemic-functional grammar and their compatibility with the GET-passive in the BoE corpus, examining suggested restrictions critically. For instance, it has been said that *get* cannot passivize cognitive or other stative (Huddleston & Pullum 2002: 1442; Cowan 2008: 405) or durative verbs (Hatcher 1949: 434). Downing (1996: 189) finds one instance each of *get liked* and *get loved*, concluding that *get* is unlikely with such mental verbs but not impossible. In her words, "Even a minimal incidence is of interest since it points to a wider range of possible combinations than had previously been contemplated" (Downing 1996: 191). Fehringer (2022: 9), too, presents counterexamples to the claim that *get* does not occur with durative verbs. According to Downing (1996: 203), the type of verb least likely to occur with *get* is the "relational" one; for example, the only instance of *getting owned* in her data focuses on "com[ing] to be possessed" ("The stocks get over-owned by Americans," Downing 1996: 190). She also suggests that verbs of perception such as *hear* or *see* are acceptable in the GET-passive only if the event has a "significant result," perhaps affecting the grammatical subject (Downing 1996: 189).

Moreover, it has been suggested that *get* cannot occur with verbs encoding "spontaneous change" or "creation" (Collins 1996: 51) but only with subjects that already exist (Lakoff 1971: 154). This idea has not been widely accepted; for instance, Banks (1986: 126) and even Lakoff (1971: 154) herself offer counterexamples. One case from our data is presented below as Example (30): the act of painting results in the creation of the subject referent (a mural). Downing (1996: 187) argues that *get* is not common with verbs of creation but is possible "when an element of causation is present," as arguably is in the sentence reproduced here as Example (31).

(30) The mural got painted freehand in one 12-hour burst (COHA/2017/magazine)

(31) A lot of so-called butter gets made from rather dubious ingredients these days. (Downing 1996: 187)

Schwarz (2017) compares the occurrence of different situation types (stative vs. accomplishment vs. activity vs. transitional act vs. momentary act, cf. Vendler 1957; Quirk et al. 1985: 200–9) in the two passive constructions over time. Her findings indicate that the most common type with *be* is accomplishment (durative situation with an endpoint), while for *get*, it is transitional act (punctual situation with an endpoint); however, differences between passive constructions and between situation types seem to neutralize over time (Schwarz 2017: 319–21). All in all, Schwarz interprets this to support the claim that the GET-passive is further grammaticalizing, which involves shedding semantic restrictions (2017: 326). Fehringer (2022: 16–17) finds the GET-passive to favor telic rather than atelic verbs. Fryd (2009: 293) takes this further, calling the GET-passive "markedly telic." What makes investigating the variable "situation type" difficult is that it is a feature of the whole clause rather than just the lexical verb, so it can only be coded at the token level and cannot easily be automated. In Chapter 6, we outline a computational approach to exploring the effect of different verb types on the choice of *get* versus *be*.

2.9 Summary

In this chapter, we have delimited the phenomenon under study—the English passive and the alternation between *be* and *get* as passive auxiliaries—and presented a broad array of factors suggested in the literature to govern the choice of the passive auxiliary. These can be broadly divided into semantic, syntactic, register, and sociodemographic factors. While some previous studies address diachronic change, only few studies explore regional synchronic variation. Choosing *get* over *be* is generally linked to a certain degree of subject responsibility and often associated with undesirable consequences for the subject, for instance, *to get robbed*, but may also have a positive outcome in some cases, such as *to get promoted*. Informal registers and genres have been shown to favor *get* along with certain types of lexical items.

In the large-scale analysis we develop, we are able to consider most of the syntactic variables, some of the semantic and stylistic variables, and only few of the sociodemographic factors. The chosen corpora do not include any naturalistic spoken data, and there is no sociodemographic information readily available about the authors beyond their geographic location (in the synchronic data from GloWbE). Some of the semantic variables can only be coded individually at the level of an entire sentence, or altogether cannot be objectively assessed, and are, therefore, not suitable for our large-scale approach. Others can be investigated through a proxy such as subject responsibility through subject animacy. Chapters 4–8 present details about variables included in our analysis, how we operationalize them, and what automated solutions enable us to carry out this study on two very large datasets. Before that, in Chapter 3, we address in more detail the issue that not all instances of *be* or *get* followed by a participle-looking form represent the passive, how previous studies have distinguished "central" passives from other related forms, and how we automate this task for the present project.

3

Centrality and the Passive Gradient

As Chapter 2 has shown, a precise delineation of the variable is far from trivial in the case of the English passive alternation. In this chapter, we describe our approach to data extraction and circumscription of the variable context. We initially take a formal approach that extracts all *be* and *get* + past participle constructions, which we describe in 3.1. The data thus extracted have good recall, that is, they identify nearly all actual passive tokens in the corpus. However, the method on its own suffers in precision in that many of the observations extracted are not, in fact, true or central passives. We discuss the issue of passive centrality in 3.2, revisit previous approaches to the problem in 3.3., and present our own, automated approach in 3.4.

3.1 Variable Extraction

We use the lemmatized and PoS-tagged downloaded versions of two corpora from the English-corpora.org website, COHA and GloWbE (see Sections 9.1 and 10.1 for more information about the corpora). In the "Word/lemma/PoS" tab-delimited format provided, each line in the text file contains a file identifier for the respective corpus text, one token from the corpus, followed by its lemma, and the PoS tag assigned by the CLAWS tagger (Garside, Leech, & Sampson 1987), in a tab-separated format, as shown in Example (32).

(32)	4078012	The	the	at
	4078012	tips	tip	nn2
	4078012	had	have	vhd
	4078012	flowed	flow	vvn
	4078012	.	.	y

Our extraction script parses the corpora line by line, that is, token by token, and identifies all cases of the lemmas *be* or *get* followed by a token tagged as a verbal past participle. We allow for the presence of a negator either preceding the passive auxiliary, as in Example (33), or following it, as in Example (34), as well as the presence of one or several adverbs in between the auxiliary and the participle, as in Example (35).

(33) I'm not getting paid $3 million. (COHA/news/1978)

(34) Teeth are not recognized as personal property. (COHA/news/1880)

(35) It's been fully accepted by the Nixon administration (COHA/news/1970)

In addition to extracting each of these *be* and *get* + past participle constructions, we also collect information about various aspects of the wider sentence context. The entire clause and sentence a token occurs in are recorded (with these being defined as any material to the left and right of the passive construction up to the next punctuation character in the first case and the next sentence-final punctuation character in the latter case). Additionally, automatic extraction includes the tense and aspect of each passive verb phrase as well as the head of the subject noun phrase (for more information on this procedure, see Chapter 4). Since several claims can be found in the literature about the (im-) permissibility and probability of prepositional phrases introduced by *by* or *to* after a passive construction (see Chapter 2), our extraction also systematically checks for the presence of these items.

The raw data yielded by this initial extraction procedure comprise 3,798,421 tokens for COHA and 16,464,513 tokens for GloWbE. The proportion of GET-passives (or at this stage rather passive-like structures) is 1.64 percent in COHA and 2.68 percent in GloWbE. The recall of the search should be good, though an automated extraction method will necessarily systematically fail to retrieve some minor types. In our case, this concerns instances where there are more or longer elements inserted between the auxiliary and the main verb. We expect optional negators and adverbs, but of course, one occasionally finds longer or other elements in this position. Cases of subject-auxiliary inversion, as in (36), escape the extraction script. In addition, in the case of coordinated participles, our script only records the first element. Hence, our extraction procedure misses instances of the passive like those underlined in Examples (37) and (38).

(36) And to whom were they written?

(37) But then parliamentary processes and traditions are well and truly blurred now. (GloWbE/Australia/general)

(38) "There is definitely concern that the stimulus money will get diffused and diluted by other political pressures within states," Mr. Kealy says. (COHA/ news/2009)

Considering the size of the dataset, we see this minimal loss of data as unproblematic, especially since it affects both *be* and *get* equally and thus does not introduce any skew. More problematic, however, is the question of precision—whether all the collected examples truly represent the English passive. This thorny matter will be addressed in the following sections.

3.2 The Passive as a Fuzzy Category

Any statistical analysis of the English passive alternation is troubled by the complexity of the variable under study. While only comprising two variants, the formal structure *be*/*get* + past participle subsumes a range of uses with different functional-semantic nuances. Only some of these allow for the choice between *get* and *be* as the passive auxiliary under conditions of (near) referential equivalence. For example, Granger (1983) finds seven different functions for *be* + past participle, only one of which is a true passive construction. Therefore, ensuring that all tokens under consideration actually allow for the selection of either *be* or *get* is essential for an accountable analysis (Labov 1982: 30).

The passive is not a clearly delimited phenomenon and represents a continuum rather than a binary distinction. Svartvik (1966: 156) refers to a "passive scale," while Quirk et al. (1985: 167) use the term "passive gradient," and others (Collins 1996: 44–5; Biber et al. 1999: 475) have described the passive as a "fuzzy" category, with prototypical and marginal members and without clear boundaries (see Aarts 2007 for a general treatment of gradience in grammar). Central members (i.e., "true" passives) are instances where the past participle has a clear verbal-eventive reading, and *be* and *get* are interchangeable to describe the same event, as in Example (39). In sociolinguistic parlance, these are the "count" (Blake 1997) cases that should enter a statistical analysis of the passive alternation.

(39) Beach enthusiasts need not to worry about getting eaten by dolphins. They only eat fish and other crustaceans. (GloWbE/Philippines/blog)

Beyond these, however, a range of further cases exist, with a blurred line between "count" and "don't count" cases. Some of these are illustrated and discussed in the following:

(40) I am very disappointed with the way your embassy has handled my case. (GloWbE/Pakistan/blog)

(41) You might get disappointed by something … but never lose your faith toward it. (GloWbE/Malaysia/blog)

(42) The last time I was disappointed by one of its systems was the Nintendo 64, and things have come on a lot since then. (GloWbE/USA/blog)

The past participle may be used with a clearly adjectival meaning as in Example (40), in which case the whole structure entails a stative reading when occurring with *be*. Since the GET-passive itself is eventive (Cheshire, Kerswill, & Williams 2005: 14), there is a semantic tension in examples like (41), which consequently cannot be treated as fully equivalent to the same sentence with a BE-passive. However, under the right contextual circumstances, even a BE-passive with a participle that commonly occurs adjectivally can receive an eventive reading, as in Example (42). A major challenge in an automated, large-scale study of the passive alternation is to extract actual cases of alternation without including too many false positives, that is, sentences where both *get* and *be* cannot be used with the same meaning.

The endpoints of this gradient are fully "verbal" and fully "adjectival" uses of the past participle. Some scholars consider even the adjectival use a type of passive—a statal or adjectival passive (e.g., Huddleston & Pullum 2002: 1436). However, at the adjectival end of the continuum, substituting *get* for *be* does not result in a semantically equivalent sentence, so we argue that these should not be included in a variationist study on the passive alternation.

In other words, in between the two ends of the spectrum lie many gray instances of *be* or *get* + past participle that may be ambiguous, featuring characteristics of both adjectival and verbal properties (Stein 1979: 29–30; Gronemeyer 1999: 6; Huddleston & Pullum 2002: 1436). Distinguishing between them can be difficult or even impossible (e.g., Dixon 2005: 166). This may be the case more so for *be* than for *get* (Huddleston & Pullum 2002: 1441). Many of these ambiguous cases are "psychological verbs" (Collins 1996: 46–7) expressing emotions, as represented in Example (43).

(43) While she is getting irritated about the python … her husband Noel is busy growing bananas. (ACE-A30–6452; cited in Collins 1996: 47)

Hatcher (1949: 433) argues that participles like *upset* and *irritated* always imply a past action because something has to upset a person before they *get upset*, but these words "feel" more like adjectives because we are usually more interested in the resulting emotional state than the causing action. This inchoative use of *get* is synonymous with *become*.

Another reason for ambiguity may be the underlying syntactic structure, that is, the presence of the preposition *by*. Dixon (2005: 166) points out that when the stimulus that causes an emotional reaction in the *experiencer* (using his terms for the semantic roles) is named, it may be introduced with either *by* or another preposition specific to the lexeme. Examples are provided in (44) and (45).

(44) I was surprised at the result. (Dixon 2005: 166)

(45) I was surprised by the result. (Dixon 2005: 166)

Dixon (2005: 166) suggests that *surprised* is an adjective in (44) and a verb in (45), where it occurs with *by*. By contrast, Svartvik (1966: 104) lists many different prepositions and even clauses that can act as "quasi-agents." In a particularly inclusive approach, he considers all combinations of a verb (except *have*) with a passive participle as passives (Svartvik 1966: 93) classifying them based on whether some kind of agent is present or could be added and their relation to a potential active sentence (Svartvik 1966: 117). Others treat the *by*-structure as ambiguous, saying that prepositions other than *by* can introduce "agent-like phrases," too (Quirk et al. 1985: 196).

Some of the adjectival cases occur idiomatically with *get*; here, neither *be* nor *become* is a viable replacement (e.g., *get drunk*, *get lost*, *get stuck*). Biber, Conrad, and Leech (1999: 481) refer to the inchoative semantic nature of such items but still classify sentences with *involved* and *stuck* as examples of the GET-passive. Quirk et al. call adjectival usages formally similar to the GET-passive "pseudo-passives" (1985: 161) or "statal passives" (1985: 170) and instances with both verbal and adjectival characteristics "semi-passives" (1985: 168). One of the most frequent uses of *get* is in a construction that is formally parallel to the GET-passive but whose grammatical subject is the agent of the action: *get started*. It is only in rare cases with inanimate subjects that *get started* can perhaps be construed as a passive sentence, as in Example (46).

(46) Senator McGovern's campaign did not really get started until September 13, when the Senator and his nonrunning mate, Edward Kennedy, drew 10,000 to 15,000 persons to a noon rally in Pittsburgh's Market Square. (COHA/1972/magazine)

In the vast majority of cases, *start* is used in the middle voice, that is, where the subject is both affected by and responsible for the action, making *getting started* nearly synonymous with *starting*. In this meaning, it cannot be conceived of as any sort of passive. There are also a handful of other idiomatic usages of *get* + past participle that do not display the passive semantics, including *getting used to*, *carried away with*, or *rid of something*. This concerns a low number of types with a fairly high number of tokens, and the easiest solution is to exclude them individually from the analysis.

There are further verbs, either reflexive or reciprocal, that are often interpreted as middle constructions when occurring with *get* (Anderwald 2018: 3). Some of these are, for instance, *dressed*, *shaved*, *married*, or *acquainted* (Hatcher 1949: 433–4). These verbs covered a high portion of the early instances of the GET-passive (e.g., Fleisher 2006), and their modern interpretation as expressing "middle voice" has influenced the collective understanding of the GET-passive more broadly (Anderwald 2018: 3). They are often named as first or prime examples of why *get* + past participle is something else than a passive construction (e.g., Mitkovska & Bužarovska 2012: 197, 204). However, Anderwald (2018: 4) argues that when the GET-passive began to emerge, these sentences were, in fact, not reflexive or reciprocal but regular, central passives. She cites historical sources that show how "conventions of getting introduced and getting acquainted have changed enormously" (Anderwald 2018: 4) from the eighteenth and nineteenth centuries, when third-party mediation was required. Similarly, *getting married* was not a mere matter between two individuals (Anderwald 2018: 6), and acts of grooming and body care, such as *getting dressed* or *shaved*, were typically assisted as they involved corsets, shaving knives, and other now obsolete or rare practices (Anderwald 2018: 7–8).

Moreover, versatile *get* also functions as a verb of causation with both adjectival and verbal participles. In this context, Wanner (2009: 99) discusses the following examples from the Frown corpus (Mair 1992–6):

(47) We can get everybody engaged. (Frown/A05)

(48) "I'll get it taken care of," Lily offered. (Frown/N03)

Such cases are often but not always excluded from investigations of the passive. As Wanner (2009), approaching the analysis from a functional-generative point of view, names the presence of an "implicit agent" as the defining characteristic of the passive, it can be argued that also causative *get* with a verbal participle can be counted as passive (Wanner 2009: 101). Similarly, Dixon (2005: 358) sees a connection between the causative and passive senses of *get*, through sentences such as (49)–(52).

(49) The boss got Cameron to fire Jay.

(50) The boss got Jay (to be) fired.

(51) Jay got themselves fired.

(52) Jay got fired.

Examples (49)–(51) carry causative meanings, but Examples (50)–(52) also contain a passive element. Dixon (2005: 358) suggests that such examples are "related." In his view, the GET-passive, in fact, involves an omission of *be* and of a reflexive pronoun. Our search strategy does not capture instances where a noun or pronoun intervenes between the *be* or *get* and the participle; consequently, Examples (49)–(51) fall outside of the envelope of variation covered in our study.

In a diachronic study of a construction undergoing significant change, the problem is exacerbated by the fact that the alternation itself is not stable over time. As the GET-passive increases in frequency, it encroaches upon territory formerly reserved exclusively for the BE-passive. In the course of this process, initially categorical environments may become open for variation. For instance, Banks (1986: 127) questions the acceptability of GET-passives with an explicit agent coded in a prepositional phrase headed by *by* in the late twentieth century. Yet, the Corpus of Contemporary American English (COCA, Davies 2008) contains hundreds of such instances; see Examples (53) and (54) for just two.

(53) But then his own daughter was getting bullied by another girl, was the victim of some sort of preteen Mean Girls bullshit and he knew who the perpetrator was. (COCA/2009/fiction)

(54) Superheroes always have origin stories. spider- Man gets bitten by a genetically altered arachnid. (COCA/2005/magazine)

3.3 Previous Approaches and Their Limitations

Previous studies on the passive have tended to rely on manual coding of instances as either central passive or not and then exclude the latter. Fehringer (2022: 5) takes a variationist approach similar to ours, aiming to only include cases where there is a genuine choice between *be* and *get* without substantial change in meaning. However, with Fehringer's (2022) dataset being much smaller than ours (N = 792, after cleaning), the choice of which observations to count could be made on a manual token-by-token basis. To give another example, Hundt, Dallas, and Nakanishi (2023) rely on sampling to make manual coding of all examined instances possible. They take a random sample of 150

BE-passives from each of the ten varieties of English they examine and code these individually (Hundt, Dallas, & Nakanishi 2023: 6).

It must be pointed out, however, that even the manual sorting of observations into central and nonpassives is not a trivial task. Different studies report different criteria for making the decision about centrality and sometimes even disagree about criteria (Granger 1983: 1).[1] Since the number of mentioned criteria is high and there are significant overlaps, we will enumerate the suggested features and tests without specifying which scholars named which features. The following sets of criteria have been used to distinguish true or central passives from other formally similar constructions (Wasow 1977; Granger 1983; Quirk et al. 1985: 167–71; Collins 1996: 45–6; Downing 1996: 181; Huddleston & Pullum 2002: 1436–7; Rühlemann 2007: 113–14, 116; Toyota 2009: 477; Honda 2012: 74–5; Collins & Yao 2013: 494; McIntyre 2013: 22; Coto Villalibre 2015: 18; Schwarz 2015: 158).

If the answer to these questions is yes, the sentence in question is a central passive:

1. Can a semantically related active sentence be formulated?
2. Can *get* be replaced by *be* without a dramatic change in meaning?
3. Is an agent mentioned or recoverable from context that is not the grammatical subject?
4. Can a *by*-PP be added to name the agent?

By contrast, an affirmative response to any of the following questions indicates a noncentral passive:

1. Can *be* or *get* be replaced by a lexical copular verb like *feel*, *seem*, *look*, *remain*, *become*, *act*, or *sound*?
2. Can the participle be followed by a preposition other than *by*?
3. Can the participle be modified by a degree adverb?
4. Can the participle be modified by *quite*, *rather*, *very*, *too*, or *completely*?
5. Can the participle be prefixed with *un*- to form an antonym?[2]
6. Can a comparative or superlative form be created of the participle?
7. Can the participle be coordinated with an adjective?
8. Does *get* carry the meaning "obtain, receive" or "reach, arrive (at a place)" in the sentence?
9. Is the active version of the sentence perfective?

Many of these criteria rely on making acceptability judgments about hypothetical utterances. However, such acceptability and these judgments have been subject to debate and change in relation to the GET-passive (e.g., Sussex 1982: 91) and are not stable and agreed upon in general. We made the same observation when coding a sample of sentences for centrality in order to train our own classifier (see next section). Making judgments on questions such as whether a coordinated adjective could be added is extremely difficult. There is no line but a gradient from acceptable and frequent to unusual and creative to weird and dubious to unacceptable and ungrammatical, and in some cases, we could not agree on a judgment among the four of us.

3.4 An Automated Approach

In treating the passive alternation as a sociolinguistic variable, we follow Cheshire's (2005: 99) position that when two alternate sentences rely on the same lexical verb and the same entities as sentence arguments, they can be considered semantic equivalents to a sufficient degree. Overall, a "tacit consensus seems to be that the condition of strict semantic equivalence can be relaxed for syntactic variables, so that a variable can be set up on the basis of an equivalence in discourse function" (Dines 1980; Coupland 1983; both cited in Cheshire 2005: 85). However, we also take measures to exclude nonpassives from our analysis, described in this section.

In the first step, we eliminate a number of lexemes that do not participate in the passive alternation. These include participles that are categorically or in the vast majority of cases adjectival and some items falsely tagged in the original corpora. This is the full list of excluded forms: *accustomed, acquainted, addicted, agitated, alarmed, alienated, amazed, annoyed, appalled, armed, attracted, awed, baffled, based, blurred, boozed, bored, born, bothered, bound to (but not bound in other contexts), clogged, committed, complicated, confused, connected, dazzled, delighted, depressed, disappointed, disheartened, divorced, drunk, embarrassed, embroiled, engaged, exasperated, excited, exhausted, frightened, frustrated, gone, hooked, hurt, impressed, inspired, interested, intrigued, involved, irritated, isolated, located, lost, married, medicaid, organised, organized, overwhelmed, overrated, over-rated, panicked, paralyzed, paralysed, pissed, prepared, rid, relaxed, satisfied, scared, shocked, situated, started, stranded, stressed, stuck, surprised, tempted, thrilled, tired, tuned, under-rated, underrated, upset, wet, worried.*

In a second step, to ensure that the modeled lexical verbs genuinely participate in the alternation, we require that each of them occurs with each of the two auxiliaries a minimum of twenty times per corpus. The boundary was set considerably above the theoretical minimum of one occurrence in order to reduce the bias stemming from *be* being much more common as a passive auxiliary than *get*. If there are on average twenty-six or thirty (depending on the corpus) BE-passives for each GET-passive, including items with even a single occurrence with *get* would create the false impression that infrequent verbs statistically favor *get* as a passive auxiliary. Ultimately, however, this restriction is arbitrarily chosen. In practical terms, it has the positive consequence of reducing the dataset and thus making processing and modeling it computationally more manageable.

To automate an evaluation of where on the passive gradient a token falls, we train a logistic regression model on a manually coded sample of sentences. Independent raters coded each token in the sample as either central passive or not central passive, employing the criteria suggested by Schwarz (2015: 158). For a passive to be classified as central,

1. the construction needs to have an active analogue,
2. the participle cannot be coordinated with an adjective,
3. the participle cannot be modified by *quite* or *rather*,
4. the auxiliary cannot be replaced by a lexical copular verb like *feel* or *seem*, and
5. an agent is present or could be added to the construction.

Two raters handcoded the same random sample of 10,000 sentences from COHA for whether they constitute true cases of alternation and can therefore be regarded as central passives. The raters agree in 8,861 cases (88.6 percent). This corresponds to a Cohen's kappa, a measure to assess inter-rater agreement between two raters on categorical data, of 0.6145, indicating substantial agreement (Landis & Koch 1977: 165; a score of 1.0 represents absolute agreement between the coders, while 0 represents none.). We further limit this COHA sample to those cases containing participles that can be found with both *be* and *get* in the full data ($n = 6{,}984$). We also added a handcoded sample of sentences from GloWbE, which was roughly equal in size ($n = 9{,}252$) for a total of 16,236 clauses. In order to maximize efficiency, and since we assume inter-rater agreement not to substantially differ for GloWbE as opposed to COHA, the different raters coded different sentences, without a further calculation of kappa.

Next, we set our sights on automating this manual annotation in order to extend it to the large datasets comprising millions of tokens. Then, we fit a logistic regression model that predicts whether an instance was coded as central or not based on a number of automatically extracted measures indicating how frequently each participle type in our data (n = 267 in COHA; n = 1,866 in GloWbE) is used in an adjectival versus a more prototypically verbal function.

Specifically, on the participle level we process the whole corpus with a Python script (available via the companion website) and consider for each participle the proportion of all its occurrences in the corpus that

1. is preceded by a degree-modifying adverb (*very, more, most, quite, rather, really, extremely, so, highly, hugely, pretty, relatively, totally, completely, utterly, reasonably*), following Dixon (2005: 167), who argues that only adjectives can be premodified by *very*;
2. occurs as the complement of a copulative verb other than *be* (*seem, feel, taste, look, smell, appear, sound, become, turn, go, grow, remain, stay, keep*);
3. occurs in coordination with a true adjective (e.g., "happy and excited," "shaken and wet"); and
4. occurs with prefixation with *un-*.

For each of these participle-level measures, higher values indicate a more adjectival and therefore less central passive use.

On the verb lemma level, we include as predictors the proportion of all occurrences that

1. consists of past participial realizations (assuming that higher values indicate verb lemmas with less dynamic properties, which implies a more adjectival, less verbal function);
2. occurs as the first (lexical) verb in the sentence (assuming that higher frequencies indicate more dynamic verbs and, therefore, more central passives). We define sentence boundaries as any occurrence of a token that is either a full stop, a question mark, an exclamation point, a semicolon, or a colon. Additionally, any time our script encounters a sequence of ten anonymized tokens (represented as "@"), we also assume a sentence boundary; and
3. occurs in the active present tense (assuming that this indicates more dynamic verbs and central passives).

Finally, on the sentence level, we consider

1. whether the construction is preceded by an adverb;
2. whether the construction is followed by a prepositional phrase headed by *by* (and thus more likely to be a central passive).

Prior to model fitting, the numeric variables were z-scored to center and scale them. The categorical variables were treatment-coded, with the baseline categories being not preceded by an adverb and not followed by a prepositional phrase headed by *by*. To illustrate, consider Examples (55) through (58) from our data. The values provided in square brackets after each example are the input values for the predictors outlined in the bullets above, in that order, prior to normalization.

(55) Mr. Romney was said by others to be presenting the proposal in "low key." (COHA, 728651, 1970, news) [0.0003, 0.0001, 0.0009, 0.0003, 0.0471, 0.0031, 0.1883, No, Yes]

(56) The United States was already deeply entangled in the labor question through the Adamson Bill of 1916. (COHA, 430805, 1918, magazine) [0.0439, 0.2085, 0.0208, 0.0058, 0.5632, 0.0279, 0.0257, Yes, No]

(57) I think the NZ Police should be thanked by the public. (GloWbE, 1726138, New Zealand) [0.0013, 0.0014, 0.0088, 0.0013, 0.0061, <0.001, 0.8122, No, Yes]

(58) A growing layer of workers and young people are completely disillusioned with the main parties. (GloWbE, 3761165, Ireland) [0.0935, 0.1863, 0.0754, 0.0002, 0.7706, 0.0144, 0.1035, Yes, No]

This model was fitted on a training set of 70 percent of the data (n = 11,366), holding out the remaining data points to evaluate the model performance on. After fitting the model, we excluded the predictors "coordination with true adjective," "prefixation with *un-*," and "first verb in sentence" because their slopes were not significant at $p < 0.05$ or pointed in the wrong direction. The final model's R^2 was 0.2081 (Tjur's pseudo-R^2), which is a fairly low value. The model output is shown in Table 3. This model predicts the log-odds of a sentence being rated as a central passive.

We evaluate the model performance on the test data (n = 4,870). The probability of an item being a central passive is 0.8099 on average (sd = 0.1248) for sentences that were rated as passives. In contrast, it is much lower (m = 0.613, sd = 0.2776) for those that were rated as noncentral passives. The following examples illustrate the range of predicted probabilities, going from 0.95 in Example (59) to 0.75 in Example (60), 0.5 in Example (61), 0.25 in Example (62), and finally one of the lowest-scoring examples in Example (63).

(59) They must be answered by all countries acting as one. (COHA, 203668, 1960, magazine)

(60) The foundation was partly washed away yesterday. (COHA, 781206, 1889, news)

Table 3 Logistic Regression Model Predicting Tokens That Were Manually Coded as Central (vs. Noncentral) Passives from Participle-, Lemma-, and Token-Level Predictors

Term	Hyp. slope	Estimate	Std. error	z-value	*p*-value	sig.	95% CI low	95% CI high
Intercept	NA	1.20	0.03	43.86	<0.0001	***	1.15	1.25
preceded by adverb (participle)	–	−0.63	0.04	−17.06	<0.0001	***	−0.70	−0.56
copulative verb complement	–	−0.59	0.04	−15.22	<0.0001	***	−0.67	−0.52
past participial realizations	–	−0.24	0.02	−10.46	<0.0001	***	−0.29	−0.20
used in active present tense	+	0.17	0.03	6.33	<0.0001	***	0.12	0.22
preceded by an adverb (sentence)	–	−0.36	0.08	−4.75	<0.0001	***	−0.51	−0.21
prepositional phrase headed by *by*	+	1.09	0.10	10.51	<0.0001	***	0.89	1.29

(61) and the document was filled with quotations from his earlier declarations. (COHA, 728412, 1970, news)

(62) From top to bottom, the estate is drenched in historical luxury. (COHA, 621976, 2000, news)

(63) The United States was already deeply entangled in the labor question through the Adamson Bill of 1916. (COHA, 430805, 1918, magazine)

Figure 1 shows the trade-off between sensitivity (ability to identify true positives) and specificity (ability to identify true negatives) of the classifier as a function of the probability threshold for classification. The best overall performance is achieved when setting the probability threshold to 0.78, where the sum of sensitivity and specificity is 1.432. We opt for the minimally more conservative threshold of 0.8099, that is, the mean probability of all central passives. At this threshold, the sum sensitivity and specificity is only marginally smaller (1.391). This choice slightly privileges specificity over sensibility, as we are interested in circumscribing the variable context as best possible and ready to afford the loss of a portion of potential valid central cases.

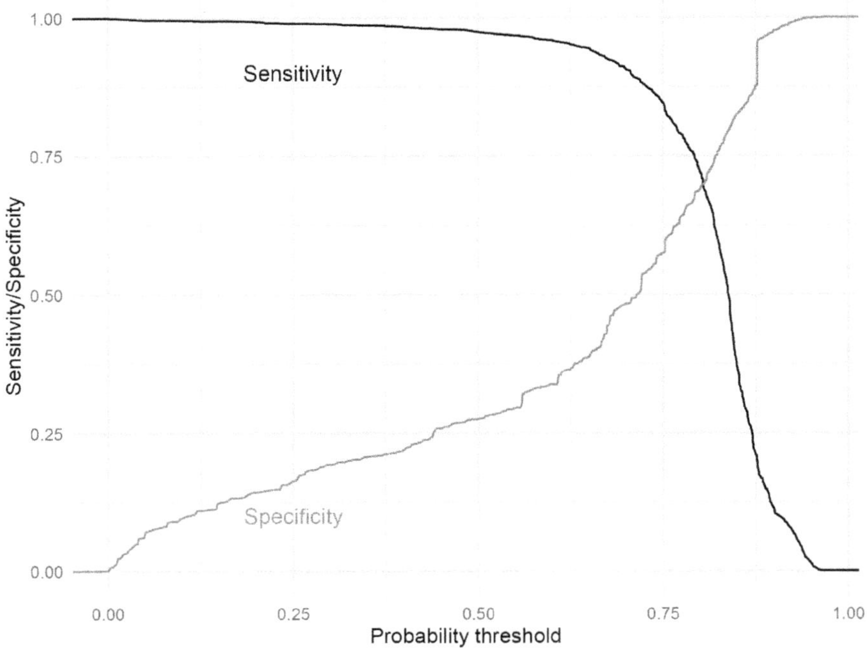

Figure 1 Sensitivity and specificity as a function of probability threshold.

Table 4 shows the confusion matrix for the classifier at this threshold for the test data. The corresponding F-score is 0.76. Our analysis will present two models per corpus, one fitted on the central and one on the complete dataset, pointing out differences in the results wherever these arise.

Originally, the COHA data contained 1,181,196 tokens and 267 distinct verb lemmas after exclusion of categorical cases, which were reduced to 662,170 and 182, respectively, after applying this threshold in order to only include central passives. In contrast, the GloWbE data initially had 9,932,636 tokens and 1,866 unique verb lemmas, while the central GloWbE passives consisted of 5,650,629 tokens of 1,280 different verbs.

Given the relatively low R^2 value of the classifier and the necessarily arbitrary threshold we define for inclusion in the central data set, we highlight the fact that no data are ultimately lost in our procedure. Retaining all data in the full model and fitting an additional one only on the central data (as defined earlier) allows us to explore the effect of centrality and thus of approaching a strict delineation of the variable context. Doing the latter in an automated way is relatively new territory, and we expect that the method stands to benefit from further testing and refinement.

Table 4 Confusion Matrix for the Centrality Classifier at Probability Threshold $p = 0.8099$

		Actual	
		Central	**Noncentral**
Predicted	Central	2497	326
	Noncentral	1216	831

3.5 Summary

In this chapter, we have discussed the theoretical and practical problem of defining the English passive and delimiting it from other formally similar sentences, finding that it might not be possible to establish a clear boundary between "central" passives and others but that we might be dealing with a cline. We looked at criteria used in previous studies for detecting central passives, which have in most cases been applied on a manual token-by-token basis. However, for our big-data approach, we need an automatized process for evaluating the centrality of potential passive sentences. We have developed this in the present section, combining exclusion of categorical cases, a manually annotated gold-standard dataset and a specifically trained classifier that distinguishes central from less central passive tokens. To our knowledge, this is the first time the question of passive centrality has been approached from this angle, and our procedure allows us to scale up a robust variationist analysis of the English passive alternation by several orders of magnitude. We see considerable potential for usage-based, corpus, and sociolinguistics in adopting such a computational approach for circumscribing the envelope of variation (Bleaman & Kommerell 2024). The distinction into central and all passives will be employed in both our regression models in Chapters 9 and 10.

4

Operationalizing Subject Responsibility

A frequently suggested semantic implication of the GET-passive is subject responsibility—the idea that the subject referent is somehow responsible for the situation befalling them (see Section 2.4). In the clearest case, the subject has initiated the action, as in Hatcher's (1949: 436–7) ever-relevant example, "Have you gotten vaccinated yet?," but more commonly, the situation results indirectly from the subject's actions, for instance, their carelessness or failure to prevent it. This contrasts with the BE-passive, where the agent, whether named in the *by*-PP or left implicit, retains responsibility. Subject responsibility is one of the main semantic variables whose influence on the passive alternation we want to investigate. In this chapter, we will describe the steps taken to operationalize subject responsibility and include it in this study, relying on the concept of animacy (Sections 4.1–4.3) and the presence or absence of an agent (Section 4.4). Using these variables is consistent with existing research. However, we recognize that both are relatively coarse approximations. An animate subject does not have to carry responsibility, and thus it is entirely possible to find animate subjects with BE-passives as well as with GET-passives. Similarly, the absence of an explicitly expressed agent in a *by*-PP does not necessarily imply full responsibility of the sentence subject. In both variables, consequently, we expect shifts in average preferences depending on the kind of passive construction rather than anything approaching categorical behavior. While recognizing these limitations, we would argue that a large-scale multivariate study is in a better position to utilize these predictors to good effect, being better able to detect subtle differences in selectional preference.

4.1 Animacy as a Prerequisite for Responsibility

Animacy is an inherent, extralinguistic property of entities, wherein the crudest distinction is made between entities conceptualized as alive and those conceptualized as not alive. Being alive comes with certain assumptions about consciousness, sentience, and the ability to move and act in the world (Yamamoto 1999: 1). Animacy influences how "salient" entities are to language users (Zaenen et al. 2004: 118). It is also encoded in the grammars of many languages (Comrie 1981: chapter 9); for example, it is reflected in the English pronominal paradigm in contrasts such as 3SG *she/he/they* versus *it* or relative *who* versus *which*. Animacy is conceived of as an anthropocentric hierarchy from human to nonhuman animate to inanimate, but finer distinctions may sometimes be relevant, for instance, between different grammatical persons, proper and common nouns (Comrie 1981: 179), or higher and lower animals (Yamamoto 1999: 12).

Animacy is intertwined with other concepts; the amount of "prominence" an entity receives in discourse depends on its animacy but also on person (first vs. second vs. third), individuation, and definiteness (Yamamoto 1999: 3–4; Zaenen et al. 2004: 118). Zaenen et al. (2004: 120) propose that animacy depends on how "human-like" an entity is perceived to be. Going along similar lines, Langacker (1991: 306–7) calls it an "empathy hierarchy" based on "likeness and common concerns." Comrie (1981: 191) suggests that what is usually seen as an effect of animacy may, in fact, largely have to do with the "topic-worthiness" of an entity.

There is a natural overlap between animacy and certain semantic roles. Agents—associated with "intentionality, control, responsibility, and consciousness"—and sentient experiencers are typically animate (Dahl & Fraurud 1996: 58; Yamamoto 1999: 5). This is also the key to how animacy is related to subject responsibility: only animate referents are capable of conscious, controlled, purposeful action and hence capable of carrying responsibility for its consequences (Dahl & Fraurud 1996: 58).

Studies tend to operationalize subject responsibility in terms of animacy of the sentence subject. This is also the path we are taking, including in our model as a factor animacy of the subject referent in order to test the alleged association between subject responsibility and *get* as a passive auxiliary. Based on ample previous literature (see Section 2.4), the expectation is that inanimate subjects disfavor *get*. There are three main challenges associated with the predictor subject animacy: (1) the automatic detection of the sentence subject, (2) the fuzziness of animacy as a category, and (3) the coding of animacy. We will discuss each of these problems and our solutions later.

Animacy can also be seen as related to the concept of the GET-passive indicating adversativity or benefit, as "adversity or advantage are relevant only to humans/animates, their associates or possessions" (Givón & Yang 1994: 139).

Therefore, this variable is related to two hypotheses in our study: we expect *get* to co-occur with animate subjects because animate subjects can (1) be responsible for events and (2) experience benefits and drawbacks.

4.2 Extracting Subject Noun Phrase Heads

The first step in testing subject animacy is to detect the subject of the passive sentences in our dataset. In many cases, the subject is simply the closest noun or pronoun to the left of the verb phrase. In pilot research (Bohmann et al. 2023), we found this to be accurate in approximately 75 percent of all cases, leaving a significant margin of error.[1] To improve precision, syntactic parsing of the sentence in question is required. For this, we rely on the DependencyParser class of Python's (van Rossum & Drake 2009) spaCy module (Honnibal & Montani 2017), which implements a modified version of Honnibal and Johnson's (2015) non-monotonic arc-eager transition system. Each extracted sentence with a passive token is parsed, and the head of the noun phrase (NP) with a dependency relation "nsubjpass" (subject of a passive sentence) is identified. In case this head is a relativizer, the script retrieves the head of the antecedent NP. To illustrate, (64) and (65) are two examples of passive sentences parsed in spaCy to identify each word's dependency relation, head element, and POS.

(64) (The, det, president, DET), (president, nsubj, was, NOUN), (of, prep, president, ADP), (the, det, nation, DET), (small, amod, nation, ADJ), (Asian, amod, nation, ADJ), (nation, pobj, of, NOUN), (was, ROOT, was, AUX), (re, acomp, was, VERB), (-, acomp, was, VERB), (elected, acomp, was, VERB), (last, amod, Sunday, ADJ), (Sunday, npadvmod, elected, PROPN), (., punct, was, PUNCT)

(65) (The, det, townspeople, DET), (townspeople, nsubj, told, NOUN), (that, nsubjpass, evacuated, PRON), (were, auxpass, evacuated, AUX), (evacuated, relcl, townspeople, VERB), (told, ROOT, told, VERB), (their, poss, stories, PRON), (stories, dobj, told, NOUN), (on, prep, told, ADP), (local, amod, news, ADJ), (news, pobj, on, NOUN), (., punct, told, PUNCT)

In (64), identifying president as the subject NP head via its "nsubjpass" dependency relation is straightforward. In (65), a meaningful interpretation of the NP head requires identifying the antecedent of *that*. Our script handles such cases, in which it processes the elements to the left of the relativizer and identifies the head of the NP premodified by the relative clause.

Machine-led syntactic parsing of complex sentences of natural language is not a trivial task. In addition to issues of accuracy, this process involves further theoretical and practical challenges, discussed later.

One shortcoming is that our procedure identifies a single noun to represent the whole subject NP. In most cases, this is unproblematic, as determiners, adjectival premodifiers, and relative clause postmodifiers tend not to change the animacy type of a noun. However, in a few cases, this will lead to downstream errors, as, for example, proper nouns are not always recognizable from their parts. For instance, *Anthony* and *Atkinson* are personal names, but *St. Anthony* and *Fort Atkinson* are place names.

Moreover, sometimes, there is no single noun that could be identified as a subject. Some sentences do not feature an overt subject; instead, the subject is deductible from the context; yet, in other cases, the subject may be an entire clause. Some examples are shown in Examples (66)–(68). The syntactic subject is given in italics.

(66) *How rapidly the Franciscans and Dominicans declined from the rigid purity of their founders* need scarcely be told. (COHA/1869/magazine)

(67) Honey, we'll just have to chance it. Well, I'm game. I mean, even if the roads are slippery and muddy they can't hold us up too long. The chances of getting hit by lightening are, well, extremely slim. (COHA/1965/TV/movie)

(68) Let the early pace run but don't get fooled by it. (COHA/1959/magazine)

The subject in Example (66) is the whole *wh*-clause that refers to a situation. Example (67) is a control construction with an arbitrary PRO, that is, an elided subject of the embedded clause. This subject can be retrieved either generically ("anyone") or anaphorically ("we"). Arbitrary PRO is a common occurrence in English control constructions, which escapes our lookup procedure. Example (68) contains an imperative clause; as a result, the subject is not named but is understood to be the addressee(s). If our script is not able to identify a subject, it provides the output "xxx"; these instances are placed in the category "unknown." The latter comprises between 16.8 and 17.4 percent of all tokens in our data sets (see Table 5 for details).

To estimate the accuracy of our subject detection procedure, we checked a random sample of 1,000 observations, one half from COHA and the other from GloWbE. In this sample, the correct subject head had been identified in 88.7 percent of cases. This, thus, represents a considerable improvement from the 75-percent accuracy achieved in the pilot study (Bohmann et al. 2023). After

Table 5 Distribution of Animacy Categories across Subject Noun Phrase Heads

	COHA full		**COHA central**		**GloWbE full**		**GloWbE central**	
	N	%	*N*	%	*N*	%	*N*	%
Inanimate	590,290	49.97	344,754	52.06	5,256,250	52.92	3,167,963	56.06
Animate	320,832	27.16	174,586	26.37	2,434,967	24.51	1,269,958	22.47
Collective	38,173	3.23	18,825	2.84	423,855	4.27	215,204	3.81
Body part	27,256	2.31	12,657	1.91	93,618	0.94	43,420	0.77
Unknown	204,645	17.33	111,348	16.82	1,723,946	17.36	954,084	16.88
Total	**1,181,196**		**662,170**		**9,932,636**		**5,650,629**	

extracting the headwords of subject NPs, the coding for animacy for the most frequently occurring types was carried out manually, as described in the next section.

4.3 Classifying Noun Phrase Animacy

The animacy gradient can be split into categories in more than one way and has been split differently in different studies. One problem here, identified by Zaenen et al. (2004: 119–20), is that "the linguistically relevant distinctions between animate and non-animate and between human and non-human are not the same as the biological distinctions." The authors classify animacy as follows: human, collectivities of humans ("a group with collective voice"), animal (nonhuman, including viruses and bacteria), place, time, "prototypical" concrete objects or substances (including body parts), inanimate and not prototypically concrete, intelligent machines, vehicles,[2] and three different tags for uncertain cases (Zaenen et al. 2004: 121–2).

Following Zaenen et al.'s (2004) classification, Hundt, Dallas, and Nakanishi (2023) distinguish between "human," "animate," and "inanimate" in a study of the passive alternation. The first category includes humans and human-like imaginary creatures. The second category encompasses nonhuman animals as well as "collectives of humans," place names standing for humans, "plants and mushrooms," and "viruses and bacteria." Alongside other inanimates, "intelligent machines and vehicles" are put in the third group (Hundt, Dallas, & Nakanishi 2023: 10–11). Note that in both cases, the coding was done by human coders separately for each sentence (Zaenen et al. 2004: 122; Hundt, Dallas, & Nakanishi 2023: 10). It is noteworthy that Zaenen et al. (2004: 122) comment on the unexpected lack of agreement between their three trained coders around some of the categories: "We had hoped that the coders would share the intuitive understanding of the developers of the categories. This is obviously not the case for all categories." The inter-coder agreement was high for humans and non-concrete inanimates, but there was more disparity in the minor categories (Zaenen et al. 2004: 122).

Dahl and Fraurud (1996: 62) explain that distinctions of animacy are inherently "fuzzy," as language may treat inanimate entities sometimes as (if) animate and vice versa. An animate entity can be represented in an inanimate form, for instance, in a drawing, or animacy can be assigned to an inanimate object such as a plush toy (Yamamoto 1999: 24). Dahl and Fraurud (1996: 62–3) list different types of nonhumans to which animacy can be "extended" in specific contexts; these include animals and mythological creatures, institutions and companies, collective nouns, countries, and personified inanimates. They add that relevant instances of animacy in grammar often result in "exceptions or dubious borderline cases" (Dahl & Fraurud 1996: 63). One such case is displayed as Example (69) below: the subject head noun *Earth* identified by our script can either refer to a mere rock in space or be personified, as a literary device or here quite concretely (also shown by the use of the human-referring relative pronoun *who*).[3]

(69) On April 22 ABC broadcasts the Earth Day Special, featuring Bette Midler as *an abused Mother Earth* who collapses in a town square, suffering from global warming, deforestation, etc., and <u>gets tended</u> by Drs. Doogie Howser (Neil Patrick Harris) and Steven Kiley (James Brolin). (COHA/1990/magazine)

Evidently, determining animacy is not always straightforward, even when investigating it qualitatively at the token level. We code animacy at the level of noun types, which is the only way to cope with a dataset of several million observations. For this approach, a major problem is polysemy. It is not unusual for a word to have multiple meanings, and these may differ in terms of animacy. For example, the noun *servers* in Examples (70) and (71) show a split between an animate and an inanimate meaning that is not uncommon with *-er* nouns (also, e.g., *planner, installer, spinner, polluters*).

(70) the hard fact that tipping really is how *servers* <u>get paid</u> (GloWbE/USA/blog)

(71) *The servers* <u>get taken down</u> with no notice for emergency maintenance. (GloWbE/South Africa/general)

There are other semantic groups that show this ambiguity fairly systematically: the same word often refers to both a people and the language they speak (e.g., *Dutch*) and an animal seen as a living being and a food item (e.g., *prawns*), and many brand names refer to the product manufactured as well as to the company as a human collective (e.g., *Ferrari*). The matter is further complicated by the use of metaphor, metonymy, and meronymy, which expand the extension of words; see Examples (72) and (73).

(72) Their whole army is in the midst of the town; *neither age nor sex* is spared: at this moment, they are even trampling upon infants (COHA/1811/fiction)

(73) Federal employees have real jobs. *This asshole* was elected. (GloWbE/USA/blog)

In (72), the abstract nouns *age* and *sex* are used to refer to groups of people, while in (73), a tabooed body-part noun stands metaphorically for an unpleasant person. In fact, many of these difficult cases concern the category "body part," and it is considered separately in our study precisely because its animacy status is unclear. Overall, our accuracy check (to be discussed later) suggests that polysemy is not a significant source of inaccuracy in our analysis.

We looked into using an existing lexicon of animacy, but the selection is narrow and application difficult. The publicly available lexicon WordNet® groups words semantically into "sets of cognitive synonyms," and a categorization of nouns into persons, animals, groups, and numerous different inanimate types could be extracted from their freely downloadable database (Princeton University 2010). However, we worry that the comprehensiveness of the WordNet® database would actually be counterproductive for the purposes of our project. WordNet® lists all meanings of a lexeme without weighing that some of them are much more common than others. For example, according to WordNet®, *pen* is ambiguous between an inanimate "writing implement" and an animate "female swan," and *Angel* could equally refer to "a spiritual being" or the Angel Falls waterfall in Venezuela (Princeton University 2010). Considering all senses indiscriminately would likely lead to an inflation of the category "unknown" and thus entail a loss of information in the predictor subject animacy. Dictionaries typically also exclude one major type of animate subject: personal names. Finally, it is unclear how well our datasets, containing diachronic data as well as non-standardized varieties of English, are represented in standard dictionaries. Hence, we decided to carry out the coding of the most frequent noun types manually. Nonetheless, it is obvious that there would be a need for this kind of resource in natural language processing, either in the form of a comprehensive dictionary or, ideally, of a robust categorization algorithm.

We distinguish between the following five categories of animacy: inanimate, animate, body part, collective, and unknown, which we discuss in the following. The "inanimate" class contains various abstract and concrete inanimate entities (e.g., *exclusions*, *rainforests*, *screenshots*, *cleanser*).

"Animate" includes proper and common nouns referring to humans, animals, and imaginary living creatures (e.g., *bloggers*, *appellant*, *Ronaldo*, *vampires*, *pug*). We depart from some other classifications in not separating humans from other animates; this decision reflects our belief that not only humans but also animals can be responsible agents of action. With the same reasoning, plants and mushrooms are excluded from this category and considered inanimate instead.

"Body parts" (e.g., *heart*, *eyes*, *feathers*, *nerve*) are a category of their own because of their meronymic relationship to animates; we expect them to be conceptualized varyingly as animate or inanimate depending on context. It will be interesting to observe whether this category differs from the others in terms of its preferences.

The category "collective" encompasses items that may refer to human and animal collectives and thus be viewed as animate (e.g., *Egypt*, *orchestra*, *treasury*, *committees*, *Barca*); see Examples (74) and (75).

(74) Washington sources said that *both Hanoi and Moscow* were asked if they fully understood what the American terms for stopping the bombing were. (COHA/1968/news)

(75) Twenty minutes later, when *the press* was invited inside, 50 men and women with full field packs stampeded toward the front door. (COHA/1996/magazine)

"Collective" includes place names and different human organizations and groupings but also words that are ambiguous between buildings and the institutions that inhabit them (e.g., *churches*, *university*, *museum*) and company names (e.g., *Facebook*). *Magazine* and *newspaper* are included in this group as well; they seem, in the majority of cases, to refer to the organization responsible for producing a particular publication rather than the printed product itself.

The final "unknown" category contains obviously polysemous items that fit multiple categories (e.g., *they* or *nobility* "nobleness," "a noble person," "nobles collectively"), words from other PoS mistagged as nouns (e.g., *thenceforth*), numbers and measurements (e.g., *seventy*, *truckloads*), and items that were so rare that they fell beyond the threshold for manual coding described below (e.g., *gerunds*, *Weyerhaeuser*). Also sentences for which our script was unable to retrieve a subject belong to this category.

The data were coded manually by one author. Capitalization may change the referent of a noun, so forms in lowercase and with an initial capital were considered separately. For instance, *Bush*, *Spears*, and *Melody* are likely personal names when capitalized and common nouns when not, and *Hurricanes* with an initial capital usually refers to the sports team Carolina Hurricanes, a collective, while lowercase *hurricanes* generally refers to weather phenomena. Even though capitalization often makes an entity more animate, this is not always the case. For example, consider the *Python* programming language and *python* the reptile, where the latter can be considered more animate. When the meaning or referent of a word was not well known, Google searches, web-based dictionaries, and the two source corpora were used as aids.

All nouns that occur at least forty times in subject position in the joint dataset (COHA and GloWbE) were handcoded, and some less common subjects were annotated if their animacy could be determined without resolution of ambiguity or further research. This amounted to a total of 43,275 noun types with the following distribution into animacy categories: 24,472 inanimates, 12,625 animates, 2,337 collectives, 505 body parts, and 3,336 words of unknown or ambiguous animacy. The unknown category is merged with the data that are untagged. The remaining data consist of 61.3 percent inanimates, 31.6 percent animates, 5.9 percent collectives, and 1.3 percent body parts. The coded data (again, excluding the unknowns) represent 16,741,074 tokens or 82 percent of the data. The extraction of subjects was done before excluding any noncentral passives. An overview of the animacy coding in both corpora is given in Table 5. Note that, for each corpus, we work with a dataset of all tokens and one with only the ones that are predicted to be central passives according to the procedure delineated in Chapter 3.

We checked the accuracy of our type-based animacy coding on a sample of 1,000 passive sentences (500 from COHA, 500 from GloWbE). Observations with the tag "unknown" represent 18.5 percent of the data and are not considered in the accuracy check. Extrapolating the results to the handcoded part of the entire dataset without the unknown and uncoded instances yields an estimated accuracy of 93.9 percent for the animacy coding. The remaining 6.1 percent display three sources of error. The first type has to do with the accuracy of subject detection. Detecting the correct sentence subject was successful in approximately 89 percent of cases (see Section 4.2). The identification of the wrong noun as the subject does not necessarily lead to the sentence receiving a wrong animacy tag (the item may be labeled as unknown or accidentally receive the correct tag), but it did result in an incorrect animacy label in 3.9 percent of the tagged observations. Further 1.3 percent are incorrectly annotated because of shortcomings in the type-based manual annotation, such as failing to consider *chamber* also as a human collective or *Shadow* as a human character in Neil Gaiman's *American Gods*. Finally, 0.9 percent of tagged sentences are lemmatized or PoS-tagged erroneously in the original data and are not combinations of *be* or *get* + past participle at all. This is displayed in Examples (76) and (77). Here, *she's* is a contraction of *she has* in (76), and *paid* should be tagged as an adjective premodifying *officials* in (77), not as a participle in a passive construction. The problem here is not in the animacy coding—such sentences should not be part of the extraction in the first place. They represent inevitable noise in such a large dataset. Overall, we consider this near-94-percent accuracy for semiautomatic coding of subject animacy high. The set of coded nouns are made available to the research community on the project website.[4]

(76) If she's already blown through $1.2 million than I WILL call her an idiot. (GloWbE/USA/blog)

(77) We're only poorly paid public officials. (COHA/1937/fiction)

4.4 *By*-Prepositional Phrase

We will end this chapter by briefly discussing a second variable often mentioned in the context of subject responsibility: the presence of a *by*-PP following the passivized verb. The referent of this prepositional phrase is usually the agent of the event, and including it in the sentence is optional. Explicitly naming an agent in this manner is often treated as incompatible with the idea of the grammatical subject carrying responsibility for the event since the *by*-PP draws attention to the responsibility of another participant (Wanner 2009: 104). Therefore, we can proceed to formulate a hypothesis about the *by*-PP. While naming the agent is uncommon in the passive in general, we expect to find it even less frequently in the GET-passive. Our second hypothesis testing subject responsibility is, hence, that the presence of a *by*-PP disfavors the choice of *get* as a passive auxiliary, as suggested, *inter alia*, by Arce-Arenales, Axelrod, and Fox (1994), Quirk et al. (1985: 161), as well as our own pilot study (Bohmann et al. 2023: 42).

To test this, we check for each instance of the passive whether a *by*-PP is included or not. We approximate this issue by checking the word immediately following the past participle. This method is perfect in neither accuracy nor recall: it will not find instances where the PP is delayed in the sentence, but it will collect some cases where the *by*-PP carries a function different than a passive agent, such as a time adverbial. In Example (78), our automatic method fails to find the agentive *by*-PP "by a brilliant doctor," whereas it assumes that *email* and *word* in Examples (79) and (80), respectively, refer to agents of action.

(78) And I've been treated for that by a brilliant doctor, and in their own words "the results have been spectacular" (GloWbE/UK/general)

(79) The winner will be notified by email. (GloWbE/South Africa/general)

(80) (which backs up my theory that the only reason the last 20 chapters of Huck Finn exists is because Twain must have been getting paid by the word) (GloWbE/USA/blog)

To evaluate the extent of false positives, we manually evaluate 1,000 clauses in our data that have been automatically identified as containing a *by*-PP, with 500 each from COCA and GloWbE. We consider only cases of genuine agent-PPs, where a paraphrase to a corresponding active clause is possible with the NP introduced by *by* promoted to the syntactic subject. A total of 885 of the clauses (88.5 percent) meet this criterion. The differences between the two corpora are relatively marginal: accuracy is at 86.2 percent for COHA and at 90.8 percent for GloWbE. The false positives are predominantly instrumental phrases that encode a procedure or means by which a result is achieved (such as the whole clause introduced by *by* in Example (81), 5.0 percent), formulaic expressions (such as "by surprise" in Example (82), 3.5 percent), temporal (such as "by 2015" in Example (83), 1.1 percent) and degree adverbials (such as "by two bits" in Example (84), 1.0 percent) and a few further individual cases, demonstrated in Examples (85) and (86), comprising 0.9 percent.

(81) Focusing of this hand-held microscope was achieved by sliding the draw tube in. (GloWbE/Philippines/general)

(82) But the English were so taken by surprise that they could not do much. (COHA/1896/fiction)

(83) The targets are to be achieved by 2015. (GloWbE/Kenya/general)

(84) these six bits are shifted left by two bits. (GloWbE/UK/general)

(85) I have goods that are laid by for years. (COHA/1853/fiction)

(86) He'd been screwed by his paws to the plank. (COHA/1981/fiction)

Based on this manual, post hoc evaluation, it appears that the problems in automatic agent-PP detection do not affect a large portion of the data but can rather be put down to inevitable “noise” that the size of the dataset offsets. Moreover, there should be no reason to assume that the inaccuracy would be greater with either *be* or *get*.

These two measures enable us to test one of the most commonly named semantic features of the GET-passive—the passive subject carrying some responsibility over the situation. We expect the GET-passive to favor animate subjects over others and disfavor sentences containing a *by*-PP.

5

Operationalizing Adversativity and Non-Neutrality

The GET-passive has often been linked to non-neutral sentences, primarily in terms of the consequences of the depicted situation. *Get* is hypothesized to be chosen as a passive auxiliary when something good or bad happens to the sentence subject (Hatcher 1949: 441; Toyota 2008: 167–8; see also Section 2.5). Some scholars, however, question whether it is the subject's perspective, and not rather the speaker's or writer's perspective toward the described event (Toyota 2008: 169–71). This can be illustrated with Example (87), where the grammatical subject of the passive is the pronoun *they*.

(87) "Well, we're not going to bother to train anybody in our industry because they'll promptly get snapped up by another industry," the Duke added. (LOB A12 107–8, cited in Toyota 2008: 169)

Toyota (2008) points out that (87) likely describes the negative impact for the speaker *Duke* (rather than for the subject *they*) and rephrases the clause with the passive construction as follows:

(88) We would be adversely affected by another industry's snapping up people in our industry. (Toyota 2008: 169)

To incorporate these semantic constraints in the present study, we employ sentiment analysis as a useful approach for gauging attitudes and affect in discourse. Sentiment analysis is a process of categorizing verbal statements into neutral, positive, or negative based on the emotions, evaluations, and opinions detected therein; some previous studies also investigate *subjectivity*, *appraisal*, *polarity*, *valence*, and *tone* (Rauh 2018: 320).

5.1 Sentiment Analysis: Previous Research

The first and still prevailing use of sentiment analysis has been in consumer behavior analysis and marketing, but it has also been applied in a variety of other domains, ranging from political science (Rauh 2018) to healthcare (Denecke & Reichenpfader 2023; Korkontzelos et al. 2016). Concretely, sentiment analysis has been used, for example, to facilitate disaster response and recovery based on activities in social media and mobile networks (Ragini, Anand, & Bhaskar 2018), to identify adverse drug reactions on Twitter and DailyStrength forums (Korkontzelos et al. 2016), and to detect populist right-wing conspiracy discourse on German online forums (Puschmann et al. 2022). Last but not least, also in sociolinguistic studies, sentiment analysis has been utilized (e.g., Schweinberger 2019; Viola 2023).

Application of sentiment analysis to sociolinguistic questions is still in its infancy. There is little doubt that emotional force of discourse can have an influence on the choice of variants in many cases, but operationalizing such an influence in quantitative terms has rarely been done. Hunt et al. (2023) consider the interrelation of one particular type of emotionally charged language—swear words—with a classic sociolinguistic variable (the pronunciation of the suffix *-ing* with velar nasal /ŋ/ or alveolar nasal /n/) from the perspective of listener perception and find a clear connection between these two phenomena. Schweinberger (2019) conducts sentiment analysis on spoken dialogues in the Irish component of the International Corpus of English (ICE). His interest, however, lies not in specific linguistic variables but in the distribution of different base emotions (fear, joy, surprise, etc.) across registers (public vs. private) and speaker demographics (gender, age, etc.).

The two studies that most directly correspond to our use of sentiment analysis—as a predictor in analyses of particular linguistic variables—are Strelluf and Hills (2021) and Viola (2023). Strelluf and Hills (2021) consider the local, non-standardized feature positive *anymore* in American English. *Anymore*, used without an indicator of negative polarity, refers "to an activity or situation that was not formerly true, but has come to be characteristic of the present" (Murray 1993: 174). An example is provided in (89).

(89) Mizzou is a dumpster fire anymore. (Strelluf & Hills 2021: n.p.)

Importantly for the present discussion, positive *anymore* is said to correlate with a negative speaker attitude. Based on a large collection of geolocated Twitter messages subjected to sentiment analysis, Strelluf and Hill (2021) show that negative speaker attitude indeed influences the choice of the expression.

Viola (2023) provides a programmatic assessment of sentiment analysis for linguistic research, which she exemplifies through a case study of the progressive aspect in Italian. Her findings indicate a statistically significant correlation between negative sentiment and choice of the progressive aspect, in line with findings from other languages, such as English and French. Yet, despite being present, the effect of this correlation is relatively small.

We consider the above findings promising for the potential of sentiment analysis for sociolinguistic research, and our own contribution seeks to advance work in this direction. When considering the passive alternation, however, an additional level of complexity arises. As the opening paragraph of this chapter has shown, there is disagreement (and sometimes ambiguity) as to the perspective from which sentiment is relevant for the choice of passive auxiliary (sentence subject vs. speaker or writer). While these perspectives may often coincide, they do not necessarily do so, as Example (90) illustrates.

(90) To review briefly, in the late 1960s, men got paid more than women (usually double) for doing the exact same job. (COHA/2004/nonfiction)

Here, the sentence subject *men* profits from the unbalanced salary (positive sentiment), but the speaker or writer likely aims to point out the inequity of it (negative sentiment).

We use sentiment analysis to examine whether the GET-passive is used more frequently in sentences that depict a non-neutral attitude toward the depicted situation on behalf of the author or the sentence subject. We try to tease these two apart by investigating sentiment both in the main verb (the activity immediately affecting the subject) and in the entire clause (representing the author's stance in discourse). Our modeling procedure further allows us to investigate the competing hypotheses of adversativity versus non-neutrality favoring *get* (Coto Villalibre 2015)—does the GET-passive occur particularly in sentences depicting unfortunate events or is a similar effect also found in sentences describing favorable events? The procedure, along with other challenges in automated sentiment analysis, specifically addressing historical corpora, will be discussed briefly in the following section.

5.2 Sentiment Analysis: Approaches and Challenges

The goal of sentiment coding is the detection of thought processes and feelings of the speaker or writer toward their discourse. Aside from the issue of categorizing and quantifying complex human emotions (Viola 2023: 3), sentiment analysis entails a number of challenges. In this section, we first illustrate major challenges before we discuss several approaches to sentiment analysis.

One general major challenge in sentiment analysis concerns the detection of semantic nuances that do not simply arise from individual lexical words but from syntactic patterns or the wider context, including matters like negation and irony (Rauh 2018: 321; van Atteveldt, van der Velden, & Boukes 2021: 132). This is illustrated in the following examples:

(91) In the music business I've seen lots of composers invited to pitch for say a TV advert on the basis that they produce the finished music themselves, for free (which can include paying for session musicians, studio time etc), and *only* get paid *if* theirs is [t]he winning pitch. (GloWbE/Great Britain/general; emphasis added by the authors)

(92) There is no reason for people to get killed in Canada. It's one of the safest countries in the world (GloWbE/Sri Lanka/general)

(93) so basically the outside world *thinks* people get treated well (GloWbE/South Africa/general; emphasis added by the authors)

An approach that only considers the values of individual words would be likely to give a positive rating to Example (91). However, considering the use of conditional *if* and the negative entailment of *only*, the overall sentiment should be considered rather negative. Similarly, in Example (92), if the scope of negation is considered, it becomes evident that despite the lexical verb *kill*, the sentiment of the sentence is not as negative, as the overall clause assumes a general safety in Canada. Yet, as one reviewer has pointed out, this example can also be interpreted conversely; the negation "no reason" may intensify the negative sentiment of *kill* rather than weaken it. This is a perfect example of how challenging the identification of sentiment is—even for human raters. Last but not least, in Example (93), the lexical verb *thinks* suggests that the following clause is not true, similarly reverting its sentiment from positive to negative.

Not only fine semantic nuances but also irony pose a particularly great challenge in automated approaches as it has no fixed lexical markers (Rauh 2018: 321). Example (94) displays a case of irony, which the automatic coding likely fails to identify. An automatic approach may detect positive sentiment based on the word *prestigious*, and in order to read the sentence as negative, extralinguistic information is required, that is, that traveling by bus is not considered "prestigious."

(94) And flying is seen as about as prestigious as taking a bus. (COHA/2003/news)

Evidently, the language user's intentions can never be directly accessed and identified without doubt. As a result, researchers have conceptualized a range of different approaches to assess sentiment. First, the analyzed unit can range from a single clause or sentence to an entire text (Sharef, Zin, & Nadali 2016: 157). Second, in quantifying sentiment, different levels of measurement can be employed: sentiment can be treated as a continuous variable, for instance, ranging from −1 (negative extreme) to 0 (neutral), to 1 (positive extreme), or as a categorical variable depicting separate levels, such as negative, neutral, ambiguous or mixed, and positive. Sometimes distinctions are made between different specific positive and negative emotions (e.g., anger, anticipation, fear, disgust, surprise, trust, joy, and sadness in Schweinberger 2019).

One approach to identifying sentiment in a sentence relies on human coders evaluating case by case what sentiments they as readers observe in a given text. These could be trained experts or crowd-sourced lay coders. Humans classifying units of language token by token are able to use co-textual and real-life contextual knowledge to detect sentiment more flexibly (Rauh 2018: 325).

Nonetheless, qualitative annotation does not always produce fully reliable results; human performance is influenced by personal biases, predispositions, and situational disturbances. As a result, individual perceptions may differ between human coders as well as from the original intentions of the author of the text (Rauh 2018: 325–6). Bobicev and Sokolova (2017) examine 1,000 forum posts annotated by three different coders in terms of various inter-annotator agreement measures, that is, percentage agreement, Cohen's (1960) kappa and Krippendorff's alpha (measures to assess inter-rater agreement between multiple raters on categorical data; Krippendorff 2004). The findings are generally less than encouraging, with reported kappa values ranging between 0.4 and 0.5, indicating moderate agreement between the three coders at best (Landis & Koch 1977). Similarly, for part of this research, we manually coded clauses from GloWbE in a ternary positive-negative-neutral distinction. Examples (95)–(97) illustrate situations where we disagreed about categorical coding, with the respective coded sentiments in brackets.

(95) players get paid whenever they complete a set of four identical tiles (GloWbE/Hong Kong/blog, neutral/positive)

(96) burping helps to let out air that might get trapped in your baby's stomach while eating (GloWbE/Canada/general, neutral/positive)

(97) i should note that i'm not getting paid for this piece (GloWbE/Australia/blog, neutral/negative)

A second commonly used method is based on sentiment dictionaries (as, for instance, done in Schweinberger 2019). In this case, human coders rate words in isolation. This results in lists of predefined, non-contextualized information about the assumed semantic and sentiment connotations of the coded lexemes, which are then used for calculating the proportion of positive and negative words of all words in a text (Rauh 2018: 320). The dictionary-based method is the least labor-intensive and hence the most cost-effective way of doing sentiment analysis (Rauh 2018: 319).

However, the accuracy of sentiment dictionaries strongly hinges on the size and quality of the dictionary and how representative it is of a given text type (Rauh 2018: 321; van Atteveldt, van der Velden, & Boukes 2021: 122). Furthermore, automatic dictionary-based sentiment coding has been shown to exhibit an inbuilt neutrality bias: it may detect no sentiment where human coders would (Rauh 2018: 326). Moreover, syntactic structure needs to be taken into consideration; a dictionary combined with a small set of syntactic rules (covering, for instance, degree modifiers and indicators of negative polarity) is usually significantly more successful than a simple lookup for each word in isolation (see, e.g., Hutto & Gilbert 2014).

A third approach relies on some form of machine learning, often in the form of supervised learning based on human-coded training data. These often represent samples of the same kind of data the classifier should be applied to. The classifier—often a variant of Naive Bayes or support-vector machines (Wankhade, Rao, & Kulkarni 2022: 5770)—is then trained and used to categorize new, unseen sentences. In comparison to human annotation, the machine-learning approach is able to upscale to large amounts of text. Provided the training data are well-chosen and carefully annotated, it may achieve "excellent accuracy" (Wankhade, Rao, & Kulkarni 2022: 5770).

Yet, implementing a machine-learning approach is also more challenging on the part of the user, who needs to understand the choices of algorithms and parameters involved. In addition, many supervised learning methods can be opaque as to the reasons for which they assign a score or classification to a given text, thus requiring careful evaluation.

Comparing human coding to dictionaries and machine-learning models, van Atteveldt, van der Velden, and Boukes (2021) conclude that trained human coding or crowd-coding still attain the best results in detecting sentiment. Machine learning outperforms dictionary-based approaches but does not meet the standards of human coding (van Atteveldt, van der Velden, & Boukes 2021: 123).

Yet, for big data, human coding is, for obvious practical reasons, not available. Our project relies on two large corpora, which necessitates the automation of most analyses. Big datasets are often inherently messy, produced by a variety of authors, in a variety of genres, and for a variety of intended readerships. Sharef, Zin, and Nadali (2016: 154) discuss the challenges of carrying out sentiment analysis on large datasets from social media, characterized by "volume, velocity, veracity, variety, value and volatility," for the purpose of strategic marketing planning. Our corpus data show some similarities to big social media data and are large in size, heterogeneous, and (in the case of GloWbE) from unverified sources. One aspect of this messiness, particularly relevant for web-based texts such as those in GloWbE (but also for parts of COHA) that contain orthographic representations of dialectal speech, is the high frequency of non-standardized words (Sharef, Zin, & Nadali 2016: 160)—which are unlikely to be included in any sentiment dictionary.

A further difficulty in investigating corpora that are not only big but also represent historical texts arises from the fact that the use and meaning of language change over time, and so do the (social) contexts in which the texts were produced. Historical texts may have been read and understood differently by readers at the time than by contemporary readers. For example, a modern reader may have a different emotional reaction to a text like Example (98) than its contemporaries did:

(98) As soon as order was restored, and all the company who had been brought in were seated, Maidwa presented one of the chief's daughters to his eldest brother, saying: "These women were given to me, to dispose of in marriage. I now give one to each. I intended so from the first." (COHA/1856/nonfiction)

As social expectations, norms, and values have changed over the course of two centuries, it raises the general question in what position present-day researchers are to decide over what they perceive to be positive, negative, or neutral emotions in historical texts. This project certainly brings us to our limits in capturing sentiment in historical data.

This section has illustrated some challenges of the process and discussed different approaches to sentiment analysis, including some specific to big data and historical corpora. In the following sections, we will describe our large-scale approach to investigating sentiment at the clause and the verb level.

5.3 Our Two-Pronged Approach to Sentiment

As mentioned at the beginning of this chapter, a situation depicted in a sentence can be evaluated positively or negatively from two separate (and sometimes differing) points of view: that of the sentence subject and that of the sentence producer. We aim to incorporate both of these viewpoints by considering sentiment at two levels as two separate variables: as a feature of the verbal participle, on the one hand, and at the level of the whole clause, on the other hand. This distinction was already seen in two example sentences, Examples (87) and (90), where a situation construed as positive for the clausal subject is framed as negative in overall terms in the author's discourse. Before discussing the more technical details of our two approaches to coding, we will present some more example sentences in order to illustrate sentiment in different instances.

We understand sentiment at the participle level as negative when the action depicted by the main verb is negative (from the grammatical subject's perspective). In order to identify sentiment at the participle level, we extracted the respective sentiment value for the participle from the dictionary provided by VADER (Hutto & Gilbert 2014), followed by the assigned sentiment on the clausal level and its corresponding confidence value. By contrast, at the clause level, we understand sentiment as negative if the overall situation is perceived as such (from the author's perspective). To identify sentiment of the entire clause, our classifier assigns the entire clause to a category (negative, neutral, positive) and calculates a confidence value (see Section 5.3.2).

Examples (99) and (100) are negative, both on the participle, that is, *robbed* and *misused*, and clause levels, that is, from the author's point of view. For illustration, we include the automatically extracted sentiment values at the participle level, where negative values indicate negative sentiment and vice versa, and at the clause level, which the classifier categorizes as negative, neutral, or positive and calculates a confidence value.

(99) You don't even have to be on the street anymore to get robbed. (COHA/1981/news; participle: -1.9; clause: negative/1.0)

(100) The new technology gets misused. (COHA/2006/news; participle: -1.82; clause: negative/1.0)

Sentences depicting beneficial events can be coded as positive on the participial and clausal levels. Example (101) represents positive sentiment on the verbal as well as the clausal level.

(101) I'm very thankful for all the op[p]ortunities I was given (GloWbE/Kenya/general; participle: 1.64; clause: positive/1.0)

Some examples classify as neutral. For instance, Examples (102) and (103) can be considered neutral both on the verb level and the clause level—the depicted events are neither obviously positive nor negative.

(102) all the time language is changing because of social backgrounds and social backgrounds cause the language to be changed (GloWbE/Bangladesh/blog; participle: -0.48; clause: neutral/1.0)

(103) In 1689 his Latin Epistola de Tolerantia was published in Holland, a corrected English translation being issued in 1690. (COHA/1941/nonfiction; participle: 0.56; clause: neutral/1.0)

In some cases, the sentiment of the participle does not align with the sentiment of the clause. Example (104) displays incongruence between the two levels: *paid*, on its own, is considered neutral; yet, the overall sentiment of the clause is negative. It is worth pointing out that concerning the previous clause sentiments, the classifier is fairly confident assigning a sentiment (rounded to 1.0), but in Example (104), which exhibits the diverging sentiment of the participle, it is less confident (at 0.88).

(104) To review briefly, in the late 1960s, men got paid more than women (usually double) for doing the exact same job. (COHA/2004/nonfiction; participle: 0.44; clause: negative/0.88)

In the remainder of the chapter, we will describe our procedure for measuring sentiment based on the two approaches we take. We rely on the dictionary approach to identify sentiment based on the participle level since, in this case, adversativity can appropriately be located in a single word, that is, the main verb participle of the passive clause. In order to identify sentiment of the entire sentence, we develop a machine-learning model trained on manually coded data.

5.3.1 Participle-Level Sentiment

For coding lexical verbs for sentiment, we needed to choose a sentiment dictionary among a number of candidates. The numerous sentiment dictionaries available use different methods of classification (binary, categorical, numeric). To aid our decision process with regard to conceptualizing sentiment, we manually evaluated two promising candidates for dictionaries, VADER (Hutto & Gilbert 2014) and AFINN (Nielsen 2011). VADER, short for Valence Aware Dictionary and sEntiment Reasoner, combines a basic dictionary with a set of simple rules to incorporate information such as negation, degree modification, and emphatic spelling into the scoring procedure. AFINN is the product of a single-person project (Nielsen 2011) and comprises 2,477 lexical items coded by its author. We tested its most current, comprehensive version, AFINN-111, against VADER. We also considered further dictionaries, such as SentiWordNet (Baccianella, Esuli, & Sebastiani 2010) and SenticNet (Biagioni 2016), but excluded these from systematic comparison since impressionistic results already indicated a high degree of divergence from our own intuitions.

In order to compare the sentiment dictionaries systematically, each author handcoded 300 randomly drawn pairs of participles from our data (with a total of 1,200 cases). Manual coding included a ternary variable (positive, negative, neutral) for each item as well as a forced choice concerning which is the more positive of the two. This handcoding was subsequently compared to the categorization provided by VADER and AFINN. These two dictionaries disagreed in 234 cases (19.5 percent). Across three of the four raters, VADER performed slightly better than AFINN with by-coder error rates between 27.5 percent and 32.8 percent and a combined error rate of 30.3 percent, while the error rate for AFINN ranged from 30.8 percent to 32.8 percent (combined across all coders: 31.8 percent). As a result, we picked VADER for the participle-level coding.

VADER's sentiment lexicon comprises entries for 9,000 candidate features (lexical items and character sequences), each of which has been independently coded by ten different human raters on a scale of -4 (fully negative) to 4 (fully positive). The full range of scores as well as their mean and standard deviation are available, but for our coding of verb-level sentiment, we rely on the mean scores.

We also take negation into account. If the clause is negated, the mathematical sign of the score is inverted. For instance, *destroyed* in Example (105) has a score of -2.2 on its own in VADER's lexicon. Since it is negated in this example, however, the participle-level sentiment score we assign is +2.2.

(105) American energy has not been destroyed by the storms of the past. (COHA/1907/news; participle: +2.2)

We acknowledge that this approach is not ideal; negating a verb does not necessarily turn it into a positive one, as one anonymous reviewer has pointed out. However, considering the amount of data, we still believe our approach to provide a valid approximation whose imprecision is at least in part counterbalanced by corpus size.

5.3.2 Clause-Level Sentiment

To account for the author's perspective, we also assess sentiment in larger syntactic units (than simply considering the participle). Entire sentences can be highly complex and often contain various sentiments, so we are extracting shorter units, aiming for the clause. This was done by simply including all words to the left and right of a passive token up to any marker of punctuation, specifically full stops, question marks, exclamation points, semicolons, colons, commas, as well as the double dash (--), used to represent an em-dash in the corpora.[1] Note that the tokenization of the corpora treats punctuation between words, such as titles (*Dr.*), or within them, such as in dates (10.02.1965) as part of word tokens, not as separate punctuation devices. These cases, therefore, do not introduce undesirable clause boundaries in the above procedure.

As human coding is not feasible for big data and sentiment dictionaries are less accurate than human coding and machine learning (van Atteveldt, van der Velden, & Boukes 2021), we turned to supervised machine learning for the clause-level-based sentiment analysis. For that we used both algorithms and linguistic features based on example data (Sharef, Zin, & Nadali 2016: 159). Supervised machine-learning approaches usually require two pre-labeled datasets, one training set and one test set. To train this classifier, human raters first handcoded a sample of tokens from our data for sentiment, following van Atteveldt, van der Velden, and Boukes's (2021: 123, 135) as well as Krippendorff's (2004: 240) recommendations to have at least two coders annotate a sample of the data. The categories "neutral," "positive," and "negative" were used. Now, the focus was on the author's perspective and the whole clause rather than the affected participant. That enabled us to code clauses such as Example (106) as negative despite the fact that the clause subject benefits from the action (and the participle has a neutral sentiment value of 0.44):

(106) To review briefly, in the late 1960s, men got paid more than women (usually double) for doing the exact same job. (COHA/2004/nonfiction; clause: negative/0.88)

Importantly, this approach sets apart sentiment detection on the clausal level and on the verb level. The context to be considered was limited to the clause featuring the passive construction, assuming that the sentiment in the immediate vicinity of a passive should be the most relevant for the choice between *get* and *be*—if sentiment indeed plays a role.

To create a classifier, we use a task-aware representation of sentences (TARS) classifier as introduced by Halder et al. (2020). This classifier can perform zero-shot text classification (i.e., assigning custom labels to text without the need for any training data), but few-shot classification vastly outperforms this method. It is available in Flair (Akbik et al. 2019), a natural language processing library for Python (van Rossum & Drake 2009). TARS allows the user to provide custom labels and is therefore not limited to sentiment analysis but useful for any kind of text classification. TARS needs two datasets: one training dataset to establish an initial classifier and one testing dataset to test and improve its performance. For the training data set, we only consider clauses where the two raters agreed on the classification. Additionally, we extract and code an evaluation dataset in order to compare the classifications made by the classifier to those made by a human rater.

The samples for handcoding are balanced across the respective relevant dimensions in each corpus. The inter-rater agreement for sentiment in the handcoded data will be discussed in the following.

For COHA, this concerns the decades (n = 19), genres (n = 5), and auxiliary variants (n = 2). The training data initially contains five instances for each of these combinations (n = 950), the testing data contains three each (n = 570), and the evaluation data two each (n = 380). However, each token can only occur in one of the datasets, so after eliminating non-distinct clauses, the datasets consist of 804, 473, and 304 tokens, respectively. In this sample, the two raters agreed on the sentiment category in 71.4 percent of cases. This corresponds to a Cohen's kappa of 0.5291 or moderate agreement.[2]

For GloWbE, the sample was balanced across country (n = 20), genre (n = 2), and auxiliary variants (n = 2). The samples were extracted to approach the COHA samples in terms of size, so the training data set contains 960, the test data 638, and the evaluation data 399 tokens. Here, the raters agreed on the sentiment category in 69.6 percent of cases. This corresponds to a Cohen's kappa of 0.4886, which indicates moderate agreement that is slightly lower than the inter-rater agreement in the COHA sample.

After having described the inter-rater agreement for the handcoded samples, we now evaluate the performance of the trained classifier on manually annotated clauses. We subsequently discuss differences in its performance between the two corpora COHA and GloWbE.

For COHA, the performance of the classifier is remarkably similar to the handcoded instances: the automatic and the handcoded classification coincide in 72.0 percent of clauses (n = 219). The Cohen's kappa is 0.5159, only slightly lower than the agreement between two human raters. The classifier and the handcoded sentiment showed comparable agreement for negative and neutral, but the classifier had a worse performance for sentences handcoded as positive, which it often categorized as neutral.

For GloWbE, the classifier performs slightly better: the automatic and the handcoded classification coincide in 76.4 percent of clauses (n = 305). The Cohen's kappa is 0.5056, which is marginally higher than the agreement between two human raters. For this sample, the classifier also performs best for negative and neutral sentences and worst for positive sentences. In comparison, the classifier does better, in this category, than in the COHA data despite still showing a tendency toward neutral classifications.

Previous research suggests that automated sentiment analysis may work better for positive than for negative sentiments (Rauh 2018: 336). This does not seem to be the case for our data; the trained classifier performs worse for positive clauses than for the other categories, and the manually coded samples show the strongest agreement for neutral and negative cases. For COHA, the raters agreed the most strongly for neutral sentences, followed by negative and positive sentences in that order. One rater, for example, showed a tendency to rate sentences as neutral that another rater perceived as positive. For GloWbE, the raters likewise agreed more often on neutral followed by negative and finally positive classifications.

We conclude that sentiment analysis is a highly subjective endeavor with many ambiguous instances, making sentiment assignments difficult. We recognize the complexity of the data, as discussed earlier, and the entailing challenges regarding both manual and automatic sentiment detection, which, as a result, may not always be accurate or unambiguous. As a consequence, our interpretation of the model may be affected by these methodological limitations. However, we believe that it is still useful to try out these approaches and that linguistic analyses will profit immensely from big data approaches like these.

As we have seen, for example, in Example (92), human raters often disagree on categorizations or agree that several categorizations are valid, so in light of this tendency, we cannot hold an automated analysis to a higher standard than the agreement that can be achieved between human raters. Encouragingly, however, our automated sentiment analysis with TARS comes quite close to this standard (for COHA) or even surpasses it (for GloWbE). We recommend researchers who work with sentiment analysis consider using machine-learning approaches, particularly those who deal with non-standardized data that is not covered by the available sentiment dictionaries.

6

Distributional Verb Semantics

The GET-passive does not occur equally readily with all verbs. Its dynamic nature (Quirk et al. 1985: 162; Huddleston & Pullum 2002: 1442; Wanner 2009: 87) is likely to favor dynamic and concrete verbs and to inhibit its use with cognitive and stative verbs. As Section 2.8 has shown, however, much of the discussion around lexical conditioning of the passive alternation to date has been engaged in the form of categorical statements and individual counterexamples. In light of the relatively low token count in previous studies on the passive alternation, the collocational behavior of lexical verbs has scarcely received detailed empirical attention. Lists of verbs that can be found particularly frequently with the GET-passive are provided in Biber, Conrad, and Leech (1999: 481) as well as in Mindt (2000: 283). Yet, both lists are rather short, include items of questionable passive status—*married*, *involved*, *stuck*, *rid*, and so on—and diverge significantly in terms of their individual entries. Rühlemann (2007) presents an empirical study of the verbs in both lists combined, analyzing each item's frequency of occurrence with the GET-passive in the British National Corpus (BNC Consortium 2007). The wide range of frequencies he finds inspire him to treat the GET-passive as an illustration of lexical grammar (Sinclair 2000; Hunston & Francis 2000).

While contributions such as these draw attention to collocational aspects of the passive alternation, they remain rudimentary at an empirical level. Their most obvious limitation is in the small number of specific words they target. Yet, even the results for these words need to be treated with care. First, only a minority of them enter into a systematic alternation with the BE-passive under conditions of referential equivalence: *hit*, *left*, *caught*, *killed*, and *mixed* are the only items in Rühlemann (2007) that unambiguously fall in this category. The second limitation refers to reporting raw frequencies, which is of limited use in determining the attraction of any particular verb to the GET-passive. Doing so accounts neither for the general frequency of a verb in the corpus nor for the ratio of its use with the GET- versus the BE-passive. Finally, there appears to be an important middle layer of abstraction that is left unattended when research considers only individual lexical items' propensity to occur with the GET-passive. Such preferences are likely not to be fully item-specific but at least partly mediated by the semantic properties of the verbs. Thus, establishing groups of words with similar semantic profiles and systematically investigating the attraction of each such group to either variant of the passive alternation promises to yield new insights into this grammatical alternation. We incorporate such an approach into our study and outline its methodological details in this chapter.

6.1 Distributional Models of Word Meaning

For an automated approach to identifying semantically related verbs in our data, we rely on well-established tools from machine learning that build on the distributional hypothesis (Harris 1954; Firth 1957). Encapsulated in Firth's (1957: 11) oft-cited statement that "you shall know a word by the company it keeps," the distributional hypothesis posits that a lexical item's meaning can, to a large extent, be derived from its patterns of co-occurrence with other words. This insight collapses the distinction between meaning and usage and thus sits well with a usage-based approach to language in general. It also opens semantics to large-scale, data-driven analysis via unsupervised learning.

To illustrate the approach on the conceptual level, consider Table 6, based on frequency data from COHA. The words *fork* and *spoon* frequently occur in discourse focusing on food and kitchen items, including words like *eat*, *food*, and *table*. Such similar contexts of occurrence indicate a shared level of semantics between the two items. By contrast, the word *automobile* occurs much less frequently with these collocates and can be found more often with *engine* and *wheel*.

Table 6 Collocation Frequencies for Selected Words in COHA, within a Context Window of Four Words to the Right and Left[1]

	eat	***food***	***table***	***engine***	***wheel***
fork	42	25	36	0	2
spoon	38	17	39	0	0
automobile	1	5	3	61	21

Table 6 is intuitively accessible and plausible, yet it only represents a minute subset of all words in COHA. For a full representation of the information contained in the corpus, all words (or at least all lexical words that occur above a certain frequency threshold) ought to be considered. The result is a very large matrix that quickly becomes intractable for human interpretation. Hence, a mathematical procedure is required to operationalize semantic relatedness as expressed in the full set of co-occurrence relationships in the corpus. In technical terms, this is a problem of dimensionality reduction. If we think of each column in the matrix (i.e., each collocate) as a dimension of the data, the initial matrix contains thousands of dimensions. The goal is to express as much of the information contained in the original matrix in terms of a much smaller set of dimensions. The result is then a distributional vector space (also called a word embedding space), in which each word is formally encoded as an abstract vector, that is, a set of coordinates in the space.

Similarity or difference between two vectors in a vector space can be expressed via a range of distance measures. One commonly used measure, which serves as an illustration here, is cosine distance. To take the examples from Table 6, the vector for *fork* would be u_{fork} = (42, 25, 36, 0, 2), corresponding to the collocate frequencies of the items in the columns. The vectors for *spoon* and *automobile* would be u_{spoon} = (38, 17, 39, 0, 0) and $u_{automobile}$ = (1, 5, 3, 61, 21), respectively. The cosine distance between u_{fork} and u_{spoon} is rather small at 0.018, whereas that between u_{fork} and $u_{automobile}$ is rather great at 0.92. Since cosine distance is bounded between 0 and 1, these values express a strong similarity between the words *fork* and *spoon* and a strong distance between *fork* and *automobile*. In other words, proximity of two items in vector space directly encodes similarity in terms of their contexts of occurrence.

Development of computationally efficient and robust embeddings of linguistic items into such vector spaces has been a significant area in the field of natural language processing over the past decades (Turney & Pantel 2010; Erk 2012; Baroni, Dinu, & Kruszewski 2014). Applications range from representations of word types to individual word tokens (e.g., Agirre & Edmonds 2007), multi-word phrases (e.g., Mitchell & Lapata 2010), topic modeling (Blei, Ng, & Jordan 2003; Manning, Raghavan, & Schütze 2008; Dinu & Lapata 2010), document retrieval (Manning, Raghavan, & Schütze 2008), and many more. For a detailed overview, see Turney and Pantel (2010).

One decisive methodological shift has been from count-based to prediction-based methods for constructing vector spaces. The former kind of method closely follows the structure of the example given above: it records all the collocate counts for all words within a predefined context window and constructs a matrix of these counts. Subsequently this matrix is subjected to dimensionality reduction applying processes from linear algebra such as singular value decomposition.

Prediction-based methods are a more recent innovation. Rather than representing all word co-occurrences and then applying dimensionality reduction, these techniques iteratively process data and train connectionist models—such as neural networks—to predict words from their surrounding context (or vice versa). The word embedding space can then be extracted from one or several embedding layers constructed by the underlying network model during training. The most successful and well-known instances of prediction-based techniques to date are Word2Vec (Mikolov, Chen et al. 2013), FastText (Bojanowski et al. 2017), and ELMo (Peters et al. 2018). Baroni, Dinu, and Kruszewski (2014) present a systematic comparison of count- and prediction-based methods and come to the decisive conclusion that the latter "obtain a thorough and resounding victory against their count-based counterparts" (Baroni, Dinu, & Kruszewski 2014: 238). It should be noted, however, that this is an area of ongoing development, and the same year in which Baroni, Dinu, and Kruszewski's paper was published saw the release of GloVe (Pennington, Socher, & Manning 2014), a competitive count-based algorithm.

Compared to formal, symbolic representations of semantic relationships, distributional approaches offer a number of attractive properties. In practical terms, they do not require manual encoding of semantic information since this information is learned directly from the data. This fact drastically reduces the human work involved in developing semantic representations and renders the result less susceptible to individual coding choices, such as which semantic relations are to be incorporated into a model (Mitchell & Lapata 2010: 1389). Distributional representations also fare well in terms of performance in applied domains, particularly where (dis-)similarity of items is of importance (Baroni & Lenci 2010; Erk, Padó, & Padó 2010).

However, these advantages come with several caveats. First, distributional models are not semantic in the strict sense in that they do not incorporate a systematic logic of sense relationships. Whereas formal representations encode the various possible taxonomic relations (such as synonymy, antonymy, hyperonymy, etc.) in explicit and systematic terms, proximity in distributional space is a much more coarse-grained notion of word relatedness, conflating such logical distinctions. One line of research into distributional models concerns isolating specific taxonomic representations in distributional space (Nickel & Kiela 2017; Mrkšić et al. 2017; Roller & Erk 2016).

Second, and related to the above, the information represented in distributional models is not just semantic but connected to word use more generally. Syntactic, stylistic, perspectival, and other information all enters into the construction of the vector space. Erk and Chronis (2023: 191) refer to the sum of this information as "word stories [which they define as] an amalgam of several things, including but not limited to affordances (ways that humans typically use an object), judgements and emotions, and the topical contexts in which words frequently appear." Inclusion of all this information is not per se out of line with the initial distributional hypothesis. As Brunila and LaViolette (2022) point out, precisely what we understand as the "company [a word] keeps," that is, the contextual information to draw on for constructing a distributional model is of great consequence. Firth's (1957) original proposal, they argue, was heavily influenced by anthropological and pragmatic perspectives, in which "context" has to be seen as situational and social rather than strictly syntagmatic-linguistic (Brunila & LaViolette 2022). It is a matter of perspective whether one considers the type of information in "word stories" as noise that detracts from the core semantic relations between lexical items or as valuable additional information about word usage, as Erk and Chronis (2023) do. However, it should be clearly noted that simple distances in a distributional model do not systematically keep apart these aspects, and thus the ontological status of relationships captured in such a model is somewhat unclear.

These complicating aspects notwithstanding, there is a growing body of work that illustrates the utility of distributional models for the study of linguistic phenomena. An early example is Sagi, Kaufmann, and Clark (2011), which focuses on semantic change in individual lexical items. More specifically, the authors construct token-level representations of all instances of the word types *deer*, *do*, *dog*, and *hound* in the sections of the Helsinki Corpus representing Middle English (1150–1500 CE) and Early Modern English (1500–1710 CE). They show that, over the time period covered, the semantic density (inverse of the average angle between vectors) for both *dog* and *do* decreases, reflecting a semantic generalization of these words. By contrast, the semantic density for *deer* increases as an effect of this word's semantic narrowing. Jenset (2013) applies a similar approach that explicitly incorporates grammatical information to trace the semantic development of existential *there* from approximately 850 to 1700 CE, and Zimmermann (2019) demonstrates the utility of word embeddings for studying semantic chain shifts, specifically the FOOD > MEAT > FLESH shift. Fonteyn and Manjavacas (2021) use distributional models to trace the development of the prepositional phrase *to death* from a resultative to an intensifying use.

In addition to research focusing on individual words or constructions, linguists have also taken an interest in more global interpretations of word vector spaces. Bamman, Dyer, and Smith (2014) present a modified version of Word2Vec's Skip-Gram approach that learns geographically distributed word embeddings. Hovy and Purschke (2018) employ a similar approach to construct city-level embeddings for the German-speaking world, and they perform clustering over these embeddings to identify German dialect areas. Their results coincide well with independently established dialect boundaries. Rosenfeld (2019) further elaborates methods for identifying the geographical signal in word embeddings, which he illustrates on the basis of a dialect map of Texas constructed from 2.3 million geolocated tweets (see also Rosenfeld & Hinrichs 2023). Bohmann (2023) uses word embeddings for the twenty global varieties of English in GloWbE to quantify cross-varietal similarity and distance between these as well as to establish clusters of varieties characterized by similar word usage.

What we aim to do in the present study is to subject all the verbal participles in our passive data to clustering based on their position in embedding spaces learned from the corpora themselves. The resulting clusters are then treated as levels of a predictor variable in our models of the alternation between *be* and *get* as passive auxiliaries. Using semantic clusters derived in this way as predictor variables in a variationist study has, to our awareness, only been done in one paper by Paolini et al. (2023). There is, however, precedence in Perek's use of distributional models in studies of changing productivity in the WAY-construction (2018) and the V *the hell out of* NP construction (Perek 2016). In this research, Perek uses distributionally derived clusters of words to illustrate the ways in which constructions open up to new kinds of items in their schematic slots over time. From this idea, it is only a small step to treating cluster membership of items as a predictor in a statistical model. In the following three sections, we will explain how we construct the respective word embedding spaces (6.2), how we identify clusters of related verbs in these (6.3), and what our cluster structure for each corpus looks like (6.4).

6.2 Establishing a Word-Vector Representation for the Passive Alternation

Our aim in the present study is not to extensively evaluate all possible options for generating word embedding models from our data. Rather, we require a robust solution that is relatively straightforward to implement both in our own workflow as well as in potential projects that might take methodological inspiration from ours. For these reasons, and given the unambiguous results in Baroni, Dinu, and Kruszewski (2014), we opt for a widely used algorithm with accessible computational implementation in Python: Word2Vec (Mikolov, Chen et al. 2013). This choice is consistent with previous research in linguistics, much of which has drawn on variants of Word2Vec with success (Hovy & Purschke 2018; Zimmermann 2019; Fonteyn & Manjavacas 2021). Word2Vec is available as part of the gensim (Řehůřek & Sojka 2010) module for Python and can thus be incorporated easily into our existing analysis pipeline. This also ensures relatively straightforward replication of our methodological steps. We recognize, however, that tools for constructing word embeddings are rapidly developing and that, ideally, the full range of available options should be systematically compared and the most successful one chosen for a given task.

Several pretrained Word2Vec embedding spaces are available, such as one based on a 100-billion-word sample of documents from the Google News dataset (Mikolov, Sutskever et al. 2013). Instead of relying on these, however, we apply the algorithm to the corpora we analyze, for the following three reasons. First, both corpora include language that diverges from the standardized nature of the synchronic written (and often published) texts that these pretrained models are derived from. In COHA, earlier stages of the language as well as some oral data complicate this picture, whereas the digitally mediated discourse in GloWbE ranges from highly standardized to extremely unregulated and messy. It thus appeared necessary to construct domain-specific embedding spaces for each corpus separately. Related to this point is the possibility of passive constructions occurring in these corpora that feature a main verb for which no entry exists in the available pretrained spaces. This issue is avoided by learning all embeddings from the data themselves.

Finally, it was necessary to mask the identity of all tokens of the lemmas *be* and *get*. Doing so required the construction of a new embedding space at any rate. This step was necessary to avoid a potential circularity of argument. We treat distance in embedding space between verbs (or rather, the clusters constructed based on such distance) as a predictor of the choice between *be* and *get* in passive constructions. If, however, these two lemmas themselves contribute to the construction of the space, there is a potential that any significant effect at the level of the verb group simply reflects the information going into the construction of the space. To put this more simply, if the algorithm learns to differentiate between verbs that occur more readily with *be* than with *get* (or vice versa), then the different verbs' position in embedding space is necessarily correlated with the choice of passive auxiliary, independent of any further semantic aspects. We address this problem by substituting all instances of the two lemmas in question with the character *X* prior to constructing the embedding space.

We explore several options for constructing the word embedding spaces for our two studies. First, one can create a word-form or a lemma space by using either the surface forms or the underlying lemmas of the tokens in the corpus as the basic unit. Second, it is possible to either draw on all such (word or lemma) units or to restrict the perspective to the lexical ones, that is, nouns, adjectives, adverbs, and verbs. We explore the four possible combinations arising from these two binary alternatives. For each, we use gensim's implementation of Word2Vec with the default training parameters, which are a minimum corpus frequency of five occurrences for an item to be considered by the algorithm and an embedding space composed of 100 dimensions. We draw on the CBOW variant of Word2Vec, in which the space is learned by predicting individual words from their surrounding items within a context window of five words to the left and right of the target word. CBOW is preferable over the alternative Skip-Gram (which inverts the direction of prediction, using the central word to predict those in the context window) since it is computationally more efficient and performs better on relatively frequent words. Yet, it is not as good at representing very uncommon words as Skip-Gram is.

6.3 Finding Groups of Semantically Related Verbs

For the purposes of our analysis, we are less interested in the precise positioning of each verb or participle in embedding space. Fully idiosyncratic associations between individual verbs and either variant of the passive alternation are accommodated in the form of random effects (see Chapter 8). However, we hypothesize that specific groups of verbs that are closely related in terms of their "word stories" (Erk & Chronis 2023) will show similar selectional preferences. This notion is captured in the many categorical statements made about the GET-passive—for instance, that it cannot occur with stative, cognitive, or durative verbs (Huddleston & Pullum 2002: 1442; Cowan 2008: 405; Hatcher 1949: 434). What we want to achieve with our distributional method is a data-driven procedure for identifying such groups of related verbs. This is achieved by means of cluster analysis.

As a family of unsupervised learning algorithms, cluster analysis aims to identify groups of data points based on a range of measured variables. Common clustering techniques in linguistics include hierarchical clustering (Ward 1963), *k*-means (Hartigan & Wong 1979), and partitioning around medians (PAM, Kaufman & Rousseeuw 1990). We explored these different options for the present project but ultimately found the most promising solutions with model-based clustering with Gaussian mixtures (Fraley & Raftery 1998). This approach models each cluster as a multivariate normal distribution and applies a soft clustering technique, where each verb or participle is assigned a probability of membership for each cluster. As a consequence, this method allows for a distribution of probabilities that reflect varying degrees of affiliation with each cluster. Verbs that are closely aligned with a given cluster are assigned high probabilities, indicating strong membership, while those on the periphery, situated between clusters, can be assigned with approximately equal probability to multiple clusters. This probabilistic assignment is plausible for the feature under consideration since the existence of any clear-cut classes of verbs is unlikely, and the assumption of more or less prototypical membership appears much more realistic. In constructing the clusters that we use as predictors in the statistical analyses in Chapters 9 and 10, we draw on the probability distributions for interpretation inasmuch as they indicate the most central words in a cluster and also reveal overlap between clusters. In the interest of keeping modeling and interpretation manageable, however, we adopt a hard cluster assignment: each verb is assigned to the cluster for which it has the highest probability. We use the Bayesian Information Criterion (BIC, Schwarz 1978), a well-established information-theoretic measure of model fit, as our model selection criterion to identify the number of clusters.

Before implementing model-based clustering, however, a final preparatory step is necessary. The raw data—the vectors for all individual verbs in embedding space—are 100-dimensional. Clustering approaches are susceptible to what has been called the "curse of dimensionality" (Bellman 1957), that is, the fact that the volume of the data space increases exponentially as the number of dimensions grows. This expansion leads to several issues that can make clustering more challenging. In high-dimensional spaces, the distance between data points becomes less meaningful because the relative difference between the nearest and farthest points diminishes. As the dimensions increase, all points in the space tend to appear equally distant from one another, making it difficult to differentiate between clusters based on distance. Further, the sparsity of data in high-dimensional spaces makes it harder to identify meaningful structures as data points become increasingly isolated. Traditional clustering algorithms like *k*-means rely on the assumption that data points are dense and well separated in feature space, which is less likely to hold in high dimensions. Finally, an increase in the number of features can lead to overfitting. Clustering algorithms may capture noise rather than meaningful patterns, leading to less generalizable results.

For these reasons, we project the initial 100-dimensional data into two-dimensional space via *t*-distributed stochastic neighbor embedding (*t*-SNE, van der Maaten & Hinton 2008). This technique for nonlinear dimensionality reduction is able to project high-dimensional data into a lower- (typically two- or three-) dimensional space. It does so by first defining a probability distribution over all pairs of observations in the original data that assigns a high probability to similar data points and lower probabilities to distant ones. In a second step, a further probability distribution over the pairs of points in a low-dimensional space is sought that minimizes the Kullback–Leibler divergence from the original distribution. The *t*-SNE algorithm is particularly good at retaining local relations among data points and arguably less well suited for retaining global structure. However, since we are more interested in identifying distinct groups of verbs and less in the relationships among these groups, the benefits of *t*-SNE outweigh these drawbacks.

Our method for identifying clusters of verbs, thus, takes as input the verbs or participles in the various vector spaces developed for COHA and GloWbE as outlined in Section 6.2. It first projects the relationships between these data into two-dimensional space with *t*-SNE as implemented in the Rtsne (Krijthe 2014) library for *R*, with the hyperparameter of perplexity set to its default value of 30. Perplexity influences the extent to which local versus global structure in the data is retained in the projection. According to van der Maaten and Hinton (2008: 2582), "The performance of SNE is fairly robust to changes in the perplexity, and typical values are between 5 and 50." We considered perplexity values within this range but did not find them to yield more interpretable results.

The two-dimensional projection of the verbs or participles thus created is then subjected to model-based clustering with the Mclust package (Scrucca et al. 2023) for *R*. We explore solutions between ten and forty-five clusters. The value of ten is chosen somewhat arbitrarily as the bare minimum of distinct verb groups one might expect when considering all English verbs. The full range of verb classes identified in Levin (1993) is fifty-six at the coarsest level, but we consider it unlikely to find such a fine distinction in our data-driven approach.

We apply the above procedure to the four representations of verbs or participles in embedding space per corpus described earlier and select the theoretically most plausible, most interpretable solution. In the case of COHA, this is a ten-cluster structure selected via model-based clustering for the participles in an embedding space constructed from all surface forms in the corpus. For GloWbE, an eleven-cluster solution is selected by the algorithm, again based on all surface forms in the data. We explain the groups of participles identified in each corpus in the following two sections.

6.4 Interpretation of the Clusters: COHA

The cluster solution for COHA identifies ten clusters out of 1,526 unique verbal participles that occur in *be* or *get* + past participle constructions prior to any data reduction to account for non- or less central passives. Table 7 gives an overview of these clusters. The first column shows the label we agreed upon after separately reviewing the clusters. The twenty most central participles in the second column are those that show the highest probability of membership in this cluster. In addition, for each cluster, Table 7 lists its size, that is, the number of participle types it comprises, as well as the mean uncertainty of items in the cluster, that is, the sum of probabilities with which an item was assigned to any of the other clusters.[2]

There are some obvious differences between the clusters in Table 7. In terms of size, they range from thirty-six members (PERMISSION AND OBLIGATION) to 299 (HOUSEHOLD ACTIVITIES). With a mean uncertainty of 0.08, PERMISSION AND OBLIGATION is a highly focused cluster that is clearly differentiated from all other verbs, whereas a mean uncertainty of 0.41 for LESS FREQUENT VERBS betrays the fact that this cluster consists of items that are not associated by shared semantics but rather by the fact that the corpus apparently does not contain much information about them. Participles in this cluster on average show a relatively high probability of membership in AGGRESSION AND INDUSTRY, itself a rather unfocused cluster with a mean uncertainty of 0.31.

In terms of labeling, some clusters, like PERMISSION AND OBLIGATION or BODILY MOVEMENT AND POSITION, suggest one core underlying semantic motivation. In other cases, a single cluster appears to capture more than one aspect of meaning. For instance, AGGRESSION AND INDUSTRY combines two terms that are not prima facie related to one another in any obvious way. In several cases, the top members of a cluster indicate one particular semantic dimension, but other participles that also have a high probability of cluster membership add new meanings. For instance, the two most central elements in BODILY MOVEMENT AND POSITION, *looked* and *stared*, are in fact verbs of

Table 7 Clusters of Participles in COHA

Label	20 most central participles	*N* types	Mean uncertainty
LESS FREQUENT VERBS	*sidetracked, interchanged, rehabilitated, stymied, pacified, tasked, renominated, heartened, dramatized, shelved, validated, rumored, demoted, reassigned, noised, ostracized, renamed, apprenticed, overwrought, misinformed*	175	0.41
AGGRESSION AND INDUSTRY	*inscribed, engraved, ushered, escorted, started, stopped, summoned, dispatched, despatched, waited, borrowed, bought, sold, stolen, confiscated, wounded, injured, watched, crippled, entered*	167	0.31
ADMINISTRATIVE	*transmitted, conveyed, communicated, addressed, presented, submitted, forwarded, mailed, delivered, introduced, received, issued, signed, recommended, filed, proposed, approved, adopted, accepted, drafted*	141	0.28
EMOTIONS	*disappointed, puzzled, embarrassed, annoyed, perplexed, excited, bewildered, alarmed, irritated, vexed, dazed, pained, shocked, dismayed, stunned, terrified, mortified, confused, mystified, frightened*	82	0.14
INTERNAL STRUCTURE OF EVENTS	*delayed, postponed, finished, completed, terminated, ended, changed, commenced, altered, modified, lost, wasted, based, spent, founded, expended, begun, lived, produced, created*	138	0.25
COMMUNICATION AND COGNITION	*taught, learned, asked, felt, inquired, said, found, answered, discovered, realized, whispered, interested, interrupted, involved, concerned, repeated, remembered, listened, recalled, continued*	186	0.23
PERMISSION AND OBLIGATION	*inclined, tempted, obliged, compelled, forced, disposed, permitted, allowed, tried, determined, attempted, expected, refused, managed, let, resolved, accustomed, wished, contrived, tended*	36	0.08

(*Continued*)

Table 7 (*Continued*)

Label	20 most central participles	N types	Mean uncertainty
PHYSICAL CHANGE	*calmed, quieted, adjusted, balanced, matched, fixed, settled, disappeared, focused, centered, faded, flushed, reflected, clouded, blurred, obscured, lit, lighted, distorted, marked*	180	0.28
HOUSEHOLD ACTIVITIES	*opened, closed, locked, shut, piled, stacked, cooled, melted, stamped, jammed, smoked, pasted, drained, folded, crumpled, tacked, wrapped, chopped, peeled, sliced*	299	0.20
BODILY MOVEMENT AND POSITION	*looked, stared, stood, sat, came, walked, moved, stepped, turned, passed, slipped, dropped, slid, stretched, pulled, handed, flashed, rolled, swung, pushed*	122	0.21

perception rather than motion or position. We briefly introduce each cluster here and explain the reasons for the label we chose.

As mentioned earlier, there is not much semantic coherence to LESS FREQUENT VERBS. For the most part, these are simply participles that do not occur with great frequency in the corpus and that thus are probably poorly represented in embedding space. For instance, the corpus frequencies of the top five items are 245, 369, 324, 290, and 257; by contrast, the participles in the other clusters, with very few exceptions, tend to show corpus frequencies in the thousands and even tens of thousands.

AGGRESSION AND INDUSTRY, as has been mentioned, fuses two distinct concepts. Here as well, the top items tell a slightly different story from those following them. The two terms *inscribed* and *engraved* are industry-related, but these are followed by a set of relatively general participles that all give direction to others (*ushered, escorted, summoned, dispatched, despatched*). *Started* and *stopped*, in their transitive use, might be subsumed under this basic dimension as well. Only with *dispatched* and *despatched* is there a sense that these items often also contain a military component. Forms like *wounded, injured*, and *crippled* or—not within the top twenty—*launched, outnumbered*, and *hunted* further corroborate this martial-aggressive aspect of the cluster. The industry side is further represented by items like *confiscated, imported*, or *manufactured*. While aggression and industry are not immediately related, it is likely that the structure of this cluster incorporates aspects of "word stories" (Erk & Chronis 2023) inasmuch as both topical complexes are likely to be discussed in similar texts in similar genres: news reports about political and economic matters.

The ADMINISTRATIVE cluster is dominated by public verbs (Biber 1988: 242), that is, those that "involve actions that can be observed publicly; they are primarily speech act verbs." Many of these speech acts are not purely assertive but performative, such as *approved, adopted, accepted,* and so on. The participles in this group, we find, are highly coherent in that they all represent official administrative acts that often have a communicative component.

A similarly coherent group is formed by the participles in the EMOTIONS cluster. Without exception, the members of this class are participles that occur primarily in adjectival function, where they denote an interior emotional state.

The participles in the INTERNAL STRUCTURE OF EVENTS cluster predominantly describe points of transition, like the initiation (*commenced, founded, begun, created*), continuation (*delayed, postponed, lived*), or termination (*finished, completed, terminated*) of a state. Some verbs in this cluster concern changes of state along dimensions other than the temporal (*altered, modified, multiplied,* the latter not a member of the top twenty), but the time dimension predominates. The two other clusters that members of this one are associated with by non-marginal probabilities are AGGRESSION AND INDUSTRY as well as PHYSICAL CHANGE (in each case with a mean probability of cluster membership of 0.11).

COMMUNICATION AND COGNITION includes many private verbs (Biber 1988: 242), which "express intellectual states (e.g., *believe*) or nonobservable intellectual acts (e.g., *discover*)." Some public verbs are also part of this cluster; however, many of these tend to refer to assertive speech acts that do not serve a performative function (*asked, said, answered, whispered*). Given the conceptual proximity to the ADMINISTRATIVE cluster—to the extent that both include public verbs—it is a little surprising that there is no strong overlap between these two clusters. The mean probability with which COMMUNICATION AND COGNITION participles are associated with the ADMINISTRATIVE cluster is only 0.03. By contrast, for the AGGRESSION AND INDUSTRY cluster the mean probability of association for COMMUNICATION AND COGNITION is 0.12, which is the highest of all remaining clusters.

The cluster PERMISSION AND OBLIGATION covers volitional and deontic items, that is, those pertaining to commitments (e.g., *determined, resolved*), desires (e.g., *tempted, wished*), rights (e.g., *permitted, let*), and obligations (e.g., *obliged, compelled*). This cluster is both the smallest and the one with the lowest mean uncertainty per participle, which is only 0.08. As such, it constitutes a tight and well-interpretable group of verbs.

Physical change, as was already noted, shares certain properties with internal structure of events. The difference is that the latter concerns mostly changes along the temporal axis (and some further abstract changes of state like *multiplied* or *strengthened*, not in the top twenty), whereas physical change consists of changes that are more concrete. Many of the core participles here denote changes having to do with visual perception, such as *disappeared*, *focused*, *faded*, or *blurred*. However, outside the top twenty participles, we also find items denoting change in temperature (*heated*, *chilled*), in tactile properties (*hardened*, *sharpened*), and mixing of substances (*permeated*, *diluted*, *contaminated*). What all these have in common is that they refer to physical rather than conceptual changes. Many of the specific participles also can be found in scientific discourse. It is consequently likely that this cluster incorporates information about discourse domain in addition to the pure semantics of its participles. While there is some degree of overlap between physical change and internal structure of events (mean probability = 0.11), then, we find that the two express related but conceptually distinct aspects.

The cluster household activities is the largest in the COHA data and is somewhat cumbersome to interpret. It comprises many words in the classes "change of state" (*opened*, *closed*, *shut*, *cooled*, *melted*, *crumpled*), "combining and attaching" (*locked*, *pasted*, *tacked*), "putting" (*piled*, *stacked*, *jammed*, *wrapped*), and "cutting" (*chopped*, *sliced*) in Levin's (1993) taxonomy. All of these have to do with the physical manipulation of objects, often in the context of household activities such as cooking or doing laundry. The roughly 100 most central participles in the cluster fit this description very well, with items like *cooked*, *boiled*, *knit*, *combed*, *shaved*, and so on. However, the cluster loses coherence when one considers the less central items. Among these can be found those associated with physical and agricultural labor (*saddled*, *plowed*, *welded*), change in physical state (*scorched*, *spattered*, *streaked*), but also some more idiosyncratic participles like *positioned* or *gunned*. Overall, the prototypical semantics captured by this cluster—concrete, physical activities associated with household tasks—is quite clear, but there is a range of further participles included.

Bodily movement and position is similar to the previous cluster in that it has a clearly interpretable core meaning, but it incorporates some additional participles as well. The most obvious issue is that the two most central items in this cluster do not directly align with its overall semantics. *Looked* and *stared* are participles of perception rather than movement or position. However, the remaining items in the top twenty and most of those beyond these do clearly encode physical position or motion. An added aspect that is not particularly apparent from consideration of the most central items alone is that this cluster also includes verbs of caused motion, such as *thrown*, *yanked*, or *towed*. Still, the notion of movement is central to all these items. The strongest overlap between BODILY MOVEMENT AND POSITION can be observed with HOUSEHOLD ACTIVITIES. The mean probability of items in the former cluster being assigned to the latter is 0.18. This finding is not surprising since these two clusters both express concrete, physical acts.

6.5 Interpretation of the Clusters: GloWbE

The cluster solution for GloWbE consists of eleven clusters, as shown in Table 8 analogous to Table 7. The cluster structure in this case is less clear-cut than in COHA, with considerable mean levels of uncertainty for all clusters. These are especially pronounced for CHANGE OF STATE (INDUSTRIAL AND SCIENTIFIC), PHYSICAL INTERACTION WITH OBJECTS (MINOR IMPACT), DISRUPTIVE IMPACT, and DISRUPTIVE IMPACT (LOW-FREQUENCY). Each of these clusters has a mean uncertainty of 0.5 or above, meaning that the average probability of cluster membership is in fact lower than the probability of nonmembership. When interpreting the clusters, it is therefore necessary to also consider their relationship to each other.

The participles in TRANSFER AND PRODUCTION describe various common actions and interactions that occur in operational, professional, and social contexts. The notion of transfer, often but not exclusively in an economic sense, is relevant in *passed*, *obtained*, *adapted*, and *equipped*. Production and creation are encoded in items such as *produced*, *generated*, and *replicated*. More than a single core semantics, the items in this cluster appear to share a discourse domain. All of them can be associated with the world of business and administration. This cluster is most similar in embedding space to PHYSICAL INTERACTION WITH OBJECTS (MINOR IMPACT). These two clusters appear conceptually differentiated, however, along an axis of abstractness versus concreteness. While the participles in TRANSFER AND PRODUCTION all appear rather abstract, those in PHYSICAL INTERACTION WITH OBJECTS (MINOR IMPACT) denote concrete physical activities.

INTERPERSONAL TRANSACTION AND COMMUNICATION includes both items in Biber's (1988: 242) class of public verbs, such as *communicated* and *highlighted*, and suasive verbs, such as *suggested*. Further items pertain to interpersonal

Table 8 Clusters of Participles in GloWbE

Label	20 most central participles	*N* types	Mean uncertainty
TRANSFER AND PRODUCTION	*flown, passed, supported, produced, performed, generated, completed, obtained, employed, pushed, pulled, utilized, utilised, replicated, adapted, carried, drawn, trained, equipped, supplied*	87	0.29
INTERPERSONAL TRANSACTION AND COMMUNICATION	*deposited, lodged, communicated, treated, partnered, coached, copied, bought, purchased, sold, helped, verified, enlisted, brought, highlighted, ushered, reviewed, published, suggested, confirmed*	97	0.37
CHANGE OF STATE (INDUSTRIAL AND SCIENTIFIC)	*compressed, bottled, acclimatized, heated, recycled, strained, overloaded, elevated, soaked, tanned, cluttered, concussed, truncated, engrossed, rounded, processed, repossessed, misplaced, registered, foreclosed*	132	0.53
CHANGE OF POSITION AND VALUE	*put, set, spread, split, shut, read, thrust, reset, wed, overrun, ran, run, cut, broadcast, typecast, cast, developed, improved, enhanced, expanded*	52	0.28
EVERYDAY ACTIONS WITH HUMAN AGENTS	*taken, took, said, found, began, kept, liked, received, collected, donated, consumed, grabbed, shouted, watched, asked, yelled, screamed, stopped, walked, stared*	100	0.31
CHANGE OF STATE (HOUSEHOLD AND WORKPLACE)	*applied, accepted, ruined, spoiled, spoilt, canned, fried, dropped, broke, broken, hired, retired, substituted, fouled, cooked, sliced, chopped, steamed, baked, grilled*	75	0.39
PHYSICAL INTERACTION WITH OBJECTS (MINOR IMPACT)	*pierced, licked, rubbed, noticed, stalked, wrapped, chewed, tickled, brushed, smudged, splashed, imprinted, pasted, scraped, plastered, whisked, packed, swayed, scrubbed, glossed*	116	0.55
ADMINISTRATION	*branded, labelled, labeled, effected, issued, proved, proven, scored, joined, taxed, stated, expressed, extended, covered, learned, taught, smashed, cracked, locked, blocked*	116	0.31

(*Continued*)

Table 8 (*Continued*)

Label	20 most central participles	N types	Mean uncertainty
LEGAL	*payed, paid, dressed, worn, identified, benefitted, benefited, rescued, saved, banned, acknowledged, applauded, condemned, confiscated, deported, debated, criticized, criticised, evicted, prosecuted*	129	0.35
DISRUPTIVE IMPACT	*swallowed, snatched, hurled, invaded, dislodged, rammed, ejected, injected, abandoned, gunned, thrashed, ambushed, diverted, hammered, sidelined, raided, obliterated, evacuated, annihilated, tackled*	89	0.59
DISRUPTIVE IMPACT (LOW-FREQUENCY)	*dinged, pummelled, steamrolled, slugged, hit, waylaid, pummeled, burgled, walloped, cought, impaled, skewered, zapped, punked, slagged, shorted, lulled, weirded, trolled, demotivated*	259	0.50

relationships and endeavors (*helped, partnered, coached*) as well as business transactions (*bought, purchased, sold*). What we see as the coherent element in this cluster is that its members denote activities typically involving two human parties. Two other clusters show noticeable overlap with this one, namely LEGAL (mean probability for members of INTERPERSONAL TRANSACTION AND COMMUNICATION: 0.10) and DISRUPTIVE IMPACT (0.16). The former is immediately plausible inasmuch as the legal domain involves transactions and communication among human agents. The proximity to the latter might be explained by DISRUPTIVE IMPACT including many acts of violence directed by one typically human party to another (see later).

The items in CHANGE OF STATE (INDUSTRIAL AND SCIENTIFIC) describe processes by which things or substances are altered. Many of the individual items bespeak a technical register (*acclimatized, concussed*), and there is likely a genre dimension involved in this cluster. There is overlap with three other clusters: CHANGE OF POSITION AND VALUE (mean probability: 0.10), CHANGE OF STATE (HOUSEHOLD AND WORKPLACE) (0.18), and DISRUPTIVE IMPACT (LOW-FREQUENCY) (0.18). The shared aspect with the former two is the element of change. The overlap with the low-frequency cluster is, we expect, rather an effect of that cluster's lack of focus than due to any real semantic similarity.

The fourth cluster, CHANGE OF POSITION AND VALUE, comprises verbs that affect objects by disassembling (*split*, *cut*), combining (*wed*), or enhancing (*improved*, *enhanced*, *expanded*) them. It also includes verbs of putting that relate to the positioning of objects (*put*, *set*, *spread*, *thrust*). Taken together, these verbs affect either the position of an object or its integrity and value. The only other cluster with which elements in this one show a noticeable amount of overlap is the one previously discussed, CHANGE OF STATE (INDUSTRIAL AND SCIENTIFIC), with the mean probability of membership for items from the present cluster being 0.14.

The 100 verbs assigned to EVERYDAY ACTIONS WITH HUMAN AGENTS are high-frequency verbs that refer to quotidian activities humans typically engage in. These include verba dicendi (*said*, *shouted*, *asked*, *yelled*, *screamed*), cognitive verbs (*found*, *liked*), motion verbs (*walked*), but also polysemous items that can occur in many different light verb constructions (*taken*, *took*, *kept*). The common denominator appears to be the everyday nature of these verbs. All of them might be expected to occur with higher frequency in relatively oral-like, informationally loose discourses. The only other cluster with which this one shows any significant overlap is PHYSICAL INTERACTION WITH OBJECTS (MINOR IMPACT) (0.11), which potentially reflects the relatively informal nature of many items in the latter.

The cluster CHANGE OF STATE (HOUSEHOLD AND WORKPLACE) contains many verbs that apply to food items, such as *canned*, *fried*, *cooked*, *steamed*, *baked*, *and grilled*. The participles *spoiled*, *spoilt*, *sliced*, and *chopped*, while not unambiguously food-related, plausibly occur in the context of cooking and groceries as well. An additional minor group of participles in this cluster is exemplified by the two most central forms, *applied* and *accepted*. These relate to the realm of employment, as do *experienced*, *educated*, and potentially *exported* and *imported*, all outside the top twenty most central elements. The most decisive overlap (mean probability of 0.23) is found with CHANGE OF STATE (INDUSTRIAL AND SCIENTIFIC). There is transparent similarity in the fact that both clusters are concerned with changes of state. What appears to set them apart are largely the areas in which these changes occur.

PHYSICAL INTERACTION WITH OBJECTS (MINOR IMPACT) is the second-most uncertain cluster. Participles in it have comparatively high probabilities of also being associated with TRANSFER AND PRODUCTION (mean probability: 0.13) and especially DISRUPTIVE IMPACT (LOW-FREQUENCY) (0.23). It is not readily apparent what motivates the association with the former, but the shared aspect of impact appears to be the motivation to the latter. In general, verbs in PHYSICAL

INTERACTION WITH OBJECTS (MINOR IMPACT) directly affect an object without fundamentally altering this object, for example, by destroying it or changing its state entirely. Both the direction of deterioration (*pierced, chewed, smudged*) and of enhancement and repair (*scrubbed, repaired*) are present, as well as impact that cannot immediately be considered either positive or negative (*licked, rubbed, wrapped*, etc.). Most items in this cluster encode actions that affect the surface rather than the core of an object (*licked, rubbed, tickled*, etc.).

The ADMINISTRATION cluster is similar to the one labeled ADMINISTRATIVE in the COHA cluster solution. Like the latter, it includes public verbs (Biber 1988: 242), and particularly such ones that encode performative speech acts in institutional contexts (*branded, labelled, labeled, issued*, etc.). While the mean uncertainty of cluster membership in ADMINISTRATION is relatively high (0.31), there is no shared tendency among its individual participles to be associated with another cluster, as the mean probability of membership in any of the other clusters is never above 0.1.

Participles in the LEGAL cluster contain both those that describe typical legal actions (*evicted, prosecuted*, and many more items outside the top twenty like *sued, admitted, convicted, persecuted*) and those that refer to criminal acts, although the latter are not among the most central participles. Examples include *harassed, raped, murdered, killed*, and *stabbed*. One issue is that the label LEGAL captures most of the participles in the cluster but is not an ideal description for many of the most central members, which include transactional (*payed, benefitted*) and declarative verbs (*debated, criticized*). Overlap can be observed primarily with DISRUPTIVE IMPACT (mean probability of 0.12), to be discussed next.

The verbs in DISRUPTIVE IMPACT describe actions that are typically more physical or destructive in nature and generally focus on broad or significant changes, often involving large-scale disruptions (*invaded, abandoned, raided*) or complete alterations (*obliterated, annihilated*). Many of these words are used in contexts involving major events, decisions, or changes, and they often cast two entities in an antagonistic relationship. This cluster has the highest mean uncertainty (0.59), and its members show attraction to several other clusters: DISRUPTIVE IMPACT (LOW-FREQUENCY) (mean probability: 0.20), LEGAL (0.11), and INTERPERSONAL TRANSACTION AND COMMUNICATION (0.15).

The final cluster, DISRUPTIVE IMPACT (LOW-FREQUENCY), has much in common with the previous one semantically, and synonymy relations can be identified for several pairs of words in both clusters (e.g., *ambushed* and *thrashed* in DISRUPTIVE IMPACT versus *waylaid* and *pummeled* in DISRUPTIVE IMPACT (LOW-FREQUENCY). The key criterion to differentiate between the two clusters appears to be one of frequency, with the items in the low-frequency cluster being much rarer than those in general DISRUPTIVE IMPACT. In addition to this obvious overlap (reflected in a mean probability of cluster membership of 0.12), there is also proximity to PHYSICAL INTERACTION WITH OBJECTS (MINOR IMPACT) (0.15) and CHANGE OF STATE (INDUSTRIAL AND SCIENTIFIC) (0.12).

6.6 Summary

To sum up the results of our distributional approach, we have identified in both corpora clusters of related verbal participles by first projecting the entire set of words in the respective corpus into embedding space and then applying model-based clustering to a two-dimensional projection of this space. Being fully unsupervised, this approach does not always produce completely clean and clear-cut results. For most clusters, it is possible to identify a core commonality among its members, which may be semantic but also related to discourse domain and frequency of use. However, in several cases, more than one aspect appears to be subsumed in one cluster. Also, and particularly in the GloWbE data, the overlap between clusters may be quite extensive. The solution developed here, then, should be taken as a heuristic and holistic approach to difference among verbal participles rather than a ground truth. Its utility, ultimately, depends on the clusters' ability to contribute to the statistical models presented in Chapters 9 and 10.

7

Varieties of English and Substrate Influence

The rise of the English language to a global position and spread around the world is a story of British imperialism and colonialism that will not be retold in this book in great detail. The consequence is a rich heterogeneity of regional dialects, in World Englishes studies called "varieties" of English that differ from one another on all levels of description—from phonological and lexical to morpho-syntactic and discourse-pragmatic. Section 2.3 provides an overview of previous literature on the passive alternation in World Englishes. This chapter will expand on that view by introducing the twenty varieties that will be investigated in our second study that considers synchronic regional variation in the passive in Chapter 10. Various factors may contribute to regional variation in the use of a linguistic variable such as the passive. Language attitudes, for one, will influence developments. In isolation, two varieties will develop differently, but language contact will also trigger changes. In multilingual and postcolonial contexts, a potential source of influence is language transfer from one of the other languages spoken in the area, whether natively or as a lingua franca. This chapter will focus on these possible substrate influences by describing the other languages spoken in these regions and the passive constructions in them. The assumption is that the structure of these local languages may influence the variety of English developing in these places. Before discussing countries one by one, we will offer a brief general introduction from the point of view of World Englishes.

7.1 Overview of the Varieties of English in GloWbE

Our regional analysis considers twenty varieties of English represented in the GloWbE corpus (Davies 2013; Section 10.1). BrE is included along with varieties from nineteen former British (or, in the case of the Philippines, American) colonies. Different types of settlements in these colonies led to different linguistic outcomes (Schneider 2011: 45). Settler colonies, with large numbers of people relocating permanently, tend to now have English as the L1 of the majority of the population. These are the "Inner Circle" in Kachru's (1985) model of three circles of English. GloWbE contains six varieties of this type: BrE, AmE, Irish English (IrE), AusE, NZE, and CanE. Jamaica was a plantation colony with European settlers from various social backgrounds and slaves from Africa working on large sugar farms under conditions that were prone to give rise to creole languages (Schneider 2011: 48), like Jamaican Creole in Jamaica. The remaining varieties stem from former exploitation colonies, where the number of permanent settlers was lower. In many of these countries, the English language still plays a role in the day-to-day running of internal business such as administration and education, and often it has developed or is developing local features and norms, even though it is not most people's home language. The following fourteen varieties in GloWbE are usually counted toward this "Outer Circle" of Englishes (Kachru 1985): IndE, Sri Lankan English (SLE), Pakistani English (PakE), Bangladeshi English (BanglE), SingE, Malaysian English (MalE), PhE, HKE, South African English (SAE), Nigerian English (NigE), Ghanaian English (GhanE), KenE, Tanzanian English (TanzE), and JamE. Geographically, South, West, and East Africa, South, Southeast, and East Asia, Australasia, North America, the Caribbean, and the British Isles are represented in GloWbE.

This neat country-level classification into English as a native (ENL or L1) or second language (ESL or L2) totters somewhat when one considers the details. For example, JamE exists on a "continuum" (Devonish & Harry 2008; Patrick 2008) with the local English-based creole, which is most Jamaicans' L1. The status of Singapore English as an L1 or L2 has been questioned (e.g., Foley 2001). In South Africa, English is spoken both as an L1 and L2 by different segments of the population. For example, the electronic World Atlas of Varieties of English (Kortmann, Lunkenheimer, & Ehret 2020) includes three varieties of South African English: White SAE is classified as a "high-contact L1 variety" (Bowerman 2020), while Black SAE and Indian SAE are "indigenized L2 varieties" (Mesthrie 2020a, 2020b). In many cases, the internal regional, ethnic, and social differences outweigh the similarities implied by labels such as "British English" or "American English"; these are wider theoretical and ontological problems in the field of World Englishes that we are not able to discuss within the scope of this project.

The selection of varieties included in GloWbE is larger than in former studies on regional variation in the passive, but some smaller varieties are still missing (e.g., Biewer 2009 on the passive in Fiji English), as well as the entire perspective of the "Expanding Circle" of Englishes (Kachru 1985), that is, countries that do not have a colonial past but where English is used as an international lingua franca. A next step could be to observe the passive alternation in such English-as-a-foreign-language environments. Currently, there is increasing interest in English in the Expanding Circle, and scholars argue for a less strict division between postcolonial and non-postcolonial Englishes in theorizing about World Englishes (e.g., Buschfeld & Kautzsch 2017).

The remaining chapter is dedicated to examining potential substrate influence on the use of the passive in the relevant varieties of English. We will proceed region by region, giving a short historical outline, naming the main languages spoken in each country alongside English, and briefly discussing the passive voice in chosen languages.

7.2 South Asia

South Asia is represented in the GloWbE corpus by Bangladesh, India, Pakistan, and Sri Lanka. The histories of these countries are intertwined with each other and with British imperialism. British influence in the area began with trade with the East India Company in the seventeenth century and expanded to direct colonial rule in the period of the British Raj in 1858–1947 (Everaert 2017: 6). English was used for communication with the British rulers and between local ethnic groups and remained important in India as a lingua franca and an official language, often mixed together with Hindi (Everaert 2017: 7). There are twenty-two "scheduled" languages recognized in the Indian constitution and ninety-nine further minor languages spoken (Census of India 2011: 3). The most widely used mother tongue is Hindi, followed by Bengali, Marathi, Telugu, and Tamil (Census of India 2011: 15). Hindi is identical in grammar to Urdu, spoken in India as well as Pakistan, so the passive in the two languages is discussed jointly later.

Pakistan was part of the British Indian Empire during the colonial period but separated from India in 1947. At this point, Bengali was the dominant language in East Pakistan, while Punjabi was the main language in the west. Following another split in 1971, East Pakistan became sovereign Bangladesh. In the western part, that is, modern-day Pakistan, the official languages are now English and Urdu; both are lingua francas in formal contexts and not spoken as L1s (Everaert 2017: 10; Rahman 2020: 282). Pakistan is a highly multilingual place; despite being an official language, Urdu, for instance, is only the fifth most common L1 after Punjabi, Pashto, Sindhi, and Saraiki (census data cited in Rahman 2020: 280).

Standard Hindi and Standard Urdu are close relatives—they have been called "really the same language" (Hoernlé 1880: vii) and are in speech "virtually the same" (Everaert 2017: 9). They differ only in the script they use and aspects of their formal vocabulary, where Urdu shows Persian and Arabic influence, and Hindi draws more on its Sanskrit roots. Hindi and Urdu have two passives. The "compound passive" is formed with an equivalent of *go* followed by a perfective past participle of the main verb; the agent is not mentioned (Hoernlé 1880: 322; Kant Agnihotri 2023: 172–6). Hoernlé calls the second passive a "potential passive" because it indicates that something can be done rather than simply that it is done (1880: 324). It is formed synthetically via suffixation and by shortening the root vowel (Hoernlé 1880: 324). In these languages, intransitive verbs can be used in the passive as well, without any grammatical subject (Everaert 2017: 121). Kant Agnihotri's (2023: 174) example sentence literally translates to "Sleeping was done on the roof last night." Overall, however, Kant Agnihotri (2023: 172) suggests that the passive is used more in English than in Hindi.

In Pakistan and India, Punjabi is spoken in the Punjab regions. The main Punjabi passive is similar to the other Indo-Aryan languages described above: an equivalent of *go* with a perfective participle of the main verb (Tolstaya 1981: 47). However, there is also a second one, consisting of an equivalent of *be* and another participle (Tolstaya 1981: 47). This passive shows narrower conditions of use, only appearing in 3SG to express obligation, but it can be used with intransitive verbs as well (Tolstaya 1981: 48).

Bengali is the second most frequently spoken language in India and the main language of Bangladesh. Another Indo-Aryan language related to Sanskrit, it is spoken by the vast majority (98 percent) of the Bangladeshi population (Tinker & Husain 2024). English is used in Bangladesh as a second language by urban and educated speakers (Tinker & Husain 2024). Bengali has two passive forms. Both utilize the "verbal noun" form of the main verb, combining it with an auxiliary equivalent to *go* (in spoken language) or *become* (more common in written language) (Beames 1891: 43–4; Khaled Saifulla pc March 2024).

The island state of Sri Lanka came under British rule later than other South Asian colonies, in the late eighteenth century, but the level of "institutionalization" of English there is high (Bernaisch 2015: 1). The major ethnic group is Sinhalese (74.9 percent), and the Sinhala language is spoken by an even bigger part of the Sri Lankan population (87 percent), while less than a third (28.5 percent) speak Tamil and less than a fourth (23.8 percent) speak English (The World Factbook 2024; the respondents could select multiple languages in this 2021 census). The number of English speakers and presence of English have, however, been increasing rapidly in recent years (G. A. Eranthi Hirunika Abeywardena pc December 2024).

Sinhala is an Indo-Aryan SOV-word-order language whose spoken and written versions differ from one another significantly, with the written code showing a significantly more complex morphological structure (Wijayawardhana, Wickramasinghe, & Bynon 1995: 103). The notion of control pervades the Sinhala grammatical system so that events are marked as either controlled or involuntary (Wijayawardhana, Wickramasinghe, & Bynon 1995: 105). The passive is a formal feature barely used in day-to-day conversation, where "the active voice is nearly always used in preference to the passive" (Gunasekara [1891] 1999: 179). Colloquial passive-like sentences involve either an inanimate subject or an animate subject in a marked case (dative, instrumental, or accusative—with different levels of control implied) coupled with passive morphological marking on the verb (Wijayawardhana, Wickramasinghe, & Bynon 1995: 110, 134). In the literary variety, there is a whole verb class where many verbs have passive meanings and additionally a compositional passive that can be formed from verbs from other classes (Matzel 1966: 134). It consists of a main verb infinitive, followed by an auxiliary meaning "get, receive" (Matzel 1966: 134, 198–9). Gunasekara ([1891] 1999: 179) points out that these are strictly speaking not passive forms but "gerunds in the accusative case" that take on the function of the passive. Nonetheless, we should observe if the fact that Sinhala has a kind of a GET-passive of its own makes it more likely for Sri Lankan speakers of English to choose *get* as a passive auxiliary in English as well. Finally, the anonymous editors of the crowdsourced "Polyglot wiki" give further insight into the cultural and interactional aspects of the passive in Sinhala:

> In Sinhala, the passive voice is commonly used to show respect and humility, especially when talking about oneself or others. It is a way of downplaying personal achievements or actions and attributing them to external factors or circumstances. In Sinhala culture, there is an emphasis on collectivism and harmony within the community. The passive voice reflects this cultural value by shifting the focus from the individual to the collective. It promotes a sense of interconnectedness and shared responsibility, where actions and events are seen as a result of collective efforts rather than individual achievements. (Polyglot Wiki 2023)

7.3 Southeast Asia

Southeast Asia is represented in the corpus by Malaysia, the Philippines, and Singapore. This region is particularly interesting because many Southeast Asian languages have a passive construction that expresses adversativity (Haspelmath 2013: 358), like the GET-passive is often claimed to do. Malaysia is a multiethnic nation with a long history of multilingualism and language contact between the largest ethnic groups Malays, Chinese, and Indians (Hashim & Leitner 2011: 551). The English language found a footing there through the missionary and English-medium-of-instruction schools established by British colonizers during their 150-year stay from the late eighteenth till the mid-twentieth century (Rahim & Manan 2014: 9). After the 1957 independence, Malay (Bahasa Malaysia) was made the official national language and the medium of instruction, while English was institutionalized as an official second language and a compulsory school subject (Rahim & Manan 2014: 15–16). Most Malays speak Malay and English, and members of other ethnic groups tend to be at least trilingual, with varying knowledge of Malay and English (Rahim & Manan 2014: 12). Malaysian English has been shaped most by its contact with Malay, particularly on the lexical plane (Lowenberg 1986: 75). Malay differs in its spoken and standard forms as presented schematically in Table 9 (I Wanna Learn Malay 2020).

Oleh corresponds to the preposition *by*, while *telah* is a perfective marker (comparable to *already* in meaning). However, in speech, the passive is coded by means of word order only. Another noticeable feature is that the agent appears to be an obligatory element in all passive sentences.

The Philippines is exceptional among English-speaking countries in that it was not a British colony but first a Spanish (1565–1898) and then an American one (1898–1946). The parent variety of PhE is, thus, AmE, and the degree of dependence of PhE on AmE has been examined (Collins 2016). The largest ethnic group Tagalog encompasses a quarter of the population (Philippine Statistics

Table 9 The Structure of Active Voice, Standard Malay Passive Voice, and Colloquial Malay Passive Voice Clauses

Voice	Word order
Active voice	[agent] [verb] [patient]
Standard Malay passive	[patient] di-[verb] oleh [agent] [patient] telah [Agent] [Verb]
Colloquial Malay passive	[patient] [agent] [verb]

Authority 2023). The official languages are English and Filipino. Filipino is a standardized version of the Tagalog language and a local lingua franca. Tagalog is an agglutinative language from the Austronesian family.

In Tagalog, the main elements of a simple sentence are not a subject and a predicate but a predicate and a topic (Schachter & Otanes 1972: 59–60). The topic may correspond to any semantic role, such as actor, goal, direction, or beneficiary (Schachter 1975: 494). Another important concept is "focus," which marks with verbal affixation "the semantic relationship between a predicate verb and its topic" (Schachter & Otanes 1972: 69). Apart from the predicate appearing first, word order is free, and semantic roles are indicated with prenominal markers (Schachter 1975: 494–5). Under these conditions, the Tagalog passive sentence is conceptualized quite differently from subject-based languages. It can be one where the goal (cf. the object) is in focus, and the actor is not mentioned (Schachter & Otanes 1972: 72–3). Schachter and Otanes's grammar of Tagalog (1972) does not even explicitly describe how to form a passive sentence, as sentences expressing passive meanings are not structurally categorically different from other sentences. Differences center around concepts of focus and aspect rather than voice.

Singapore, in Schneider's words (2011: 50), "owes its existence as a political entity to British colonial activity." Modern Singapore was founded by British governor Stamford Raffles and was part of the British-ruled Straits Settlements from the mid-nineteenth to mid-twentieth century (Schneider 2011: 50). Then, it briefly belonged to the federation of Malaysia until its independence in 1965. The four official languages are English, Malay, Mandarin Chinese, and Tamil. English has spread in Singapore through the educational system, often as a medium of instruction (Foley 2001: 12–13). Educated elites speak Standard Singapore English, but alongside it, a popular colloquial variety Singlish has developed, showing strong substrate influence from Mandarin Chinese and Malay (Foley 2001: 13–14).

Bao and Wee (2003) discuss passive constructions in SingE but do not mention the GET-passive. GloWbE data, however, suggest that the GET-passive does also occur in SingE. According to Bao and Wee (2003: 11), SingE speakers have the choice between the BE-passive, a past participle without any passive auxiliary, and two constructions that show substrate influence. The first of these features the Malay auxiliary *kena*:

(107) First time jetting off alone, and first time my flight <u>kena canceled</u>. (GloWbE/Singapore/general)

The lexical meaning of *kena* is being "caught" or "hit" or "coming into contact" with something. It can be used to indicate adversativity in active as well as passive sentences in Malay and SingE (Wiktionary 2024). As a passive auxiliary, *kena* may be followed by a base form of the main verb or, more commonly and especially with irregular verbs, the past participle (Bao & Wee 2003: 2; Kim & Sato 2013: 298). Its use shows semantic restrictions: *kena* only occurs with dynamic and adversative verbs and with subjects affected by the denoted action (Bao & Wee 2003: 2–3). We find the KENA-passive (spelled as <kena> or <kenna>) in GloWbE (Davies 2013) in the Singaporean and Malaysian components; the erratic instances of *kena* in the other subcorpora are proper name usages. Examples (108)–(111) give insight into the verbal usage of the word.

(108) I kena asked when it's my turn to get married already (GloWbE/Malaysia/general)

(109) I kena the same thing in May. That week really sway, lost $80 like this, kena 2 accidents, all in 1 week. (GloWbE/Singapore/general)

(110) Damn kid associated him wearing baju kurung and visiting my place as a Hari Raya visit lor omg how adorable is this anak! Minta kena tendang keluar tingkap! (GloWbE/Singapore/blog)

(111) For this reason, kena is said to [be] a marker of the adversative passive. (GloWbE/Singapore/general)

Example (108) shows *kena* as an adversative passive auxiliary in an English sentence; Example (109) demonstrates a nonpassive usage; Example (110) shows the verb in a non-English context and Example (111) as part of a metalinguistic statement.

The total number of KENA-passives in GloWbE, however, barely reaches one hundred. Two-thirds of these stem from the Singaporean corpus and one-third from the Malaysian subcorpus, where *kena* is, in fact, mostly used in Malay contexts (cf. Example (110)). With such a low number of instances, it does not seem likely that competition with *kena* is a factor curtailing the use of the GET-passive in SingE and MalE. We rather expect the existence of a local adversative passive to feed the use of the other adversative passive, making *get* a more likely choice in these varieties.

The other SingE passive shows influence from the Chinese substrate. Bao and Wee (2003: 1) call it the GIVE-passive and present the following example:

(112) John give his boss scold.
"John was scolded by his boss."

The GIVE-passive is also adversative and used with dynamic verbs, but in this construction, the agent is obligatory (Bao & Wee 2003: 5). Moreover, the subject is seen as sharing the responsibility for the event and hence must be animate, and the lexical verb always appears in the base form (Bao & Wee 2003: 6). This passive is influenced by passive constructions in Mandarin, Hokkien, and Cantonese dialects of Chinese, discussed next, which also have an adversative passive where the agent becomes the object of the passive verb (Wang 1982; Matthews & Yip 1994; both cited in Bao & Wee 2003: 6–7; Haspelmath 2013: 359).

Chinese is a highly analytic topic-comment language. Our example of the passive comes from Mandarin Chinese. Zhu and Huang (2023: 327–32) call it the BÈI-construction, after the "passive marker" *bèi*, which immediately precedes the optional passive agent and the formally unchanged transitive main verb:

subject/patient + *bèi* + object/agent + verb + other elements

Zhu and Huang (2023: 331) state that the BÈI-construction's main function is to express an adverse meaning, although nowadays it can be used for neutral or even beneficial meanings as well. The adversative meaning makes sense considering that the meaning of *bèi* as a lexical verb, before it was grammaticalized, was "to suffer" (Zhu & Huang 2023: 332). Finally, there are further markers that can be used in place of *bèi* in speech—transliterated as *gěi* "give," *jiào* "shout, call," and *ràng* "permit, let"—which rely on the topic-comment structure where the patient is the topic and the "rest of the sentence serves as the comment to express the passive meaning" (Zhu & Huang 2023: 337).

7.4 East Asia

As the last Asian region, East Asia is represented by Hong Kong. Britain annexed the island in 1842 following the first Opium War with China. During the nineteenth century, there was not yet any mentionable bilingual English-speaking community in Hong Kong (Evans 2015: 405). The 1898 New Territories lease gave Britain the authority over the territory of Hong Kong for ninety-nine years, interrupted only by Japanese occupation in 1941–6 (Schneider 2007: 135). The twentieth century marked an increase in the population of Hong Kong especially in the form of Chinese refugees (Schneider 2007: 135). British rule ended in 1997, and Hong Kong is now a special administrative region of China. The recognition of Hong Kong English has been slower and more careful than that of many other New Englishes, and not all scholars agree that English usage in Hong Kong is widespread and distinctive enough to merit the label of a variety (e.g., Benson 2000: 373, 379; Evans 2015: 391). Census data from 2011 suggest that 42.6 percent of the Hongkongese population have some competence in English, with a rising trend in the preceding decades (Census and Statistics Department 2012; cited in Evans 2015: 392). English native speakers—mainly British expatriates—are a small minority in comparison to the (non-native) Chinese majority with Cantonese as preferred medium of communication (Benson 2000: 373).

The Cantonese passive is very similar to the Mandarin BÈI-construction described above, except that the agent is an obligatory member (which can be replaced by an equivalent of *person* or *thing* if unknown) (Matthews & Yip 1994: 149–50). They also briefly describe further Cantonese passives: the "indirect passive" has the experiencer as the subject, the "resultative passive" focuses on a resulting state, and "adjectival passives" modify nouns (Matthews & Yip 1994: 151–2). Matthews and Yip (1994: 150), however, point out that the passive is less common in Cantonese than in English. A reason may be that English uses the passive to highlight the patient, while Cantonese can accomplish the same via topicalization (Matthews & Yip 1994: 73). Last but not least, the semantic restriction of adversativity possibly also accounts for this (Matthews & Yip 1994: 150).

7.5 Australasia

Australasia is represented by Australia and New Zealand. Australia was a British penal colony from 1788 onward. The Australian colonies started gaining more autonomy in the second half of the nineteenth century and became a self-governing Commonwealth of Australia in 1901 when six colonies formed a federation (Parliament of Australia 2022). During the 150 years of colonization, the indigenous Aboriginal population decreased by an estimated 80 percent in violent conflict with the invaders but also due to the introduction of formerly unknown diseases and alcohol (Flood 2019: 34). In present-day Australia, 72 percent of the population report English as their primary home language, and the rest are divided between many different immigrant languages, while only 0.3 percent speak an indigenous Australian language at home (Australian Bureau of Statistics 2022).

New Zealand was colonized late: the indigenous Māori people signed a treaty with the British in 1840 to become part of the British Empire. New

Zealand acquired a Dominion status in 1907 and full independence in 1947. Contemporary New Zealand is an ENL country, where in 2013, English speakers accounted for 90 percent of the population, while Te Reo Māori speakers constituted 3 percent (Ministry for Ethnic Communities 2024). The question of substrate influence is, therefore, substantially less relevant for Australia and New Zealand.

7.6 East Africa

East Africa is represented by Kenya and Tanzania. The colonial period in Kenya began with the late-nineteenth-century establishment of the East Africa Protectorate, continued with the Colony of Kenya in 1920, and ended in independence in 1963. The area of today's Tanzania was ruled by German colonists from the 1880s until it came to British hands in 1919, till independence in 1961. The archipelago of Zanzibar was added in 1964 (Schmied 2013: 454). In East Africa, Kiswahili is the official and national language and the most widely spoken lingua franca, while English is "clearly in minority language," for example, in Tanzania (Schmied 2013: 454). Kiswahili is an agglutinative language, and its verbs are passivized by adding a suffix to a verbal base (-*wa*, exact form dependent on the phonological form of the base); the patient is made the subject and the agent, if included, is introduced with *na* "and, with" (Ojiambo 2022).

7.7 Southern Africa

Southern Africa is represented by the Republic of South Africa. The Cape region was colonized first by the Dutch and from the turn of the nineteenth century by the British, with masses of colonists arriving in 1820. South African history is marked by wars in the nineteenth century and racial segregation favoring the white minority over the Black majority and speakers of color in the twentieth century. In today's postapartheid South Africa, the largest ethnoracial group is Black African people (81.4 percent), followed by speakers of color (8.2 percent), white (7.3 percent), Indian or Asian people (2.7 percent), and others (0.4 percent) (Statistics South Africa 2024).[1] South Africa recognizes twelve official languages in its constitution, with the most widely spoken ones being isiZulu (spoken at home by 24.4 percent of the population according to the 2022 census), isiXhosa (16.3 percent), Afrikaans (10.6 percent), Sepedi (10.0 percent), English

(8.7 percent), Setswana (8.3 percent), and Sesotho (7.8 percent). The remaining five languages are spoken or signed by less than 5 percent each (Statistics South Africa 2024). For a more detailed sketch of the sociolinguistic profile of South Africa, see Mesthrie (2002). The two most widely spoken languages, isiZulu and isiXhosa, are Nguni languages from the Bantu family and largely mutually intelligible (University of Cambridge Language Centre Resources n.d.). In both languages, the passive is constructed synthetically: an allomorph of the suffix *-w-* is added after the verbal stem, and the agent is prefixed to mark it as such (Nthoba 1995; Mike 2020).

The third most spoken tongue in South Africa is an Indo-European language. Afrikaans is the language of the white Afrikaners that developed from seventeenth-century Dutch (Donaldson 1993: xiii). The Afrikaans passive is formed with the past participle and either *word* "become" or *wees* "be" as an auxiliary, depending on tense (*word* for present and future, *wees* for past) (Donaldson 1993: 257). The agent can be expressed with a phrase headed by *deur* ("by, through") (Donaldson 1993: 259). Similarly to English, the participle may sometimes, depending on context and lexical verb, be interpreted as an adjective rather than a passive verb (Donaldson 1993: 259).

7.8 West Africa

West Africa is represented by Ghana and Nigeria. After centuries of trade, West Africa was colonized by the British and the French in the nineteenth century. Contact and trade with Europeans—first in gold, then in slaves, then in cocoa (Boateng et al. 2024)—led to a West African Pidgin developing in the area that has Ghanaian and Nigerian subvarieties. When Ghana gained independence in 1957 as the first country in Sub-Saharan Africa, English was chosen as the official language (Boateng et al. 2024). The largest ethnic group is the Akan (45.7 percent), but at least seventy-five further languages are used by smaller ethnic groups (Boateng et al. 2024).

The Akan language relies on its fairly rigid word order to mark syntactic roles (Abrefa & Ansah 2021: 110). In the passive, an "impersonal" dummy pronoun functions as the subject, while the patient or theme is still the object, and the verbal form is identical to the active (Abrefa & Ansah 2021: 108, 113).[2]

Nigeria has three major languages associated with specific ethnic groups, religions, and regions—Yoruba, Hausa, and Igbo—and hundreds of minor languages (Jowitt 2019: 3). English is the official language, important in education and administration (Jowitt 2019: 3). Along with Nigerian Pidgin (NigP) in the south and Hausa in the north (Jowitt 2019: 11), English is used as a lingua franca between ethnic groups. Hausa belongs to the Afroasiatic language family, while Igbo and Yoruba are Niger-Congo languages.

Devices for expressing the passive in all these languages are quite similar to Akan. Yoruba, like many African languages, does not have a passive proper (Ashiwaju 1968: 48). Instead, passive meanings are expressed by using an indefinite pronoun (*a* or *nwọn*, both translatable as "they") as the subject of an active verb (Crowther 1852: 27; Ashiwaju 1968: 48); the verb form does not change, and the patient remains the object.

Similarly, in Hausa, passive-like sentences are also expressed by an impersonal pronoun that acts as the subject (Newman 2000: 271). Hausa also has another form that can be seen as a passive. It relies on a particular "grade" of verbs—grades are "morphological classes" (Newman 2000: 627) of verbs that have a specific phonological shape and may come with semantic or grammatical features. Grade 7 "sustentative" verbs usually carry meanings corresponding to the English passive, with the additional connotation of an action being (im)possible or being done "thoroughly or well" (Newman 2000: 665–7).

According to Obi-Okoye (2008; cited in Amadi 2018: 52), Igbo has no passive. Yet, the semantically equivalent structures are similar to other West African languages, with an equivalent of the dummy pronoun *it* as subject used to topicalize the patient (Amadi 2018: 52–3).

Finally, NigP—another source of influence on NigE—employs similar means for expressing passive meanings. There is no bona fide passive voice but a number of constructions may express relevant meanings; for example, 2SG and 3PL pronouns *yù* and *dèm* can be used as subjects of active sentences to avoid specifying the agent (Faraclas 1996: 186). In West African Pidgin, *get* is a verb of static possession (equivalent to *have*) (Faraclas 1996: 65), as illustrated in Example (113).

(113) A no get red klot. (Faraclas 1996: 65)
"I have no red clothes."

7.9 The Caribbean

The Caribbean is represented by Jamaica. The Britons arrived there in 1655, taking over the island from Spanish colonizers. Jamaica was a plantation colony where slaves from Africa outnumbered the settlers, leading to the development of an English-lexifier creole (Sand 2013: 210). In Jamaica, slavery was abolished in the nineteenth century, and independence was gained in 1962. English is named as the official language in the Jamaican constitution, but it coexists with Jamaican Creole (JamC) in a situation that has been described as a continuum (Devonish & Harry 2008; Patrick 2008), with most speakers more competent in the creole (Sand 2013: 210). JamE is increasingly influenced by the neighboring AmE in addition to the colonial model, BrE (Mair & Sand n.d.), and even highly educated JamE retains influences from JamC (Hinrichs 2006: 36). In JamC, a passive meaning can be expressed without any formal marking with the "basic passive" (see Example (114)), but there is also a GET-passive with uninflected *get* followed by an uninflected main verb, as in Example (115) (Winford 1993: 140–2).

(114) Plentii soldja kil laas nait. (Winford 1993: 140–2)
"Many soldiers were killed last night."

(115) Plentii soldja get kil laas nait. (Winford 1993: 140–2)
"Many soldiers got killed last night."

Haspelmath (2013: 358) points out that *get* often acts as a passive auxiliary in English-based contact languages. Consequently, the (post-)creole continuum situation in which JamE exists can be hypothesized to dispose the variety favorably toward the GET-passive.

7.10 North America

North America is represented by Canada and the United States. The British settled there in multiple waves of immigration and progressively conquered the land and massacred the indigenous people in the course of the seventeenth and eighteenth centuries (Schneider 2011: 49). The British settlers expanded westward and to Canada. Canada was among the first colonies to gain independence—it has been self-governing since 1867 and fully autonomous since 1931. In the 2021 Canadian census, 58.4 percent named English as their L1 and 20.9 percent named French, while 24.2 percent chose some nonofficial immigrant language, and fewer than 200,000 people (0.01 percent) listed one of the indigenous languages (Statistics Canada 2022). As French does not play a major role in multilingual contexts outside of the province of Quebec, we do not expect substrate influence from French to play a role. However, in general, there may be tension between American and British influence in Canada.

In the United States, the colonies declared independence in 1776. Then, after a civil war and further internal turmoil in the nineteenth century, the United States started expanding, gaining control of Puerto Rico, Guam, and the Philippines as a result of the 1898 Spanish–American War (Schneider 2011: 51), thus becoming an imperial power themselves. Later, the United States has been a popular destination for migration. The United States receives the most international immigrants worldwide, with India, China (Hong Kong), Mexico, Cuba, and the Philippines as the most frequent countries of origin (Zong, Batalova, & Hallock 2018). With immigrants accounting for 13.7 percent of the US population (US Census Bureau 2024), the label "AmE" clearly does not describe an ENL-only environment. However, we assume that, similar to Canada, no local substrate language has a significant impact on American English.[3]

7.11 Europe

Finally, Europe is represented by Ireland and the UK. In the British Isles, parts of the population speak Celtic languages in addition to English: Welsh in Wales, Scottish Gaelic in Scotland, and Irish Gaelic in Northern Ireland and the Republic of Ireland. In recent statistics, 91.1 percent of the population in England and Wales have English as their "main language"; after that, the most widely spoken ones are immigrant languages (Polish, Romanian, Punjabi) (Statista 2024). In the Republic of Ireland, 40 percent of the population self-reports to be able to speak Irish, but more than half of them do not speak it well, use it "only within the education system" (Central Statistics Office 2023), or never use it at all. Therefore, we do not expect any other language to influence these varieties of English significantly.

After this overview of the GloWbE countries and the relevant languages, we will present a synopsis of all the variables considered in our two models in Chapter 8.

8

The Structure of the Proposed Models

The chapters so far have traced the development of the English passive voice and have described the process of extracting relevant tokens and narrowing them to the appropriate contexts. They also introduce some of the relevant predictors that may influence the variation between *be* and *get*, specifically relating to subject responsibility, adversativity, and non-neutrality, as well as verb semantics. This chapter describes the model structure of the mixed-effects logistic regression model fitted on diachronic (8.1.1) and the model fitted on synchronic data (8.1.2). It also introduces additional relevant hypotheses such as the notion of lexical persistence and describes further variables such as the F-measure (as an indicator of formality). The chapter concludes by motivating the choice of statistical model and outlining the modeling procedure (8.2).

8.1 Overview of Predictors

8.1.1 The Diachronic Study

The following predictors are included in the models fitted on data from COHA. For categorical variables, we list all levels in brackets and underline the reference level.

To evaluate diachronic change, we include the year (continuous) to which each observation is dated. The increase of the GET-passive is well attested (cf. Section 2.3), and we expect it to be visible in our data.

Additionally, we include an interaction term between year and each of the other predictors. This allows us to test whether this linguistic change is accompanied by a leveling of constraints, which has been suggested elsewhere (Labov 1994, 2007; Croft 2000; Bybee 2010) and which we may also observe in our data. The GET-passive may initially be limited to certain contexts and in more recent decades be used more widely.

We hypothesize that less formal genres and texts will favor *get* and more formal genres and texts will disfavor it. For formality, we use two predictors:

1. The text genre (categorical: fiction, magazines, newspapers, nonfiction books, and TV and movies) is extracted as part of the COHA file metadata.
2. For measuring formality on the level of individual texts, we use the F-measure (continuous) developed by Heylighen and Dewaele (2002).

For Heylighen and Dewaele (2002: 298–9), informality means "context-dependence," encompassing deictic expressions, anaphora, and implicature relying on shared personal or encyclopedic knowledge, as well as different interactive and emotional elements. This contrasts with formal language, characterized by neutrality, structural complexity, and the need to make all "necessary references, assumptions, and background knowledge" (Heylighen & Dewaele 2002: 298) explicit to avoid ambiguity and inaccuracy. How much context participants share depends on their relationship and, for instance, the chosen modality. Written texts, in general, have to remain interpretable for a bigger audience over longer time spans and across more diverse settings; as a result, they tend to depend less on context and more on formal, explicit expression (Heylighen & Dewaele 2002: 295). Heylighen and Dewaele's (2002: 306–10) F-measure tries to capture this difference in a way that can be practically and quickly applied to large text corpora yet validly measures at least some of the aforementioned features and corresponds to intuitions about formal and informal texts. It is based on the assumption that words from some word classes are used more in context-dependent expressions while others are needed for context-independent discourse. Specifically, Heylighen and Dewaele (2002: 334) consider a higher use of nouns, adjectives, prepositions, and articles to represent formal language and the use of pronouns, verbs, adverbs, and interjections to represent contextual language.

In addition to the word classes mentioned in Heylighen and Dewaele (2002), COHA contains numerals, possessives, and negators. In our view, numerals clearly have rather fixed, context-independent meanings. The possessive category shall be treated similarly to other pronouns and negators similarly to other adverbs. We believe the same logic applied to adverbs being grouped with deictics can be applied to negators. Empirically, the negator *not* has been demonstrated to co-occur with verbs and pronouns (Bohmann 2019: 94–5), which lends further support to this interpretation. The authors do not include conjunctions in their calculation as they do not signal deixis or the formality of an item but represent a "measure of the complexity of sentence structure" (Heylighen & Dewaele 2002: 318).

Concretely, we calculate the F-measure using the following formula, which adds the aforementioned three word classes to Heylighen and Dewaele's (2002: 309) proposition. The symbol % stands for decimal fractions (0–1) representing the proportion of words from that word class of all words in that text.

F = (noun % + adjective % + preposition % + article % + numeral % – verb % – adverb % – pronoun % – possessive % – interjection % – negator % + 1)/2

This results in an F-measure between 0 and 1 that is independent of text length, applicable in numerous languages, and reflects the fact that formality is a continuum. A higher F-score indicates more formality. We employ this measure to texts in COHA relying on the word class tags in the annotated version of the downloadable corpus, calculating an F-measure for each text and associating it with each passive in that text. We hypothesize that texts with a higher F-measure are less likely to contain GET-passives than texts with lower F-measures.

To operationalize subject responsibility, we consider two variables:

1. The animacy of the subject referent (categorical: animate, inanimate, collective, body part, <u>unknown</u>) and hypothesize that the GET-passive is used less frequently with inanimate referents.
2. We extract *by*-prepositional phrases (categorical: present, <u>absent</u>) immediately following the verb phrase. We expect the presence of an agent to mitigate subject responsibility and hence favor the BE-passive.

See Chapter 4 for more details on each of these.

We approach adversativity and non-neutrality through two independent variables:

1. Participle sentiment (continuous).
2. Clause sentiment (categorical: <u>neutral</u>, positive, negative).

See Chapter 5 for a full discussion of how these measures were extracted and calculated and how the classification was arrived at.

We also test whether different semantic verb groups (categorical, ten levels in the full data and nine levels in the central data, with the largest group as baseline) show distinct selectional preferences in relation to *be* and *get*. For more information about the process, see Chapter 6. The resulting semantic clusters are presented in Section 6.4.

We code each observation for a number of morpho-syntactic features assuming that more complex grammatical structures favor the BE-passive:

1. Complementation with a *to*-infinitive (categorical: present, absent). We approximate this by simply checking for the presence or absence of *to* immediately after the participle. Following Xiao, McEnery, and Qian (2006: 112), we expect *to*-infinitival adjuncts to strongly favor be (see 9.3.6.5 for a fuller discussion). Note, however, that our approximation is unable to systematically differentiate between adjuncts, *to*-infinitives that act as complements of the participle and *of*-PPs.
2. Tense, aspect, and modality (categorical: present, present progressive, preterite, *to*-infinitive, modal + infinitive, gerund or non-finite *-ing*, past perfect, present perfect, modal + perfect, past progressive): previous studies have found the perfect and other complex verb forms to disfavor the GET-passive.
3. Subject person (categorical: first, second, third, other, i.e., unknown).
4. Intervening adverb (categorical: present, absent).
5. Polarity (categorical: negative, positive): we check whether the passive clause contains a negator.

Finally, we include a variable that keeps track of which auxiliary was used in the previous passive in the text. This measures priming or lexical persistence of sorts (categorical: *be*, *get*—note that this variable was coded as *be* for the first token in each text) and addresses the following question: is a writer who used one auxiliary in the previous instance more likely to use the same auxiliary in the current construction (Bock 1986; Branigan, Pickering, & Cleland 2000)? The inclusion of persistence as a predictor variable is not directly motivated by any specific hypothesis regarding the passive alternation in particular but rather by the fact that it is likely a "universal of language use and processing" (Scherre & Naro 1991: 30) that "can enhance the explanatory power of linguistic model building" (Szmrecsanyi 2006: 207). In light of the complexity of our model and the lack of a specific expectation about priming in the passive alternation that goes beyond a general persistence effect, we draw only on the relatively simple operationalization outlined above and disregard complexities such as the role of distance between prime and target or the influence of *get* or *be* occurring outside passive contexts (β-persistence as per Szmrecsanyi 2006: 2).

Nonetheless, there is one particular question about persistence that our study is able to shed light on, and that is whether an item's frequency interacts with its susceptibility to persistence. Since the diachronic part of our study covers a period of drastic frequency increase of the GET-passive, the interaction of persistence with year can help address this particular relationship. An interaction between frequency and persistence is mentioned as a productive target for future research by Szmrecsanyi (2006: 211), and some recent literature on priming has specifically incorporated frequency. Based on four corpus studies of syntactic alternations, Jaeger and Snider (2007) find that infrequent structures are more strongly affected by persistence than frequent ones. Likewise, Wei et al. (2016: 6) maintain that priming "is modulated by the baseline frequency of alternative structures, with the less frequent structure being more sensitive to structural priming effects." Such effects have generally been linked to mechanisms of implicit learning (Ferreira & Bock 2006; Bernolet & Hartsuiker 2010). Most of this work has been based on synchronic comparisons between different structures of different frequencies. Our data offers a diachronic view of one alternation, the ratio of whose variants shifts over time. If we find an interaction between time and the effect of priming, this will serve as further construction-internal evidence for the position that the "less frequent structure primes more strongly" (Jaeger & Snider 2007: 41).

We fitted two models on the data from COHA: one that limits the tokens to more central passives (refer to Chapter 3 for a description of this process) and one that includes all extracted tokens. The latter model includes as an additional predictor the probability of a token to be classified as a central rather than a peripheral passive (continuous), which also interacts with year. This variable is based on the classifier we trained to situate each token on a continuum from central to peripheral or more verbal to more adjectival passives (refer to Chapter 3 for details on this procedure).

Continuous variables are standardized, that is, their z-scores are used, to allow for better comparisons of predictors on different scales. Categorical variables are sum-coded, with the baseline levels underlined in the descriptions earlier. Generalized variance inflation factors are < 5 for all predictors, so the predictors are not strongly collinear and can all remain in the model.

8.1.2 The Synchronic Study

We include the same predictors in our model on GloWbE when possible. Specifically, we again use the F-measure (continuous) as an indication of the formality of a text (Heylighen & Dewaele 2002) to establish whether more formal texts favor *be* over *get*. Unlike in the COHA model, a genre variable was not included as a predictor. While GloWbE has a "genre" variable, this distinguishes only between blogs and "general" websites (this category includes some blogs as well) and is not particularly relevant for our purposes (Bohmann 2024).

To operationalize subject responsibility, we include the same two variables:

1. the animacy of the subject referent (categorical: animate, inanimate, collective, body part, unknown) and
2. *by*-prepositional phrases (categorical: present, absent) immediately following the verb phrase.

We hypothesize that *get* is less likely to be used with inanimate referents and with *by*-prepositional phrases.

To operationalize adversativity and non-neutrality, we include these variables:

1. the participle sentiment (continuous) and
2. the clause sentiment (categorical: neutral, positive, negative).

All previously listed variables are entered into an interaction with the country in which a passive token is attested, whereas all following variables are only tested as main effects. This is due to the complexity of the interactions and the lack of concrete hypotheses related to them.

However, we are also interested in the main effects of the country (categorical: twenty levels, the United States as a baseline), comparing the twenty English-speaking countries that GloWbE contains data from. Prior research on the different preferences for *get* across varieties of English has mostly focused on much smaller corpora such as ICE or not included other important predictors or interactions between them. British and American English have been researched extensively, while results from other countries are sparser and sometimes contradictory.

We also test whether different semantic verb groups (categorical: eleven levels, with the largest group as baseline) show distinct selectional preferences in relation to *be* and *get*. For more information about the process, see Chapter 6. The resulting semantic clusters are presented in Section 6.5.

Analogous to the COHA data, we code each observation from GloWbE for a number of morpho-syntactic features assuming that more complex grammatical structures disfavor the GET-passive:

1. Complementation with a *to*-infinitive (categorical: present, absent).
2. Tense, aspect, and modality (categorical: present, present progressive, preterite, infinitive, modal + infinitive, gerund or non-finite *-ing*, past perfect, present perfect, modal + perfect, past progressive): previous studies have found the perfect and other complex verb forms to disfavor the GET-passive.

3. Subject person (categorical: first, second, third, other).
4. Intervening adverb (categorical: present, absent).
5. Polarity (categorical: negative, positive): we check whether the passive clause contains a negator.

As with the COHA data, we include the identity of the preceding passive auxiliary token in order to account for persistence or priming effects (categorical: *be*, *get*). Unlike in the diachronic study, however, we do so merely to control for this effect. We have no hypotheses that persistence should display any variety-specific effects.

Analogous to the analysis of the COHA data, we fit two models on the GloWbE data, too: one is limited to central passives, and the other includes all tokens. The model on the full extraction includes the probability of a token to be classified as a central rather than a peripheral passive (continuous) as an additional predictor.

Prior to model fitting, the data are prepared as before, that is, the continuous variables are standardized by z-scoring them, whereas the categorical variables are sum-coded (baseline levels are underlined in the description earlier). The generalized variance inflation factors are below 5, which indicates no issues with collinear predictors.

8.2 Motivating Multilevel Models

This project uses logistic mixed-effects models. The fundamental justification for mixed-effects models is that many kinds of data violate the assumption of independence, that is, data points needing to be independent from each other. For instance, in experimental research, a field that has adopted these models more readily, each participant usually contributes more than one data point, so these data points are not independent but may cluster together. Mixed-effects or multilevel models deal with this issue by distinguishing between fixed and random effects. Fixed effects are the predictors that are necessary to test hypotheses. In other words, we assume that these variables could have a systematic and predictable effect on the dependent variable. Random effects, on the other hand, "have a non-systematic, idiosyncratic, unpredictable, or 'random' influence" (Winter 2019: 39) on the outcome. Returning to the example of experimental data, some participants may react more or less strongly to an experimental manipulation than others and may also differ in general properties such as their reading speed. Therefore, participant is usually included as a random effect. Mixed-effects models can help account for the variance caused by such factors, improving the fixed effect predictions.

While multilevel models are commonplace in modern psycholinguistic research, corpus linguistics has lagged behind somewhat in adopting them—despite corpus data being generally less balanced than data from psycholinguistic experiments. Beyond that, the inherent hierarchical structure of most corpus data needs to be considered when fitting models, which a multilevel model can achieve by including random effects. For our models, we add a random intercept for participle and all unique combinations of year and genre with random slopes for year in the COHA models and a random intercept for participle in the GloWbE models. This allows the models to consider each participle's unique association with *be* or *get* and, in the case of COHA, how this develops over time.

We prepare the data for modeling using *R* (R Core Team 2023) in *RStudio* (Posit Team 2023) with the tidyverse package (Wickham et al. 2019) and analyze them in the programming language *Julia* (Bezanson et al. 2017) using the packages listed in Table 10.

Table 10 Overview of the Used Packages

Programming language	Package	Function
Julia	CSV.jl (Quinn 2015); DataFrames.jl (Harris et al. 2012)	Reading in .csv files and working with data frames
	MixedModels.jl (Bates et al. 2013)	Fitting mixed-effects models
	RCall.jl (Lai et al. 2015); JellyMe4.jl (Alday & Tristan-Siegfried 2020)	Moving data back and forth between *Julia* and *R*
	Effects.jl (Alday, Kleinschmidt, & Arslan 2024)	Extracting model predictions after model fitting
R in *RStudio*	Quarto (Posit PBC 2023)	Describing the data, automatically inserting tables and graphs into the document, formatting
	kableExtra (Zhu et al. 2021)	Formatting summary tables
	directlabels (Hocking 2024)	Labeling graphs of the model predictions more clearly

9

Diachronic Developments in the English Passive Alternation

The English passive has been undergoing dramatic grammatical and pragmatic changes up until the present day that have not gone unnoticed by the linguistic community, with the decline of the standardized BE-passive and the rise of the innovative GET-passive documented in many corpus-based studies. The present analysis is, however, the first one to quantify the influence of different stylistic, structural, and semantic factors on the choice of the passive auxiliary in a mixed-effects model that considers all these variables and their interactions jointly, based on a large diachronic dataset of English. The findings of this endeavor are presented, visualized, and explained in this chapter. We begin by briefly introducing the data used in Section 9.1 and evaluating the fit of our two regression models (one with the whole dataset and one with only the central passives, as explained in Chapter 3) in Section 9.2, after which the predictions based on those models are discussed one by one for each relevant factor in Section 9.3.

9.1 The Corpus of Historical American English

The Corpus of Historical American English (Davies 2010) is a large diachronic corpus representing five genres and nearly two centuries of American English. Many studies utilizing COHA have excluded the 1810s and 1820s, as the amount of data from these decades is much smaller than in the following years from the 1830s up to the present day; the latest update in 2021 added a new decade (the 2010s) and a whole new genre (TV and movies from the 1930s onward) and, in fact, dropped the 1810s from the corpus altogether. The corpus now comprises 475 million searchable words. They are divided between five broad text types: fiction (including prose, poetry, and movie and play scripts), popular magazines, newspapers (from the 1860s onward), nonfiction books, and TV and movie subtitles; see Davies (2010) for a more detailed distribution over time and genres. What constitutes a single text in COHA depends on the text type—it may be as long as an entire novel or as short as a poem.

COHA has been used in various linguistic studies for insights into grammatical change (e.g., from "it is I" to "it is me" in Kuya 2021), semantic change (e.g., the amelioration of *terrific* in Núñez Pertejo 2017), and overtime developments in the use of language structures (e.g., "many a noun" construction in Hilpert 2012) or pragmatic phenomena (e.g., apologies in Jucker 2018), to give a handful of examples of studies relying on COHA. It is widely accepted as an authoritative resource in diachronic investigations into written American English.

In our study, we consider the whole COHA dataset except the 1820s due to the sparsity of data from that decade (seven million words). We also note that, working with the offline, full-text version of the corpus, our data are not identical to the searchable online interface. For reasons of copyright restrictions, a sequence of ten words is anonymized (replaced by *@*) for every 400 words in the offline version. This unavoidable loss of 2.5 percent of the data and the exclusion of the 1820s leave us with a total of 456 million words of data for this diachronic part of the analysis.

9.2 Model Fit and Output

We fit two mixed-effects regression models on the data from COHA: one on the full set of extracted tokens (refer to Section 3.1 for a description of this process) and one limited to only the central passives (see Section 3.4 for how we distinguish peripheral from central passives). Both models incorporate predictors relating to formality, subject responsibility, adversativity, and non-neutrality, among others, all in interaction with the year of occurrence (refer to Chapter 8 for a complete description of the model structure). The interactions between year and each of the other predictors allow us to examine whether the rise of *get* is accompanied by a leveling of constraints (Labov 1994, 2007; Croft 2000; Bybee 2010), with this auxiliary initially restricted and later used more freely, or whether the predicted probability of the GET-passive increases at similar rates across different contexts.

Table 11 shows the model summary for the model fitted on the full dataset, while Table 12 shows this information for the central passives.

Table 11 Output of Mixed-Effects Logistic Regression Model Predicting *Get* (vs. *Be*) based on the Independent Variables Described in Chapter 8, *N* = 1181196, COHA, full data

Term	Estimate	Std. error	*z*-Value	*p*-Value	sig.
Intercept	−4.6281	0.1827	−25.3266	<0.0001	sig.
year (z-scored)	1.0344	0.1076	9.6101	<0.0001	sig.
genre: magazine	0.2724	0.0384	7.0971	<0.0001	sig.
genre: nonfiction	−0.2391	0.0476	−5.0252	<0.0001	sig.
genre: fiction	0.4048	0.0301	13.4603	<0.0001	sig.
genre: TV/movies	−0.0080	0.0648	−0.1238	0.90146	n.s.
F-measure (z-scored)	−0.6523	0.0228	−28.6600	<0.0001	sig.
animacy: animate	0.7900	0.0309	25.5850	<0.0001	sig.
animacy: inanimate	−0.5627	0.0353	−15.9344	<0.0001	sig.
animacy: body part	−0.6546	0.0787	−8.3229	<0.0001	sig.
animacy: collective	−0.0266	0.0745	−0.3573	0.720843	n.s.
clause sentiment: negative	0.2162	0.0205	10.5638	<0.0001	sig.
clause sentiment: positive	0.1964	0.0298	6.5999	<0.0001	sig.
participle sentiment (z-scored)	0.0489	0.0216	2.2587	0.023899	sig.
participle sentiment (squared)	0.1216	0.0824	1.4753	0.14013	n.s.
cluster: aggression and industry	−0.6340	0.2765	−2.2927	0.021863	sig.
cluster: administration	−0.7837	0.3039	−2.5786	0.00992	sig.
cluster: internal structure of events	−0.7435	0.3315	−2.2432	0.024886	sig.
cluster: bodily movement and position	0.0057	0.2474	0.0229	0.981757	n.s.
cluster: household activities	0.8324	0.2139	3.8919	<0.0001	sig.
cluster: physical change	0.8132	0.2867	2.8368	0.004557	sig.
cluster: less frequent verbs	1.4906	0.3616	4.1221	<0.0001	sig.
cluster: permission and obligation	−1.2394	1.1922	−1.0396	0.298531	n.s.
cluster: emotions	1.5354	0.6087	2.5226	0.01165	sig.
PP with by	−0.4662	0.0373	−12.5114	<0.0001	sig.
PP with to	−0.1950	0.0272	−7.1754	<0.0001	sig.
polarity: negated	−0.0429	0.0319	−1.3433	0.17917	n.s.
tense/aspect: present progressive	1.2805	0.0851	15.0541	<0.0001	sig.
tense/aspect: infinitive	0.4042	0.0308	13.1146	<0.0001	sig.
tense/aspect: present perfect	0.5511	0.0339	16.2698	<0.0001	sig.
tense/aspect: preterite	−0.7189	0.0307	−23.4017	<0.0001	sig.
tense/aspect: modal + infinitive	−0.1442	0.0375	−3.8449	<0.0001	sig.

(*Continued*)

Table 11 (*Continued*)

Term	Estimate	Std. error	*z*-Value	*p*-Value	sig.
tense/aspect: gerund/nonfinite -ing	0.5009	0.0427	11.7381	<0.0001	sig.
tense/aspect: past perfect	−1.5535	0.0665	−23.3650	<0.0001	sig.
tense/aspect: past progressive	0.5550	0.1020	5.4440	<0.0001	sig.
tense/aspect: modal + perfect	−0.8591	0.1166	−7.3700	<0.0001	sig.
adverb premodification	−0.3093	0.0239	−12.9642	<0.0001	sig.
subject person: third	−0.4559	0.0214	−21.2945	<0.0001	sig.
subject person: first	0.2607	0.0401	6.4959	<0.0001	sig.
subject person: second	0.2547	0.0345	7.3875	<0.0001	sig.
previous auxiliary: GET	0.6735	0.0212	31.7109	<0.0001	sig.
probability of central passive (z-scored)	0.3351	0.0552	6.0739	<0.0001	sig.
year (z-scored) & genre: magazine	0.1073	0.0346	3.1029	0.001917	sig.
year (z-scored) & genre: nonfiction	−0.2689	0.0434	−6.1890	<0.0001	sig.
year (z-scored) & genre: fiction	−0.2152	0.0271	−7.9455	<0.0001	sig.
year (z-scored) & genre: TV/movies	−0.0754	0.0568	−1.3260	0.184853	n.s.
year (z-scored) & F-measure (z-scored)	0.0905	0.0189	4.7865	<0.0001	sig.
year (z-scored) & animacy: animate	−0.1206	0.0273	−4.4194	<0.0001	sig.
year (z-scored) & animacy: inanimate	0.1930	0.0310	6.2355	<0.0001	sig.
year (z-scored) & animacy: body part	−0.0238	0.0695	−0.3424	0.732066	n.s.
year (z-scored) & animacy: collective	−0.0075	0.0658	−0.1134	0.909723	n.s.
year (z-scored) & clause sentiment: negative	−0.0017	0.0185	−0.0946	0.924636	n.s.
year (z-scored) & clause sentiment: positive	−0.0018	0.0272	−0.0676	0.946119	n.s.
year (z-scored) & participle sentiment (z-scored)	−0.0033	0.0190	−0.1755	0.860714	n.s.
year_z & sentimentParticiple_2_z	−0.0424	0.0422	−1.0051	0.314844	n.s.
year (z-scored) & cluster: aggression and industry	−0.0040	0.1408	−0.0283	0.977456	n.s.
year (z-scored) & cluster: administrative	0.0431	0.1553	0.2774	0.781453	n.s.
year (z-scored) & cluster: internal structure of events	0.0065	0.1675	0.0387	0.969115	n.s.

(*Continued*)

Table 11 (*Continued*)

Term	**Estimate**	**Std. error**	***z*-Value**	***p*-Value**	**sig.**
year (z-scored) & cluster: bodily movement and position	−0.1699	0.1273	−1.3347	0.181962	n.s.
year (z-scored) & cluster: household activities	−0.4344	0.1098	−3.9570	<0.0001	sig.
year (z-scored) & cluster: physical change	−0.2196	0.1447	−1.5174	0.129164	n.s.
year (z-scored) & cluster: less frequent verbs	−0.1560	0.1919	−0.8131	0.416139	n.s.
year (z-scored) & cluster: permission and obligation	0.4618	0.6331	0.7295	0.46571	n.s.
year (z-scored) & cluster: emotions	0.3398	0.3082	1.1023	0.27033	n.s.
year (z-scored) & PP with by	0.0992	0.0282	3.5159	0.000438	sig.
year (z-scored) & PP with to	−0.0334	0.0238	−1.3999	0.161555	n.s.
year (z-scored) & polarity: negated	0.1000	0.0280	3.5739	0.000352	sig.
year (z-scored) & tense/aspect: present progressive	−0.3821	0.0755	−5.0586	<0.0001	sig.
year (z-scored) & tense/aspect: infinitive	0.3664	0.0286	12.8029	<0.0001	sig.
year (z-scored) & tense/aspect: present perfect	−0.1071	0.0314	−3.4103	0.000649	sig.
year (z-scored) & tense/aspect: preterite	0.3396	0.0278	12.2054	<0.0001	sig.
year (z-scored) & tense/aspect: modal + infinitive	0.0862	0.0349	2.4675	0.013606	sig.
year (z-scored) & tense/aspect: gerund/nonfinite -ing	0.2370	0.0374	6.3458	<0.0001	sig.
year (z-scored) & tense/aspect: past perfect	−0.4063	0.0651	−6.2422	<0.0001	sig.
year (z-scored) & tense/aspect: past progressive	−0.1069	0.0932	−1.1472	0.251298	n.s.
year (z-scored) & tense/aspect: modal + perfect	−0.2416	0.1142	−2.1164	0.034311	n.s.
year (z-scored) & adverb premodification	−0.1563	0.0208	−7.5138	<0.0001	sig.
year (z-scored) & subject person: third	−0.0131	0.0195	−0.6715	0.501923	n.s.
year (z-scored) & subject person: first	−0.0188	0.0370	−0.5084	0.611175	n.s.

(*Continued*)

Table 11 (*Continued*)

Term	Estimate	Std. error	*z*-Value	*p*-Value	sig.
year (z-scored) & subject person: second	−0.0608	0.0318	−1.9129	0.055757	n.s.
year (z-scored) & previous auxiliary: GET	−0.1394	0.0185	−7.5335	<0.0001	sig.
year (z-scored) & probability of central passive (z-scored)	0.1028	0.0314	3.2728	0.001065	sig.

To evaluate the model fits, we calculate the adjusted McFadden pseudo-R^2 for both models using the log-likelihood and degrees of freedom of the full model divided by the log-likelihood of a null model. The result is subtracted from 1 and returns a number between 0 and 1. While the interpretation of pseudo-R^2 is not as straightforward as R^2 calculated for models that predict numeric data (where it indicates the variance in the dependent variable that can be accounted for by the model), higher values indicate a better and lower values a worse model fit.

As null models, we define a logistic regression without random effects so that the choice of auxiliary is predicted only by the intercept as well as a mixed-effects logistic regression where this alternation is predicted by the intercept as well as the random effects used in the models. This way, we can distinguish between the model fit when only the fixed effects compared to when the fixed and random effects are accounted for.

We fit both these null models on the central and the complete dataset and observe that for the central model, the adjusted McFadden pseudo-R^2 is 0.1443 for the fixed effects only and 0.4238 for fixed and random effects, while the corresponding values for the model on the complete data are 0.1525 and 0.3923, respectively. These values, in particular the R^2 for fixed effects only, are moderately low, which we attribute to the messiness generally inherent in large corpora as well as the uncertainty associated with some of our automatically extracted tokens and independent variables.

It is not surprising that the random effects play a considerable role here. This indicates that the participle itself matters considerably in the passive alternation, with some verbs preferring either *be* or *get* and that the tendency toward either option may be modulated by the year of occurrence. Additionally, there may be individual preferences on the level of the speaker or writer for one auxiliary over the other or in terms of how individuals may react to variables such as a highly formal versus a more informal genre. These could have been accounted for by random intercepts

Table 12 Output of Mixed-Effects Logistic Regression Model Predicting *Get* (vs. *Be*) based on the independent variables described in ch. 8, $N = 662170$, COHA, central data

Term	Estimate	Std. error	*z*-Value	*p*-Value	Sig.
Intercept	−5.4653	0.2361	−23.1525	<0.0001	sig.
year (z-scored)	1.0336	0.1498	6.9003	<0.0001	sig.
genre: magazine	0.3484	0.0580	6.0075	<0.0001	sig.
genre: non-fiction	−0.2689	0.0768	−3.5025	0.000461	sig.
genre: fiction	0.5180	0.0450	11.5114	<0.0001	sig.
genre: TV/movies	−0.0398	0.0922	−0.4316	0.666022	n.s.
F-measure (z-scored)	−0.6891	0.0342	−20.1406	<0.0001	sig.
animacy: animate	0.8850	0.0539	16.4244	<0.0001	sig.
animacy: inanimate	−0.6050	0.0626	−9.6718	<0.0001	sig.
animacy: body part	−0.8479	0.1487	−5.7038	<0.0001	sig.
animacy: collective	0.0013	0.1322	0.0096	0.992322	n.s.
clause sentiment: negative	0.1239	0.0310	3.9978	<0.0001	sig.
clause sentiment: positive	0.3176	0.0448	7.0810	<0.0001	sig.
participle sentiment (z-scored)	0.0069	0.0300	0.2317	0.816804	n.s.
participle sentiment (squared)	0.0441	0.1137	0.3878	0.69815	n.s.
cluster: aggression and industry	−0.0109	0.3168	−0.0345	0.972453	n.s.
cluster: administration	−0.4645	0.3513	−1.3221	0.18613	n.s.
cluster: internal structure of events	−1.5352	0.5572	−2.7551	0.005868	sig.
cluster: bodily movement and position	0.5134	0.2655	1.9336	0.053161	n.s.
cluster: household activities	0.7405	0.2661	2.7832	0.005382	sig.
cluster: physical change	0.0164	0.5312	0.0309	0.975313	n.s.
cluster: less frequent verbs	2.1116	0.5945	3.5519	0.000382	sig.
cluster: permission and obligation	−0.4927	1.1443	−0.4306	0.666784	n.s.
PP with by	−0.3011	0.0405	−7.4388	<0.0001	sig.
PP with to	−0.2492	0.0438	−5.6898	<0.0001	sig.
polarity: negated	0.0330	0.0491	0.6728	0.50108	n.s.
tense/aspect: present progressive	1.1974	0.1353	8.8505	<0.0001	sig.
tense/aspect: infinitive	0.5924	0.0523	11.3375	<0.0001	sig.
tense/aspect: preterite	−0.4150	0.0524	−7.9142	<0.0001	sig.
tense/aspect: modal + infinitive	0.1166	0.0609	1.9136	0.055666	n.s.
tense/aspect: gerund/non-finite -ing	0.6933	0.0689	10.0558	<0.0001	sig.
tense/aspect: past perfect	−2.3375	0.1656	−14.1189	<0.0001	sig.
tense/aspect: present perfect	0.6833	0.0571	11.9710	<0.0001	sig.

(*Continued*)

Table 12 (*Continued*)

Term	Estimate	Std. error	*z*-Value	*p*-Value	Sig.
tense/aspect: modal + perfect	−1.1315	0.2254	−5.0194	<0.0001	sig.
tense/aspect: past progressive	0.1424	0.1846	0.7710	0.4407	n.s.
adverb premodification	−0.5456	0.0829	−6.5823	<0.0001	sig.
subject person: third	−0.4869	0.0329	−14.8151	<0.0001	sig.
subject person: first	0.2772	0.0638	4.3449	<0.0001	sig.
subject person: second	0.2692	0.0526	5.1130	<0.0001	sig.
previous auxiliary: GET	0.7050	0.0300	23.4640	<0.0001	sig.
year (z-scored) & genre: magazine	0.0395	0.0487	0.8104	0.417705	n.s.
year (z-scored) & genre: non-fiction	−0.1978	0.0670	−2.9522	0.003155	sig.
year (z-scored) & genre: fiction	−0.2661	0.0378	−7.0404	<0.0001	sig.
year (z-scored) & genre: TV/ movies	−0.1028	0.0759	−1.3540	0.175736	n.s.
year (z-scored) & F-measure (z-scored)	0.0757	0.0273	2.7751	0.005519	sig.
year (z-scored) & animacy: animate	−0.1201	0.0454	−2.6455	0.008157	sig.
year (z-scored) & animacy: inanimate	0.2781	0.0521	5.3412	<0.0001	sig.
year (z-scored) & animacy: body part	−0.1301	0.1271	−1.0236	0.306038	n.s.
year (z-scored) & animacy: collective	0.0622	0.1095	0.5677	0.570216	n.s.
year (z-scored) & clause sentiment: negative	0.0785	0.0267	2.9417	0.003264	sig.
year (z-scored) & clause sentiment: positive	−0.0757	0.0392	−1.9286	0.053778	n.s.
year (z-scored) & participle sentiment (z-scored)	0.0140	0.0257	0.5445	0.586118	n.s.
year_z & sentimentParticiple_2_z	−0.0010	0.0565	−0.0180	0.985643	n.s.
year (z-scored) & cluster: aggression and industry	0.0054	0.1557	0.0345	0.972503	n.s.
year (z-scored) & cluster: administrative	0.0000	0.1788	0.0001	0.999897	n.s.
year (z-scored) & cluster: internal structure of events	0.4919	0.3270	1.5042	0.132539	n.s.
year (z-scored) & cluster: bodily movement and position	−0.0948	0.1307	−0.7256	0.468079	n.s.

(*Continued*)

Table 12 (*Continued*)

Term	Estimate	Std. error	*z*-Value	*p*-Value	Sig.
year (z-scored) & cluster: household activities	−0.2281	0.1338	−1.7048	0.088226	n.s.
year (z-scored) & cluster: physical change	−0.3247	0.2686	−1.2088	0.226742	n.s.
year (z-scored) & cluster: less frequent verbs	−0.3530	0.3373	−1.0465	0.295318	n.s.
year (z-scored) & cluster: permission and obligation	0.4349	0.5576	0.7800	0.435373	n.s.
year (z-scored) & PP with by	0.1213	0.0320	3.7896	0.000151	sig.
year (z-scored) & PP with to	−0.0099	0.0362	−0.2739	0.784137	n.s.
year (z-scored) & polarity: negated	0.0754	0.0410	1.8364	0.0663	n.s.
year (z-scored) & tense/ aspect: present progressive	−0.3096	0.1127	−2.7468	0.006018	sig.
year (z-scored) & tense/ aspect: infinitive	0.2438	0.0453	5.3869	<0.0001	sig.
year (z-scored) & tense/ aspect: preterite	0.1962	0.0445	4.4134	0.00001	sig.
year (z-scored) & tense/ aspect: modal + infinitive	−0.0286	0.0535	−0.5349	0.592691	n.s.
year (z-scored) & tense/ aspect: gerund/non-finite -ing	0.1293	0.0572	2.2600	0.023818	sig.
year (z-scored) & tense/ aspect: past perfect	−0.0870	0.1434	−0.6068	0.544005	n.s.
year (z-scored) & tense/ aspect: present perfect	−0.2351	0.0497	−4.7342	<0.0001	sig.
year (z-scored) & tense/ aspect: modal + perfect	−0.1018	0.1980	−0.5141	0.607209	n.s.
year (z-scored) & tense/ aspect: past progressive	0.0776	0.1531	0.5069	0.612256	n.s.
year (z-scored) & adverb premodification	−0.2271	0.0713	−3.1829	0.001458	sig.
year (z-scored) & subject person: third	−0.0076	0.0290	−0.2638	0.791972	n.s.
year (z-scored) & subject person: first	0.0079	0.0568	0.1384	0.889898	n.s.
year (z-scored) & subject person: second	−0.0511	0.0470	−1.0865	0.27726	n.s.
year (z-scored) & previous auxiliary: GET	−0.1296	0.0253	5.1310	<0.0001	sig.

for each corpus text and additionally random slopes to catch individual variation in terms of how strongly each writer reacts to influences such as formality. However, this was not possible due to the large number of levels this variable contains, even though the model was run on high-powered machines in *Julia*, a programming language that provides extremely fast numeric computing.

It should also be noted that while the pseudo R^2 is similar for the model fitted on the central data and the model fitted on the full data, this implies that a larger amount of data does not automatically result in a better model fit; in this case, perhaps due to the messier nature of the complete dataset.

9.3 Model Predictions

We will now discuss the model predictions and all significant findings for each independent fixed effect considered in our study. It is important to understand that when discussing the factors one by one below, the model predictions do not apply to the overall likelihood of a certain auxiliary but only to the likelihood once other factors are accounted for. We start with the general overtime developments and then proceed to discussing register, various semantic factors, and morpho-syntactic variables, and finally persistence and the probability of a central passive. We will focus on the predictions the models make only for significant slopes and apply $p < 0.025$ as the alpha level. This represents a Bonferroni correction of the conventional alpha level of $p < 0.05$ due to one of our two models being fitted on a subset of data that the other model is run on.

9.3.1 Overall Frequency Developments

We begin by presenting descriptive statistics of the two variants in the relevant time period. Figure 2 contains the overtime raw counts of each variant on the left and the normalized frequencies per year on the right, accounting for the fact that the amount of data per decade varies. The smoothed lines average over fluctuations over time. Figure 2 shows from which decades we have the most passive clauses and illustrates that despite the developments, the BE-passive remains the more popular variant. Figure 2 is suitable for an overall comparison of the two passives and their relative frequency over time. The steadily rising line for *get* implies a clear overall tendency for more acceptance of *get*, particularly from the 1950s onward. At the same time, the use of *be* was stable or slightly on the rise until *c.* 1900 and has since then been rapidly decreasing.

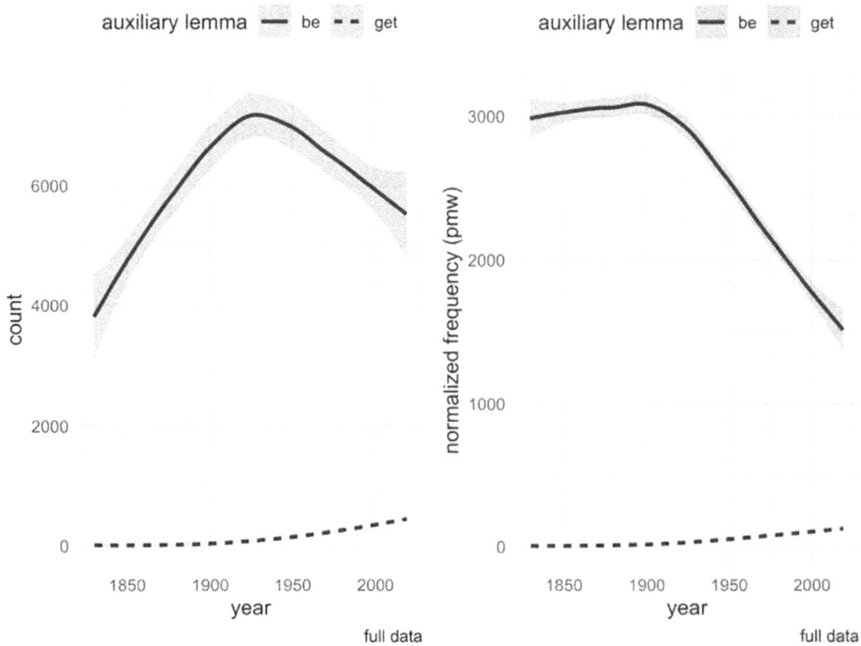

Figure 2 Raw and normalized frequency of BE- and GET-passives in COHA (full data).

The claim that the GET-passive has been becoming more and more frequent over time has been made in numerous previous studies. Based on the frequency developments in Figure 2, our logistic regression models without doubt support this claim. In the model based on the central passives only, the probability of *get* being chosen as a passive auxiliary has increased more than ninety-fold between the two extremes of the timeline represented in the data (1830 and 2017). In the past century, that is, from 1920 till 2017, the increase has been tenfold. Year is a highly significant factor in predicting the auxiliary in both models with $p < 0.0001$. The next sections will show which factors are most strongly associated with a higher probability of language users choosing the GET-passive.

9.3.2 Formality

One factor expected to significantly influence the use of the GET-passive is the formality of the discourse situation and the text. We operationalize formality via two predictor variables: the F-measure and genre. While these two factors do not correlate in a way that would constitute unhealthy collinearity, we do not expect them to be fully independent either.

Heylighen and Dewaele's (2002; see also Section 8.1.1) F-measure relies on proportions of word classes in a text; a higher F-value is a sign of formality and is hence expected to correlate with a higher probability of *be*. This measure tracks formality at the level of a text (e.g., in COHA, in a single newspaper article, book, or movie script). In addition to the F-measure, the data are divided into five text types, of which nonfiction writing can be conceived as more formal, while TV or movie scripts and fiction (which can be expected to contain some scripted dialogues) are less formal. We expect journalistic writing (newspapers and magazines) to be situated in between these extremes in terms of formality.

9.3.2.1 F-Measure

Both the main effect of F-measure and its interaction with time are significant in the same direction in both the full and the central models. As Figure 3 shows, the full model predicts that the less formal the text is, the higher the probability of a GET-passive is. The graph shows particularly well the developments in the more recent decades. The model predicts a probability of 0.0088 for the most formal (compared to 0.0757 for the most informal) texts for data points from the most recent year in the corpus (2017). Examples (116) and (117), from texts with

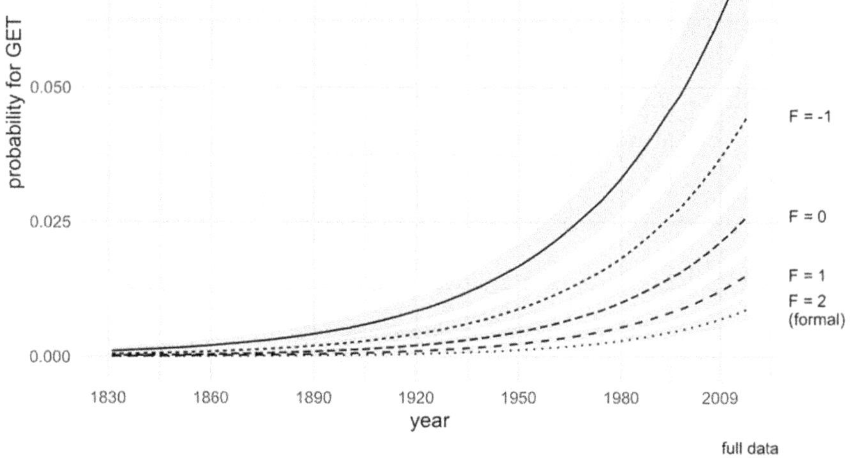

Figure 3 Predicted probability of GET-passives by year and F-measure (full data).

a normalized F-measure of 2 and -2, respectively, give an indication of the kind of stylistic range covered by the predictions plotted in Figure 3.

(116) The great danger involved in a general or sympathetic strike is the possibility that the original grievances which are the primary causes of the strike, and which are, in this case, meritoricus, may be lost sight of because of the charge that the general strike is a challenge to Government and to the existence of Government. (COHA/1926/magazine; F = 2.0)

(117) but I had been suspended so many times they just had to kick me out. (COHA/2005/magazine; F = -2.0)

It is noteworthy that if we observe the ratio of probabilities in the earliest decades in the data, the probability of *get* in informal contexts used to be even higher, as the GET-passive was initially almost exclusively an informal affair. This cannot be seen so easily in Figure 3—the overall frequency of the GET-passive has grown so steeply over the relevant time period that the difference between the lines for F-measure in the earliest years appears only marginal in the graph depicting the overall data. In fact, however, the ratio of probabilities of *get* between F = 2 and F = -2 is actually larger left on the curve. It seems that formality matters, but overall less so now than when the construction started establishing itself. In its incipient stages, *get* was used practically only in less formal texts. This no longer is the case, yet informality still predicts more GET-passives.

9.3.2.2 Genre

Before discussing the predictions of our model regarding genre, we want to again present some descriptive statistics to contextualize our model against the broad tendencies in the data. Figure 4 visualizes the raw frequencies of both passives across the five genres represented in COHA in the central data, while Figure 5 shows the frequencies normalized to one million words. These graphs show how, over the past 100 years, the frequency of the BE-passive has declined across all text types, while *get* has been slowly rising, especially in fiction and TV or movie scripts. Nonetheless, *be* remains the overwhelmingly more common option except in TV or movie scripts, where the passive is overall infrequent. It can be useful to keep these overall patterns in mind when interpreting the output of the regression models, which observe the influence of factors in isolation. Some of the findings regarding genre may seem surprising (particularly the fact that TV or movies do not show a higher probability of *get*) until we remember that what we observe here are the effects of genre with formality held constant. In reality, however, we should note that the genres newspaper, nonfiction books,

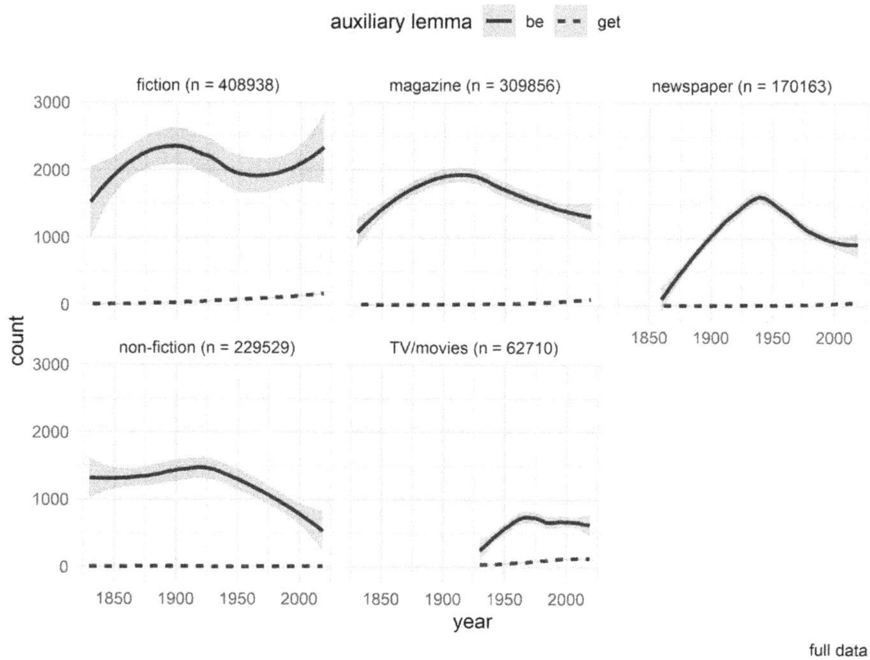

Figure 4 Frequency of BE- and GET-passives across genres in COHA (full data).

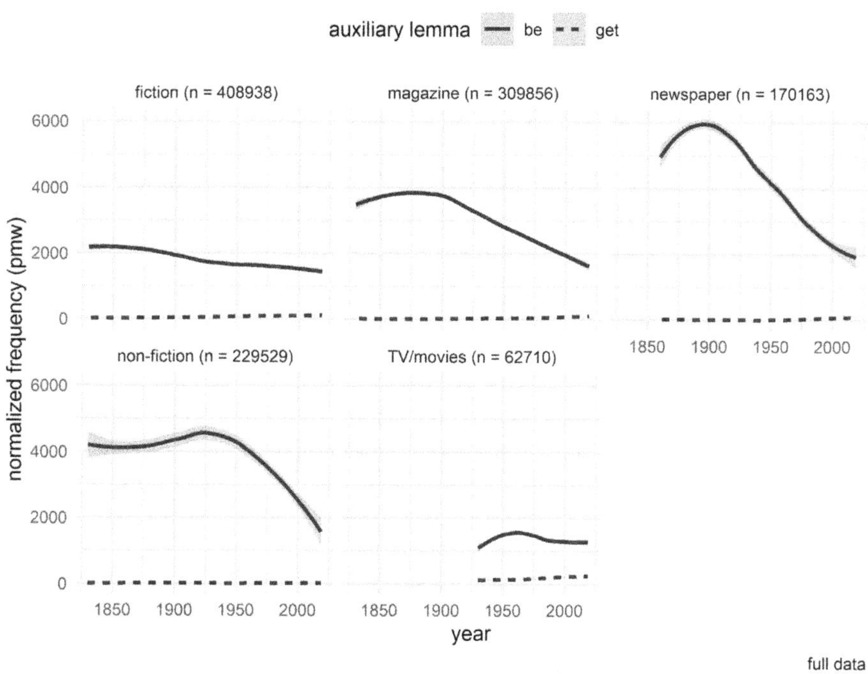

Figure 5 Normalized frequency of BE- and GET-passives across genres in COHA (full data).

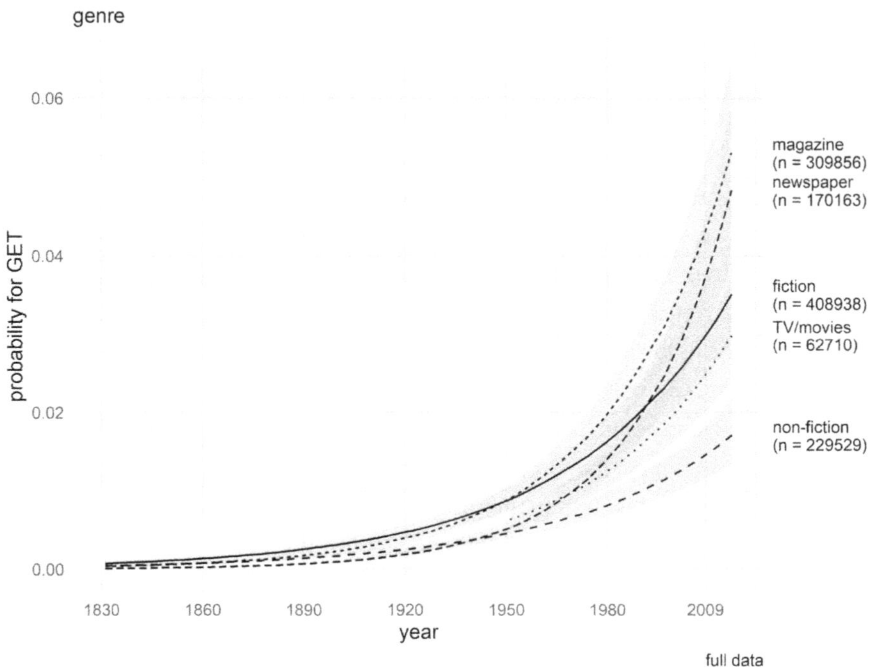

Figure 6 Predicted probability of GET-passives by year and genre (full data).

and magazines are more formal, as indicated by their average F-measure, than fiction and much more formal when compared to TV or movies. We will discuss the findings relating to the text genres next.

The full regression model (Figure 6) shows significant interactions between time and genre, with nonfiction and fiction showing a lower probability of *get* and magazines showing a higher probability over time in comparison to the baseline category newspapers. Fiction is the genre with the highest probability of *get* until *c*. 1950, when magazines take over as the top genre for the GET-passive. Also newspapers surpass fiction in the predictions based on the newest COHA data (1990s onward). Nonfiction and fiction see an increased probability of *get* over time as well, but the lines are flatter. In the central model, the same tendencies prevail, except that developments for magazines are no longer significantly different from newspapers, but both genres experience a similar growth in the probability of *get*.

The more rapid spread of the GET-passive in journalistic writing can perhaps be explained through the concept of "agility" (Hundt & Mair 1999). Hundt and Mair (1999: 236) develop the argument that genres differ in terms of how "open to innovations" or "prone to retain conservative forms" they are. The scholars identify press discourse as most "agile" in this sense and learned writing as most "uptight" (Hundt & Mair 1999: 236). Grammatical change can thus be "mediated through genre" (Hundt & Mair 1999: 236), and it makes sense that newspapers and magazines are the two genres in which an innovative feature such as the GET-passive displays the sharpest rise in the probability of use. In addition to this general receptiveness toward innovation, news writing in particular has been described as undergoing a stylistic reorientation, with a "definite trend away from the cool distancing of traditional written style and towards a kind of spontaneous directness which (though often contrived) is clearly supposed to inject into journalistic discourse some of the immediacy of oral communication" (Leech et al. 2009: 239). The overall association of the GET-passive with orality and informality fits squarely with this trend, and as such, the particularly steep rise of the variant in newspaper and magazine writing in the second half of the twentieth century appears plausible.

Both predictors taken together do suggest a continuing significance of register and (in)formality as factors conditioning the use of the GET-passive. The association between a low F-score (indicating informality) and *get* has been weakening over time, but only slightly, considering the general increase in probability for *get*. Predictions for journalistic genres now favor the GET-passive most strongly, but the text type most averse to this innovation is still the most formal one, comprising nonfiction texts. It is noticeable that the predicted probability of the GET-passive has not increased in parallel across the five genres.

9.3.3 Subject Responsibility

As explained in detail in Chapter 4, we test the claim that the sentence subject of the GET-passive bears some responsibility over the depicted situation by exploring the influence of two predictors: subject animacy and the presence of a *by*-prepositional phrase.

9.3.3.1 Subject Animacy

In both models, the interaction between subject animacy and year is significant ($\beta = -0.1206$, SE = 0.0273) for animate and ($\beta = 0.193$, SE = 0.031) for inanimate subjects. Additionally, p is < 0.025 for the main effect for subjects classified as body parts ($\beta = -0.6546$, SE = 0.0787). The behavior of the unknown category (containing ambiguous, polysemous, and infrequent subjects) closely mirrors the average tendency in all of the data, making it an optimal baseline category.

As Figure 7 demonstrates, animate subjects have the highest predicted probability of *get* as a passive auxiliary. This tendency has slightly weakened over

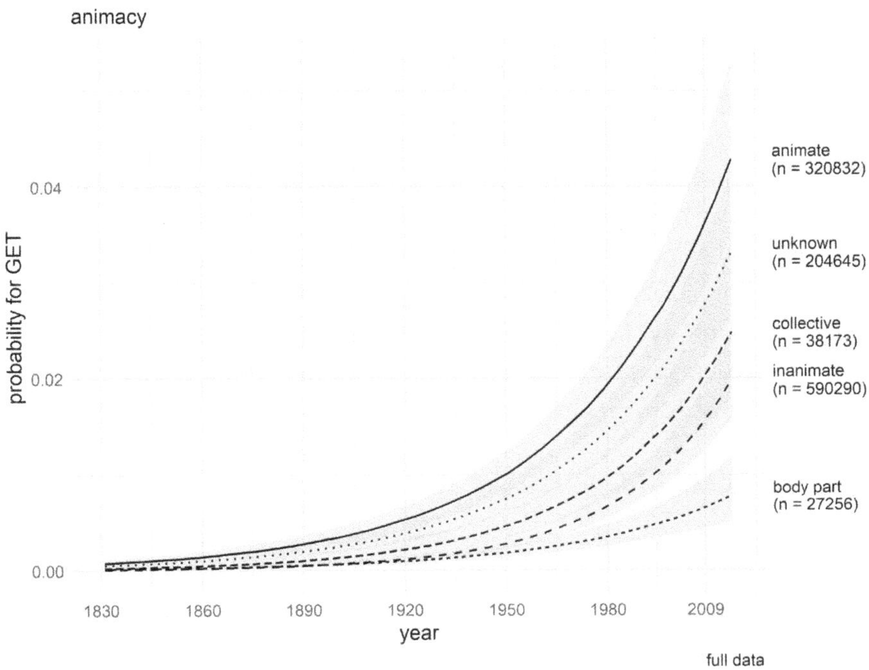

Figure 7 Predicted probability of GET-passives by year and subject animacy (full data).

time, considering the general increase in probability for *get*. In contrast, body parts are predicted to rarely occur with *get* and to favor *be* even more strongly than the passive in general—a pattern that remains almost unchanged over time. The inanimate and collective categories cluster together in-between the animates and the body parts and below the general tendency. While inanimate referents vastly prefer the BE-passive, the predicted probability of *get* has increased slightly over time. One would expect inanimate subjects to disfavor the GET-passive if, as Givón and Yang (1994: 120) argue, "the vestment of purpose, control and responsibility in the surface subject are necessary ingredients of the GET-passive." Our results suggest lower probabilities for the GET-passive with inanimate subject referents, but this tendency does not strengthen over time. Originally, we had assumed that the body-part category might meronymically signify animate entities, but this seems not to be the case, as their behavior is far from that of animate subjects and, in fact, they are the category showing the lowest probability of *get*. As we expected, collectives situate in between the animate and inanimate categories in the model, but their behavior is more similar to the latter. Animate subject referents show by far the highest predicted probability of the GET-passive.

What this means for the hypothesis of subject responsibility is that the GET-passive can be said to at least retain traces of this semantic property, although it is clearly not categorical and is slightly weakening over time. Whenever a passive occurs with a subject capable of intention and conscious action—that is, an animate entity—the likelihood of it being realized as a GET-passive increases. This constraint has only slowly been bleaching over time in the process of grammaticalization (Heine 1993: 89). Interestingly, the kinds of subject related to animate entities—collective nouns, such as *government*, *family*, or *Switzerland*, and body-part terms—do not align with the predictions for simple animate subjects. One explanation to account for this unexpected behavior might be that subject responsibility perhaps presupposes an individual and fully identified subject.

9.3.3.2 Prepositional Phrases with By

We tested the potential effect of the presence of a prepositional phrase with *by* under the assumption that this indicates an additional constituent that mostly encodes the agent. In turn, this could mitigate subject responsibility and, therefore, be associated with a higher probability of *be* as a passive auxiliary since GET-passives have been argued to disfavor overtly expressed agents (see Section 2.4). Our two models show similar results: the interaction with year is significant in both models, with a higher estimate for the central model, which we expect to contain tidier data ($\beta = 0.1213$, SE = 0.032 for the central compared to $\beta = 0.0992$, SE = 0.0282 for the full model).

The main effect indicates a higher predicted probability of a GET-passive if no *by*-PP is found compared to tokens that contain a *by*-PP. This result is in line with the claims made in previous research (Section 2.4). When plotting the interaction (Figure 8), we observe that this tendency persists over time, but the model indicates a weakening of this constraint that starts in the second half of the twentieth century when confidence intervals begin to overlap. This could indicate that the GET-passive may lose its proposed aversion to overtly expressed agents and develop into a more general passive variant. However, as the account of subject animacy suggests as well, this process appears to be progressing slowly and at present to be at a rather incipient stage.

9.3.4 Adversativity versus Non-Neutrality

According to the adversativity hypothesis, the GET-passive should occur in negative contexts, while the related non-neutrality hypothesis suggests that it actually favors both negative and positive contexts over those that do not

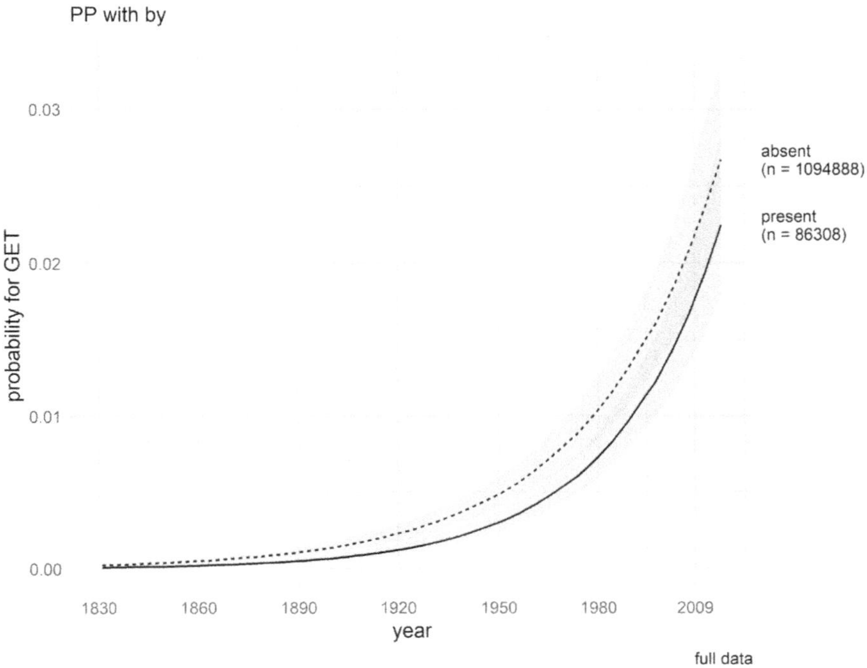

Figure 8 Predicted probability of GET-passives by year and by *by*-PP (full data).

entail any overt sentiment or value judgment (see Section 2.5). To test these hypotheses, we include sentiment of both the participle (numeric) and clause (categorical: neutral, positive, negative) in the models. One motivation for this was our desire to try to distinguish the origo of the relevant sentiment: the assumption is that while the sentiment associated with the participle applies directly to the passive subject, the sentiment of the whole clause relates rather to the stance taken by its producer, and the two may sometimes differ (see Section 5.3 for example sentences and a description of the method). Moreover, the clause sentiment considers semantic features that arise from the syntax and lexicon of the broader sentence, such as the scope of negation and realis versus irrealis mood. These issues may be illustrated by Example (118).

(118) they had thought they would be killed and felt lucky to be alive (COHA/1974/news; participle: -3.5; clause: positive)

The participle *killed* in Example (118) receives a negative score (-3.5) because being killed is an adverse event to the sentence subject. The sentence on the whole, by contrast, is assigned a positive sentiment score as it contains positive words such as *lucky* and *alive*, and more importantly, it depicts a hypothetical

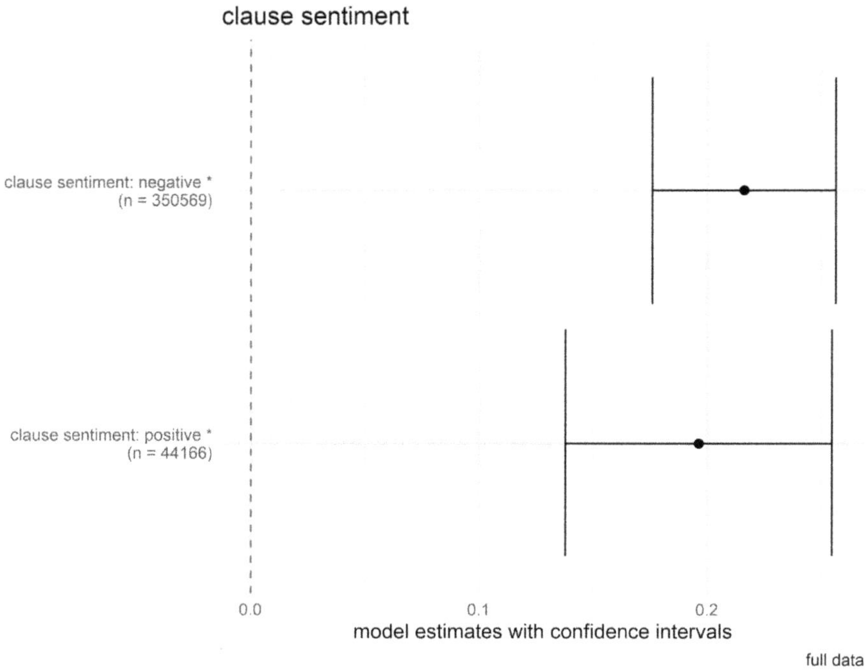

Figure 9 Predicted probability of GET-passives by clause sentiment (full data).

situation that not being realized can be seen as a source of relief from both the subject's and the writer's perspective. For more information on sentiment analysis and our way of conducting it, see Chapter 5.

Our models show clear results regarding sentiment. The slopes for participle sentiment do not reach significance in either model, not even as main effects. In contrast, clause sentiment was significant at $p < 0.025$ in the model on the full data (for negative sentiments: $\beta = 0.2162$, SE = 0.0205; for positive sentiments: $\beta = 0.1964$, SE = 0.0298), while the interactions with year were significant in the central model (for negative sentiments: $\beta = 0.0785$, SE = 0.0185; for positive sentiments: $\beta = -0.0757$, SE = 0.0272).

Figure 9 shows that the predicted probability of *get* in the full data. Positive values on the x-axis represent more *get*, while negative values represent more *be*. The probability of *get* is considerably higher for positive or negative clauses than for neutral ones, while no meaningful difference between predicted probabilities for the two non-neutral types can be observed. In other words, the GET-passive seems to favor non-neutral contexts. Regarding the diachronic development, Figure 10 shows the same division in the central data between neutral clauses with lower predicted probabilities for *get*, and positive and negative clauses

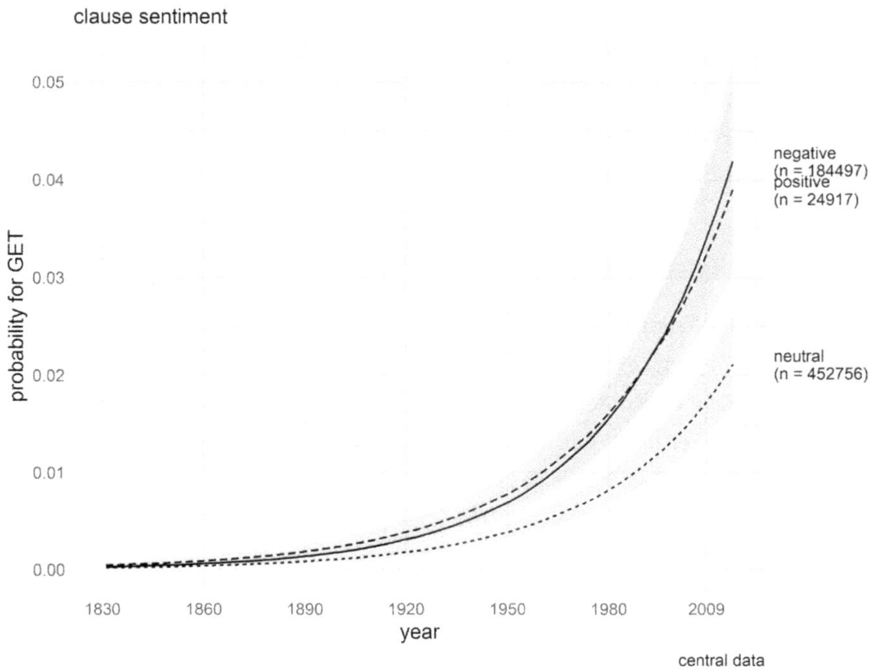

Figure 10 Predicted probability of GET-passives by year and clause sentiment (central data).

grouping together with much higher predicted probabilities for *get*. Additionally, the tendency for *get* in negative sentences has increased more steeply compared to the neutral ones. Here, the interaction between year and clause sentiment is only significant in the model fitted on the central data, hence why Figure 10 visualizes these predictions.

Adversativity is one of the most hotly debated aspects of the passive alternation. Its effect is cited in virtually all work on the GET-passive; however, it has rarely been addressed in empirically satisfactory terms. Where attempts at doing so have been made, they have typically been based on relatively small samples of impressionistically coded sentences and without a distinction between the sentiment from the perspective of the subject versus that of the speaker or writer. Our method is both able to upscale the analysis to achieve much more robust results and to add a differentiation between the subject's and the sentence producer's perspectives. While this may make a difference in some cases, we suppose that often, the two perspectives do not differ, and it is factors like considering more context and more types of sentence negation that make the clause-level sentiment analysis more reliable. With the results reported above, it becomes possible to further specify the claims about adversativity and non-neutrality made in the literature: it is non-neutral rather than strictly adverse contexts in which the GET-passive tends to be favored. For detecting non-neutrality, the whole clause context should be considered (refer to Chapter 5 for a discussion of this issue).

9.3.5 Verb Semantics

The inclusion of semantic clusters of main verbs in our models is motivated by the concept of "lexical grammar" proposed by Sinclair (2000) and applied to the GET-passive by Rühlemann (2007). The premise is that grammar and lexis are not separate entities, but they feed into each other (Rühlemann 2007: 112). This means that certain kinds of verbs might be more likely to occur in a certain grammatical construction, such as the GET-passive, while others may disprefer it. We explore this topic by including a distributional semantic clustering of verbs as a factor in our models. We have no specific hypotheses attached to semantic clusters; this part of the analysis is exploratory. The clustering method and the resulting clusters are described in Chapter 6. It is important to note that the semantic clustering is based on all verbs in the relevant corpora, while not all of them have made it to the models. As explained in Section 3.4, we have excluded from the analysis verbs of very low frequency, verbs that do not occur with both auxiliaries at least twenty times, as well as participles that categorically do not constitute passive sentences.

Ten clusters are identified in the full COHA model, of which nine survive to the central model. The predictions based on the two COHA models are visualized in Figures 11 and 12. Positive values on the x-axis, that is, toward the right, indicate a higher probability of *get*, while negative values, that is, toward the left side, signal a preference for *be*. The verb clusters are ordered so that groups with a higher probability of *get* appear above those with a lower probability. In this discussion, we will focus on the main effects in both models. Interaction with year is nonsignificant for all clusters, with the exception of the cluster HOUSEHOLD ACTIVITIES for the full dataset, where the model predicts a weaker association with *get* over time.

The largest cluster in terms of token frequency was selected as the baseline category on this basis. It is the cluster containing verbs of COMMUNICATION AND COGNITION, such as *asked*, *discovered*, *interrupted*, *told*, and *published*. In the full model, seven semantic clusters differ significantly from the baseline, while two clusters do not. One of these two clusters contains verbs of BODILY MOVEMENT

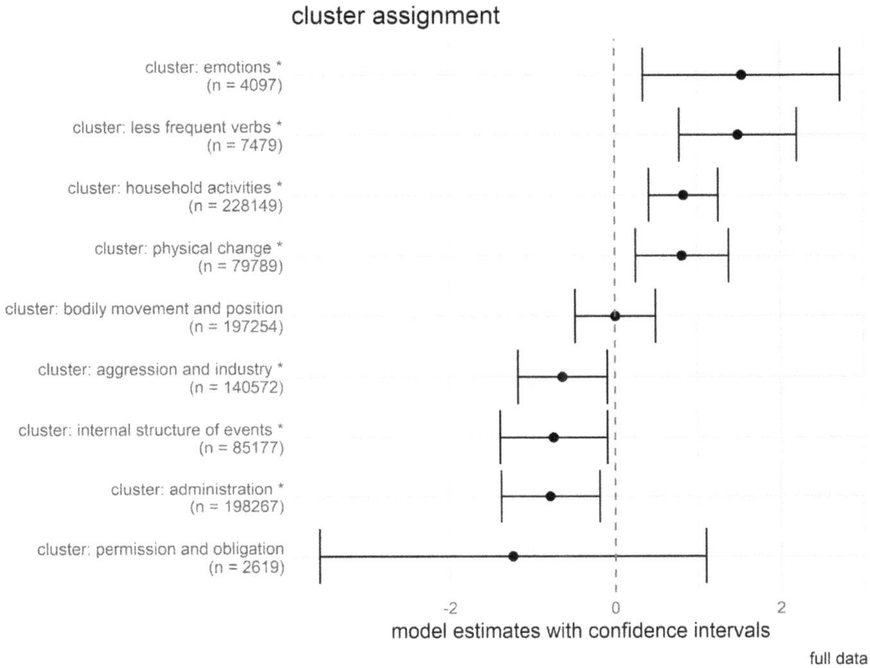

Figure 11 Predicted probability of GET-passives by verb cluster (full data).

AND POSITION, such as *moved*, *dropped*, *rolled*, *shoved*, and *knocked*. Of the verbs in the other nonsignificant cluster, titled PERMISSION AND OBLIGATION, only one made it to the final model: *planned*. This scarcity of data explains the wide confidence interval. A closer scrutiny reveals that instances of this verb following *get* cannot be considered passives, as illustrated in Example (119), and therefore, this cluster should be ignored altogether.

(119) I'm gonna have a heart attack from all the exciting activities we got planned for you this season! (COHA/2018/TV/movies)

In the full model, *get* is predicted most likely to occur with verbs from the categories EMOTIONS, LESS FREQUENT VERBS, HOUSEHOLD ACTIVITIES, and PHYSICAL CHANGE in that order, while *be* is predicted most likely to occur with the clusters ADMINISTRATION, INTERNAL STRUCTURE OF EVENTS, and AGGRESSION AND INDUSTRY in that order. The central model shows fewer statistically significant differences. LESS FREQUENT VERBS and HOUSEHOLD ACTIVITIES are still predicted to co-occur more with *get*, while INTERNAL STRUCTURE OF EVENTS is the only cluster predicted to particularly favor *be*. It should be noted that in the smaller and tidier central model, the cluster we label EMOTIONS

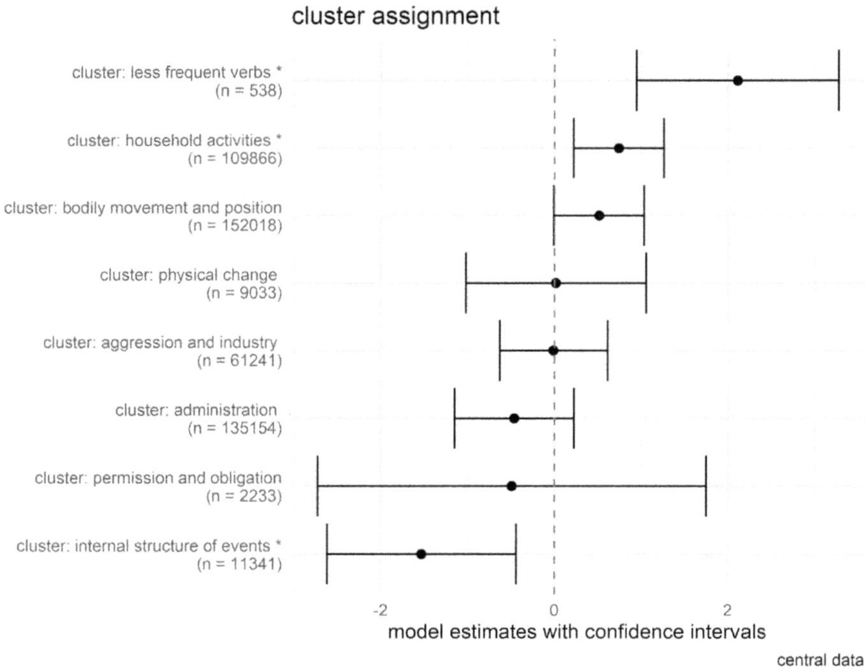

Figure 12 Predicted probability of GET-passives by verb cluster (central data).

in the full model disappears altogether. Remember that the central model is meant to exclude participles that do not constitute true passives, which is the case for many words of emotion. The centrality criteria, indeed, eliminate all the remaining participles in the EMOTIONS cluster (*flustered*, *distracted*, *offended*, *discouraged*). This cluster is missing from the central model, and it should not be discussed further in the context of the full model either, as in most contexts, these participles do not form passives.

We will now look more closely at the clusters that significantly favor *get*: LESS FREQUENT VERBS (both models), HOUSEHOLD ACTIVITIES (both models), and PHYSICAL CHANGE (only significant in the full model). The low-frequency cluster constitutes verbs like *sidetracked*, *noised*, *reelected*, *cheated*, and *educated*. We feel that the verbs in this group do not really share a semantic component and strongly suspect that they are placed in the same cluster primarily because of their quality of being less frequent. This assumption is supported by two facts. Firstly, the certainty of these verbs belonging together is much lower than overall: 0.74 for the top verbs in this cluster and 0.94 or higher for the top verbs in the other nine clusters. Secondly, the verbs in this cluster are indeed less frequent in COHA than verbs in other clusters, at least for the verbs considered in the model. The mean frequency is 575, while it is almost twice as high (1,024) for the second least frequent cluster. The label LESS FREQUENT VERBS seems justified. Unfortunately, the non-semantic basis of this cluster and the overall structure of the data make it likely that the association of this cluster with *get* is a statistical artifact. Because we only include verbs that occur with both auxiliaries, the prevalence of BE-passives in the dataset (forty-five BE-passives for each GET-passive in COHA) makes any infrequent verb that happens to occur with *get* at all seem like it relatively prefers *get*. Most infrequent verbs favoring *be* will not make it to the dataset at all, creating the effect that low-frequency verbs as a group prefer *get*. We tried to balance this out by excluding very low-frequency verbs: only items that occur at least forty times in total are considered in the COHA model. It seems that in this large dataset, the statistical association between low-frequency verbs and the GET-passive still comes up, and we want to be careful to assign any further significance to it.

The cluster HOUSEHOLD ACTIVITIES is a semantically more coherent cluster that significantly predicts the choice of passive auxiliary as a main effect in both models, showing a higher probability of *get*. In the full model, interaction with year is significant, as the link with *get* weakens over time. This is the cluster with the highest number of verb types after the cleanup. It contains participles such as *locked*, *wrapped*, *cleaned*, *washed*, and *packed*. We associate many of these physical and mundane activities with household chores and labeled this group HOUSEHOLD ACTIVITIES. However, if we take a look at instances of these verbs with the GET-passive, it is clear that actual contexts of usage may not be the household, even if this is a key feature in determining cluster membership; see example sentences (120)–(122).

(120) it started an investigation, and one of them got nailed. He was sent up for two years. (COHA/1965/fiction)

(121) Joey, I got roped into this cultural party thing this weekend. (COHA/1990/TV/movies)

(122) Then the bed linens get washed once a week. (COHA/1994/TV/movies)

Nailed is here essentially an informal synonym for *caught*, while *rope someone into something* is a metaphorical expression for "persuade." The household context does come up, as well, as in (122).

The cluster PHYSICAL CHANGE includes verbs such as *fixed*, *filled*, *heated*, *stirred*, and *buried*. This cluster shows a higher probability of *get* in the full model, but this effect disappears in the central model. We suppose that this is because the association with *get* is driven by participles that can appear as passives but, in fact, more often taken on adjectival or other nonpassive readings; see Examples (123)–(126), where the first sentence of each pair allows for a passive reading and the second implies an inchoative, nonpassive meaning.

(123) But if we want to know, say, how levels of ambition or insecurity get adjusted by early experience, we must first ask why natural selection made them adjustable. (COHA/1995/magazine)

(124) She said by the time she got adjusted to being 20 she was 30 (COHA/1971/fiction)

(125) If the fish is kept on ice until used, it will retain much of its freshness; let it once get heated and nothing will bring back the delicate flavor. (COHA/1880/nonfiction)

(126) "We've agreed not to let the debate get heated, though," says Barrie. (COHA/2006/magazine)

We will now briefly explore the remaining three clusters that significantly correlate with *be*: INTERNAL STRUCTURE OF EVENTS (both models), AGGRESSION AND INDUSTRY (only full model), and ADMINISTRATION (only full model). Some of the participles associated with INTERNAL STRUCTURE OF EVENTS include *delayed*, *finished*, *changed*, *saved*, and *transferred*. These are the only verbs significantly associated with *be* in the tidier central model. Example sentences are given in the following:

(127) This will be delayed for some few days, to give our friends in St. Augustine * time to get off. (COHA/1821/nonfiction)

(128) The grades of all the officers were changed, substituting those of the old monarchy. (COHA/1851/magazine)

In the full model, also AGGRESSION AND INDUSTRY and ADMINISTRATION are more associated with *be*. The name AGGRESSION AND INDUSTRY betrays that it is difficult or impossible to find a single semantic label that applies to most of the verbs in this group. We have, on the one hand, verbs of industrial processes such as *sold*, *started*, *stopped*, and *hired*, and on the other hand, verbs of aggression and violence, such as *wounded*, *slaughtered*, *beaten*, and *killed*. Based on the adversativity hypothesis, we could have expected these verbs to prefer *get*, but as part of this larger cluster, they do the opposite. Remember that examining sentiment at the participle level in COHA showed no association between negative verbs and the GET-passive (Section 9.3.4).

The cluster ADMINISTRATION contains verbs such as *delivered*, *introduced*, *signed*, *adopted*, and *drafted*. Such verbs connected to more technical and formal contexts seem to prefer *be* as the passive auxiliary; see Examples (129) and (130).

(129) A crowd of bills were introduced this morning. (COHA/1878/newspaper)

(130) The more formal procedure is being adopted to combat bureaucratic tendencies that had manifested themselves. (COHA/1938/nonfiction)

However, the predicted association of these clusters, AGGRESSION AND INDUSTRY and ADMINISTRATION, with the BE-passive disappears in the tidier central model, so too much weight should not be put on it.

Overall, these findings provide at most moderate support to the idea that some lexical groups may be associated with syntactic structures. Disregarding the single-verb, low-frequency, and emotion groups, there is one cluster associated with each auxiliary in the central model, and two and three clusters associated with *get* and *be* in the full model, respectively. The verbs showing a higher probability of *get* tend to be concrete, physical activities, while verbs from contexts such as industry and administration and verbs of more abstract change of state display a higher predicted preference for *be*.

9.3.6 Morpho-syntax

We include in our models also a number of morpho-syntactic factors to observe whether the GET-passive occurs in equally varied grammatical contexts as the BE-passive, including different levels of structural complexity. Diachronically, we want to investigate the degree to which the GET-passive has neutralized and grammaticalized over the years.

9.3.6.1 Negation

The first syntactic feature to observe is the polarity of the clause: whether the verb phrase is negated or not. In the full model (Figure 13), the interaction between year and polarity is significant, in that we see relatively more *get* in negated sentences over time. However, the confidence intervals are fairly large and overlapping, and in the tidier central model, polarity is not significant at all. Therefore, it does not make sense to posit this syntactic constraint as meaningful in conditioning the passive alternation. Thus, our diachronic study corroborates

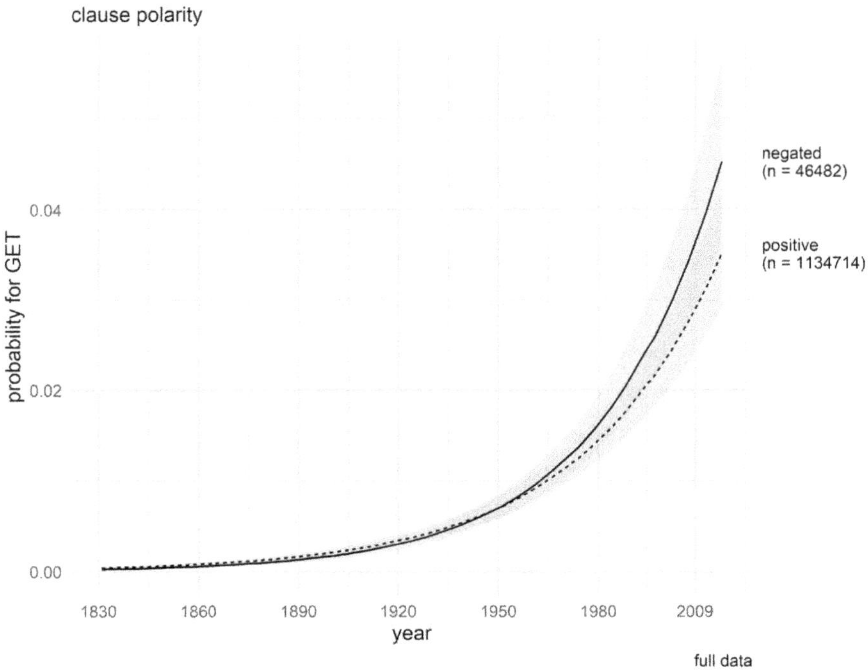

Figure 13 Predicted probability of GET-passives by year and clause polarity (full data).

Fehringer's (2022: 16) findings that negation does not significantly correlate with *be* versus *get* in a larger set of data.

9.3.6.2 Tense, Aspect, and Modality

In contrast to polarity, the effect of tense, aspect, and modality (TAM) on the alternation is more consequential. As can be seen in Figure 14, the division of variation is roughly three-way: *to*-infinitives and *-ing*-forms comparatively favor *get*, the simple present (together with the present perfect and past progressive) is in the middle in line with the general, TAM-independent predictions, and forms of past reference (both preterite and two out of three perfect forms) significantly disfavor *get*. All levels of the variable enter into significant interactions with year, apart from the past progressive in both models, modal + perfect in the full model, and modal + infinitive in the central model. Over time, we see some tendencies strengthening, like infinitives' and gerunds' stronger tolerance for *get* and the past perfect's dislike for it, but in all other cases, we see the predictions curving closer to each other over time and TAM rather somewhat losing in power in conditioning the passive alternation.

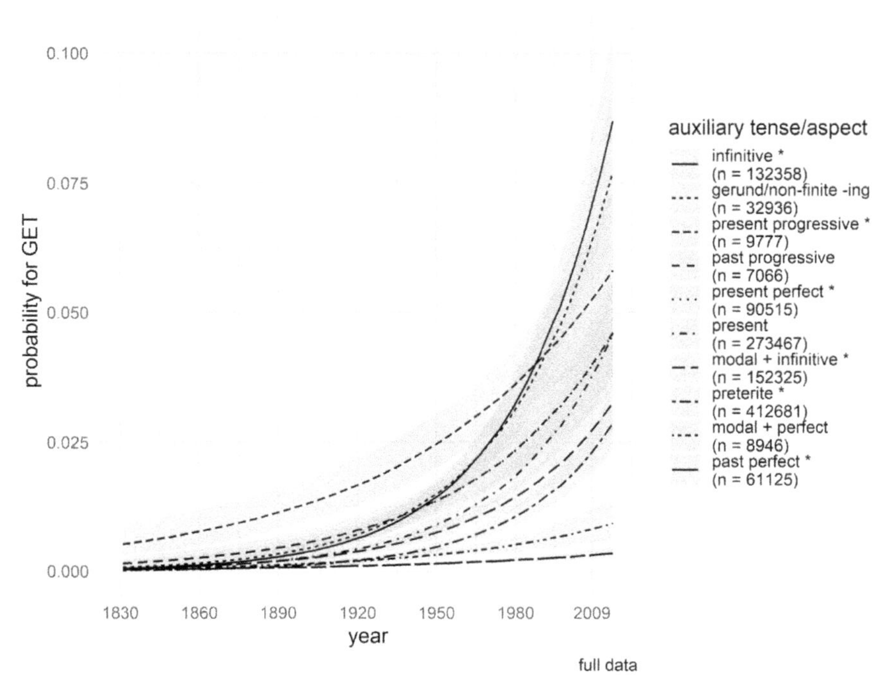

Figure 14 Predicted probability of GET-passives by year and tense and aspect (full data).

Our findings corroborate some previous claims about the GET-passive but shed new, critical light on others. One noteworthy development is that of the present progressive, which was long the most favorable context for *get*, but in the newer data, the use of *get* as passive auxiliary in this construction has not increased along the same lines. The overall success of *get* in this construction may be explained by the fact that using *get* with the present progressive avoids the clumsy double-*be* needed in the progressive BE-passive (cf. Smith & Rayson 2007: 132). This awkwardness—*horror aequi* (Rohdenburg 2003)—is most acute in combinations of modals and the progressive (resulting in "be being"; Quirk et al. 1985: 166), but this form could not be included because there are not enough instances to support a model of this complexity. Examples of the present progressive with the two auxiliaries are provided in (131) and (132).

(131) Patrol found the body of a dead woman in Washington Park. We're getting called in. (COHA/2017/TV/movies)

(132) I'm not a reactionary puppet of the imperialist state, or whatever else men in my position are being called these days. (COHA//fiction)

The weakening of this relative preference for *get* may then mean that language users are getting used to the combination of two forms of *be*. Indeed, Smith and Rayson (2007: 136) show that the present progressive BE-passive grew in frequency in twentieth-century BrE, during a time that otherwise saw a drop in the BE-passive (Schwarz 2017: 314).

Our model based on COHA agrees with previous studies that the perfect and the GET-passive rarely co-occur (Schwarz 2017: 317; Fehringer 2022: 11). The type of verb phrase most averse to taking *get* as an auxiliary is the past perfect passive, exemplified in (133). In this case, the complexity of the inflected form *gotten* might act as a deterring factor.

(133) It had been over six months since he'd left the Great Plains and nearly a year since his wife <u>had gotten bitten</u> by a squirrel with rabies and died. (COHA/1995/fiction)

Regarding TAM, our findings differ starkly from Fehringer's (2022) mixed-effects study on the conditioning of the passive alternation. Fehringer's (2022) study suffers from her smaller dataset forcing her to group multiple TAM forms together and only focus on the very broad lines. Progressive passives are not considered separately as their number is "very small" (Fehringer 2022: 11), and multiple forms are lumped together under the title "other," including combinations with modals, past perfect, modal + perfect, and infinitives (Fehringer 2022: 15). Fehringer (2022: 16–17) finds present and past forms to relatively favor *get*, while "other" forms disfavor it. In our study, almost all past forms disfavor *get*, while the probability of *get* in an infinitival construction increases dramatically over the years and ends up being the highest of all in the model for the newest COHA data. Example (134) shows a sentence with this pattern.

(134) We gotta get them married before their kid is old enough <u>to get drafted</u>. (COHA/1973/TV/movies)

We believe that our larger dataset and finer categorization provide for more reliable findings than earlier studies and allow for a nuanced picture to emerge. We do perceive a broad converging tendency, where over time, the significance of TAM in conditioning the passive alternation is decreasing, and different forms perform more similarly than before. Nonetheless, there are a couple of exceptions: the *to*-infinitive and other nonfinite verb phrases emerge as contexts preferring *get* and the past perfect as strongly dispreferring it. Explanations for these patterns might be sought in stylistic preferences rather than syntactic constraints, including language users' potential bias for the forms *getting V-ed* over *being V-ed* and *been V-ed* over *gotten V-ed*.

9.3.6.3 Subject Person

Regarding the subject person variable, both models show significant main effects but no significant interaction with year. Both models predict the same tendencies: While first- and second-person subjects are associated with higher log-odds for GET- over BE-passives, third-person subjects lean more toward *be* (both in comparison with the "other" category, which comprises instances where a subject could not be identified or categorized and in relation to first- and second-person pronouns). The predictions for the full model are visualized in Figure 15; positive values on the x-axis indicate a higher likelihood for *get*, while negative values indicate a higher likelihood for *be*. This finding replicates the results by Toyota (2008: 162–3) on subject person in passive sentences, who also found *get* to group with first- and second-person subjects.

We suggest that the relatively clear distinction between first- and second-person pronouns, on the one hand, and third-person pronouns, on the other,

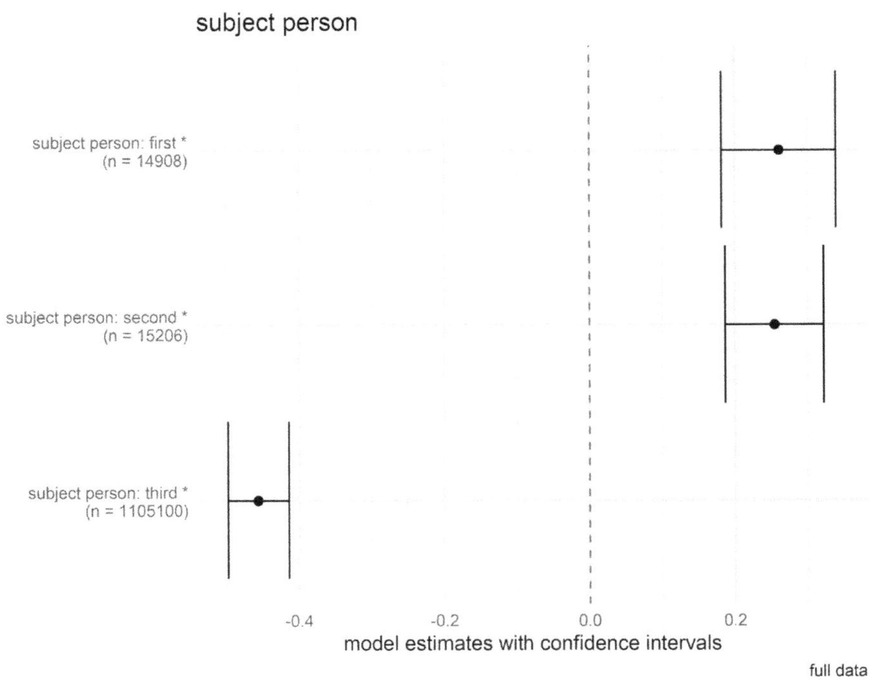

Figure 15 Model estimates for GET-passives by tense and aspect (full data).

can perhaps be read as a register effect. Both first- and second-person pronouns are indicators of involved, conceptually oral discourse (Koch & Oesterreicher 1985), patterning along with features such as contractions, indefinite pronouns, and amplifiers (Biber 1988; Bohmann 2019). As such, they typically occur most frequently in spontaneous conversations where interlocutors are directly involved in interpersonal discussions. By contrast, third-person pronouns are associated with narrative and reporting registers (Biber 1988; Bohmann 2019), where there is a clearer distance between the situation of speech production and the situation being discussed. In sum, the results for subject person may indicate that the GET-passive is favored in involved, interpersonal contexts.

9.3.6.4 Adverb

The presence of an intervening adverb in between the auxiliary and the main verb (see Example (135)) is considered in our models as a further feature of sentence complexity. Furthermore, some previous literature (Carter & McCarthy 1999: 53; Xiao, McEnery, & Qian 2006: 116) posits that the GET-passive does not allow for adverbial modification. Carter and McCarthy (1999: 53) argue that "adverbial focus on the verb might serve to defocus the subject/patient," which they treat as incompatible with the downgrading of the agent and highlighting of the patient they assume to be the distinctive feature of the GET-passive. Xiao, McEnery, and Qian (2006: 116) follow this line of argumentation and corroborate it with empirical evidence.

(135) From letters received we learn that this is being seriously considered by at least two promoters. (COHA/1927/magazine)

The effect of intervening adverbs emerges as significant in its interaction with year in both models (full model: β = -0.1563, SE = 0.0208; central model: β = -0.2271, SE = 0.0713). As Figure 16 shows, the development of this constraint over time is particularly noteworthy. While the absence of an intervening adverb is the context with a higher probability of *get* throughout, this tendency strengthens markedly with the general rise of the GET-passive. This observation runs somewhat counter to the general tendency for innovations to lose constraints as they spread (Labov 1994, 2007; Croft 2000; Bybee 2010). A qualitative look at the data, with a search for the pattern *get* + adverb + past participle in COHA mostly yields instances where the participle should be interpreted as an adjective and not a passive verb. It seems that the GET-passive very rarely appears with an intervening adverb.

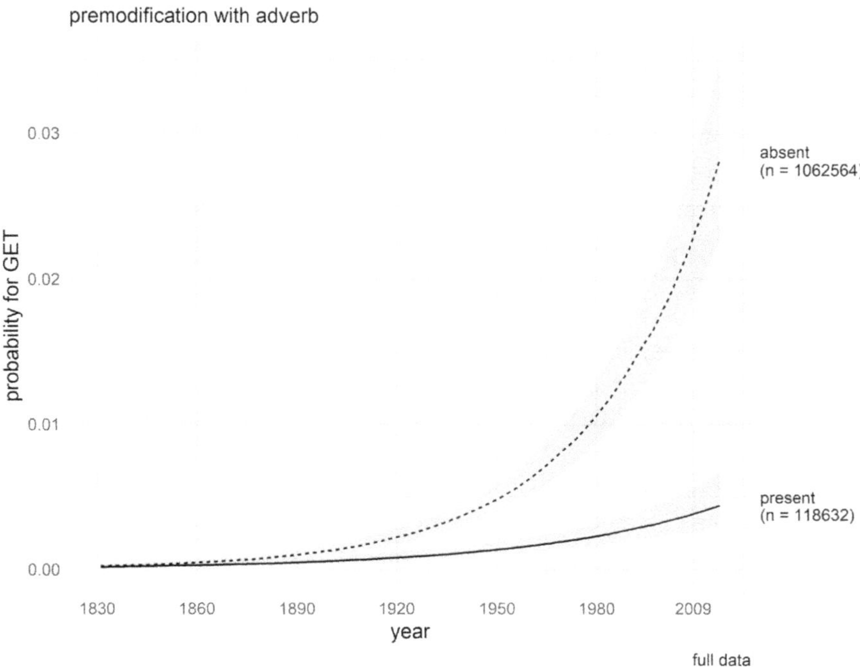

Figure 16 Predicted probability of GET-passives by year and premodification with an adverb (full data).

9.3.6.5 Non-Finite Complement Phrases with To

As a final morpho-syntactic feature, we also tested whether nonfinite complement phrases with *to* play a significant role in predicting the choice of *be* versus *get*. Xiao, McEnery, and Qian (2006: 112) suggest that only BE-passives can take such nonfinite complements. Participles that do not select infinitival constructions, such as *to paint*, but occur with such, are likely adjectival. If, however, the verb selects an infinitival complement and occurs with such, it may be verbal (Richard Zimmermann pc May 2020). This is illustrated in the following examples, where (136) depicts the variant in a rather adjectival sense, which is arguably restricted to *be* only, and (137) displays a rather verbal sense that is variable with *get*.

(136) He was dressed in grotesque tights, his face was painted to look like a funny, wizened little old man, and he wore blue silk shoes which a costumer on the Bowery had assured him were once worn by Fanny Davenport in Gismonda. (COHA/1909/magazine)

(137) Boy, you're getting paid to think, not get calluses on your ass. (COHA/1973/TV/movies)

Interestingly, COHA also presents a case of variation in a context that has been previously described as being restricted to *be* only. The verb *to kill* does not select an infinitival complement and yet occurs with *get* in a nonfinite complement, as illustrated in Example (138). This construction is, however, highly infrequent and occurs only once in COHA (with the search string "GET killed to VERB" in the web-based search interface). Its *be*-counterpart, as in Example (139), is more common, yielding thirty-nine hits in COHA (with the search string "BE killed to VERB").

(138) I won't get killed to make you a record. (COHA/1948/TV/movies)

(139) They had died of, or were killed to prevent the spread of, a sort of swine fever. (COHA/1957/fiction)

In each model, only the main effect significantly correlates with the choice of *be* versus *get*, predicting a decreased probability of *get* in these contexts, aligning with previous assumptions that the GET-passive does not easily allow for *to*-infinitival clauses (β = -0.2492, SE = 0.0438 for the central and β = -0.195, SE = 0.0272).

9.3.7 Persistence

As explained in Section 8.1.1, we check whether the presence of *get* as an auxiliary in the preceding sentence results in a higher predicted probability of *get* in the current sentence. This is the case in both models, with the interaction with year also significant at $p < 0.025$. As Figure 17 shows, the predicted probability of *get* is always higher when the previous auxiliary used in the text was also *get*. Less immediately perceptible is the fact that, over time, the influence of the preceding auxiliary weakens, as indicated by the negative sign of the coefficient for the interaction term in both the full (β = -0.1394, SE = 0.0185) and the central model (β = -0.1296, SE = 0.0253).

The general finding that realization of the preceding passive with *get* in the same text significantly increases the likelihood of the following token also being realized as *get* confirms the notion that "language users are creatures of habit whose behavior can be characterized as inertial" (Szmrecsanyi 2006: 1). This phenomenon, referred to as "persistence" by Szmrecsanyi (2006), is widely attested under the label of priming in the cognitive linguistic literature (Levelt & Kelter 1982; Bock 1986; Bock & Loebell 1990; Branigan, Pickering, & Cleland 2000; Tamminga 2016; Clark 2018). The present findings add to the growing body of research documenting priming effects in naturalistic production

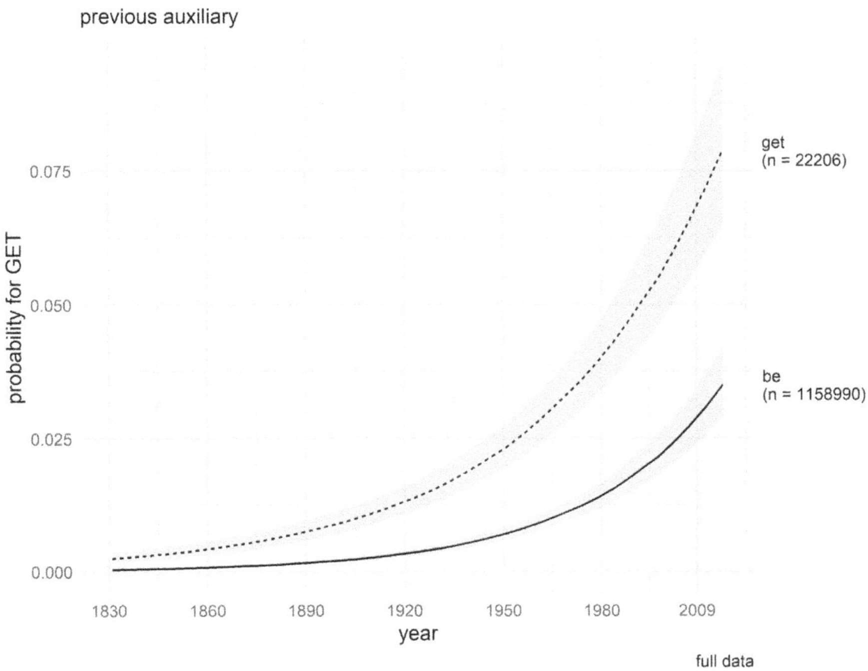

Figure 17 Predicted probability of GET-passives by year and previous auxiliary (full data).

(Sankoff & Laberge 1978; Poplack 1980; Gries 2005), including studies of the English passive (Weiner & Labov 1983; Estival 1985).

What is interesting from a diachronic perspective is the relative weakening of the priming effect over time. We interpret this not as a tendency specific to the GET-passive but rather as indicative of a potential interaction between a variant's overall frequency and its susceptibility to priming. A reduction of priming effects as a function of increased frequency has been demonstrated at the lexical level by Ostergaard (1998) and La Heij et al. (1999). Wei et al. (2016: 1) further claim that "structural priming in comprehension is modulated by the baseline frequency of alternative structures, with the less frequent structure being more subject to structural priming effects." Our result here appears to corroborate this tendency from the perspective of production as well: as the GET-passive becomes more frequent over time, its susceptibility to priming weakens.

9.3.8 Probability of Central Passives

Finally, we aim to establish the influence of the centrality of a passive on the choice of auxiliary. This predictor was only included in the model on the full

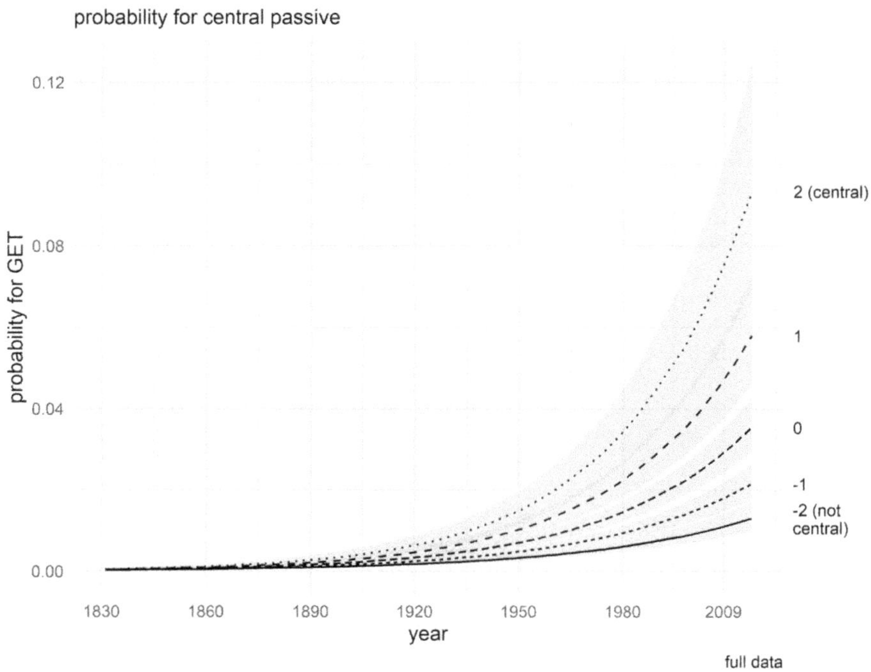

Figure 18 Predicted probability of GET-passives by year and probability of central passive (full data).

data, and both the main effect and the interaction with year were significant at $p < 0.025$ ($\beta = 0.1028$, SE = 0.0314). While the predicted probability of *get* for peripheral items has barely increased over time (Figure 18), it has steeply increased for the most central passives. In other words, *get* is predicted to occur more likely with passives that are classified as more central, that is, less adjectival.

This finding shows that, while many constructions involving *get* are on the rise in the time span covered in the corpus, the most productive environment for the change we are interested in is clearly true passives, that is, clauses involving a verb that can be read as dynamic and for which an active-voice counterpart could be found. Many less central *get* or *be* + past participle constructions still allow for both auxiliaries to be present, but not within a strictly defined variable context, that is, under conditions of referential equivalence. Examples (140) and (141) show a pair of sentences with a contrast between *be* and *get*, but neither of them contains a passive construction. These are not the grammatical contexts where rise of the GET-passive is most pronounced. This effect gives further support to the notion that we are looking at a true linguistic variable and that it is worthwhile to carefully circumscribe the variable context.

(140) The only way to insure peace is to be prepared for war. (COHA/1970/news)

(141) This is zombie shit going down, and we got to get prepared. (COHA/2019/TV/movies)

This finding provides both post hoc justification for the efforts we took to approach the issue of passive centrality in an automated approach as well as some perspective on the model output regarding the other predictors discussed earlier. While the model on the full and the central data are largely in agreement, it is the central model's findings that should be accorded more weight. Finally, there is a pointer here for future research into the passive alternation: it is important to dedicate some time and thought to deciding which observations to include in the analysis and which to treat as "don't count" cases (Blake 1997).

10

Regional Variation in the English Passive Alternation

In this chapter, we will complement the diachronic analysis put forward in Chapter 9 with a synchronic view of variation in the passive, adding the dimension of regional variation in a second pair of multivariate models. This analysis is based on another large corpus, introduced in Section 10.1. Before discussing the findings of the regression analyses in Section 10.4, we will observe the distribution of the two passive constructions across the corpus components in Section 10.2 and evaluate the fit of the models in Section 10.3.

10.1 The Corpus of Global Web-Based English

We chose the Corpus of Global Web-based English (GloWbE, Davies 2013; Davies & Fuchs 2015) for exploring regional variation in the passive because it is one of the largest datasets representing a high number of English-speaking countries. As with COHA, we are using the downloaded raw data and our own extraction script instead of the web search interface. The corpus amounts to 1.9 billion words in total, stemming from 1.8 million web pages from 340,000 websites. Each of the twenty country components contains between 35 and 387 million words (see Table 13) for a distribution of the data over the twenty countries). Similar to other corpora from the English-corpora.org website, 2.5 percent of data are lost in the offline version for copyright reasons, so we have 1.84 billion words at our disposal for this analysis. A text in this corpus—a relevant unit in our analysis of register—corresponds to a single web page. The mean length of a text in GloWbE is 1,035 words (median: 580). While this estimate comes with a large standard deviation (2,428), only about 1 percent of texts in GloWbE are shorter than fifty words.

Table 13 The Composition of the GloWbE Corpus

Country	Abbreviation	Number of words
United States	AmE	386,809,355
Canada	CanE	134,765,381
Great Britain	BrE	387,615,074
Ireland	IrE	101,029,231
Australia	AusE	148,208,169
New Zealand	NZE	81,390,476
India	IndE	96,430,888
Sri Lanka	SLE	46,583,115
Pakistan	PakE	51,367,152
Bangladesh	BanglE	39,658,255
Singapore	SingE	42,974,705
Malaysia	MalE	42,420,168
Philippines	PhE	43,250,093
Hong Kong	HKE	40,450,291
South Africa	SAE	45,364,498
Nigeria	NigE	42,646,098
Ghana	GhanE	38,768,231
Kenya	KenE	41,069,085
Tanzania	TanzE	35,169,042
Jamaica	JamE	39,663,666
Total		1,885,632,973

Source: Davies and Fuchs (2015: 6)

The data stem from blogs and other websites such as online newspapers. Blogs were targeted in order to collect "fairly informal" web language (Davies & Fuchs 2015: 26). In introducing the corpus, Davies and Fuchs talk about a 60:40 split between blogs and other websites, but in terms of word counts, the share of blogs is actually between 36 and 48 percent depending on the subcorpus (Loureiro-Porto 2017: 455–6), and these two parts of the corpus may not differ greatly when it comes to actual linguistic features (Bohmann 2024: 176). Loureiro-Porto (2017: 255) calls blogs a "speech-like" text type; however, we see even among web-based genres other texts that are more interactive and spontaneous. Admittedly, these tend to be nonpublic data, which are very difficult to collect and use from a practical and ethical point of view. Using written data only may lead to underestimating the use of the GET-passive, as this has been shown to be an informal variant more common in speech (see Section 2.6).

Davies and Fuchs (2015) demonstrate how GloWbE can be used for examining lexical, morphological, and syntactic variation, variation in meaning, and features of discourse and culture between English-speaking countries. Released in 2013, the dataset has been utilized in some but not many studies, and much of its potential is still untapped. Studies have focused on lexical features, but some do consider morpho-syntax as well. To give some examples, Anesa (2019) uses GloWbE in tandem with the International Corpus of English (ICE) to examine lexical "cross-contamination" between different World Englishes, that is, the spread of lexemes that originate in a specific variety to other English-speaking societies. The feature frequencies are invariably low, and the spread seems macro-regional rather than global (Anesa 2019). Wagner (2017) examines lexical collocations, specifically combinations of intensifiers and adjectives (e.g., *totally new*), grouping varieties into six regional clusters. Collins (2021: 300) takes interest in hypercorrection and examines five morpho-syntactic features, pointing out that sources like GloWbE are indispensable in investigating phenomena such as hypercorrection, which are, by definition, infrequent. Some studies employ only some GloWbE components (e.g., Terassa 2017 considers morphological simplification in three Asian Englishes), use GloWbE to support findings from other sources (e.g., from ICE in Terassa 2017; Anesa 2019; from ICE, COCA, and experimental data in Horch 2016 on conversion), or take a very narrow focus, for example, on a single lexical item.

Among the few syntactic studies conducted on GloWbE data, Heller and Röthlisberger (2015) constitute an encouraging example. As part of a larger research project into "probabilistic grammar(s) in varieties of English around the world" (Szmrecsanyi et al. 2016), Heller and Röthlisberger (2015) examine syntactic patterns in GloWbE in comparison with the ICE corpus, which has been the most frequently used dataset in corpus-linguistic studies on World Englishes. They investigate two classic grammatical alternation patterns, the dative and the genitive alternation. Using mixed-effects logistic regression and samples from nine varieties of English, Heller and Röthlisberger (2015) observe the influence of various predictors on the choice of construction and compare these across the two corpora. They find "an amazing similarity between ICE and GloWbE in the patterning of the alternations: [the predictor] Corpus does not really matter" (Heller & Röthlisberger 2015: 41). Loureiro-Porto's (2017) findings, however, stand in contrast with this assessment. In a comparison of modal verbs in BrE in GloWbE with the three traditionally sampled corpora ICE, BNC, and F-LOB, Loureiro-Porto (2017: 454) finds the latter three to be much more similar to one another than to GloWbE. She proceeds to conclude that GloWbE "cannot be taken to represent British English as a whole, but only British English as used on the net" (Loureiro-Porto 2017: 455). It must certainly be kept in mind that GloWbE represents a narrow selection of web-based genres, and the use of the passive is sensitive to stylistic factors.

Overall, the non-supervised sampling process of the corpus can be mentioned as a shortcoming. GloWbE was collected with the help of Google "Advanced Search" queries targeting frequent English-language combinations of grammatical words to extract random URLs of blogs and other websites based in different countries (Davies & Fuchs 2015: 4). We lack information about the constitution of the subcorpora, beyond the split between blogs and other websites (that also contain some blogs), and about sociodemographic factors. We do not know how well the data represent the respective populations, for example, whether the South African data proportionally represent both the white minority and the majority that is Black and of color. These questions may have a significant impact on the passive alternation, as for instance in the United States, the use of the GET-passive has been shown to correlate with ethnicity (see Section 2.3). We hope that the large size of the dataset mediates the problems so that the data can be considered representative of the English-speaking internet-using population from each country.

Working on web-based big data brings certain challenges. The texts originate in a variety of partly unedited sources and feature a range of intentional and unintentional non-standardized orthography, lexicon, and grammar. While human coders may be able to correctly decipher these, automatic annotation tools are not in the best position to do so (Eisenstein 2013). This messiness is a feature of web-based text that will influence a part of the data but will still leave most of it untouched and usable for analysis. Overall, in striking a balance between size and tidiness (Hansen 2018: chapter 11; Bohmann 2024), we are prioritizing the former in the present case studies. This is necessary in order to have enough observations to carry out multivariate analysis despite the relative infrequency of the GET-passive in comparison to the BE-passive.

After introducing the data, we are now ready to examine our second pair of regression models, focusing on synchronic regional variation in the English passive alternation.

10.2 The Passive Construction in GloWbE: A Descriptive View

The first two graphs (Figures 19 and 20) offer us a valuable overview of the structure of the GloWbE corpus as well as the first descriptive findings concerning

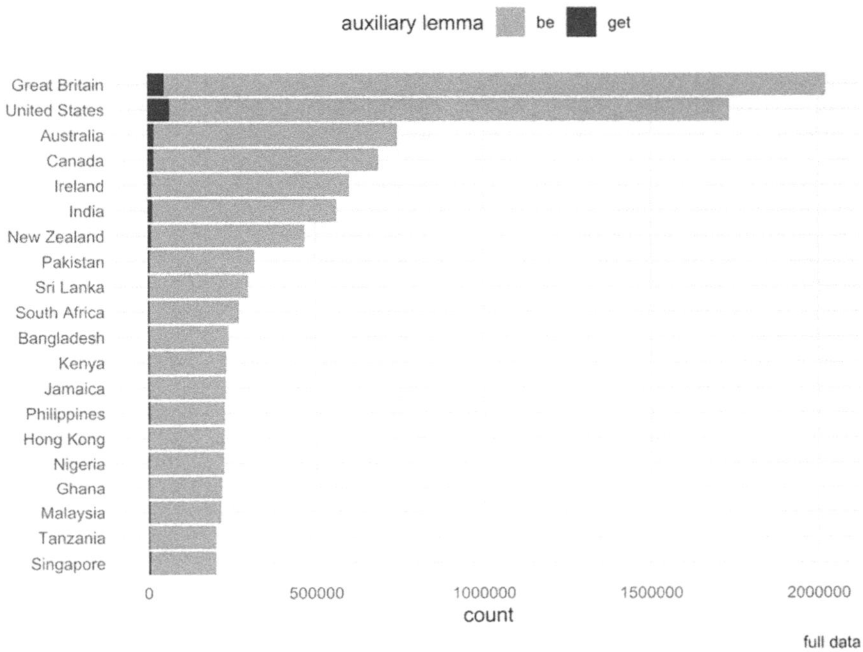

Figure 19 The raw frequency of BE- and GET-passives in different GloWbE countries (full data).

the passive alternation therein. These bar charts show the raw frequencies of the *be* versus *get* + past participle construction in the different country components of the corpus. They make it obvious that GloWbE contains much more data from the six "Inner Circle" L1 varieties of English, especially AmE and BrE, than from the fourteen "Outer Circle" L2 varieties. They also highlight the imbalance between *be* and *get* and the fact that despite its diachronic decline, the BE-passive remains much more frequent than the newer variant with *get*. In some varieties, the proportion of the GET-passive looks quite negligible in these graphs. In the full GloWbE dataset, passive constructions display forty times more *be* than *get*, and in the (more restricted) central passive GloWbE dataset, passive constructions occur more than forty-five times more often with *be* than with *get*.

More illuminating than simply observing the raw numbers is to turn our attention to normalized frequencies that take into consideration the gross differences in size between the GloWbE components. The proportional division into passive constructions involving *be* versus *get* is illustrated in Figures 21 and 22, representing the full and central datasets, respectively. The countries are ordered so that those with the most GET-passive appear on top. The ordering is

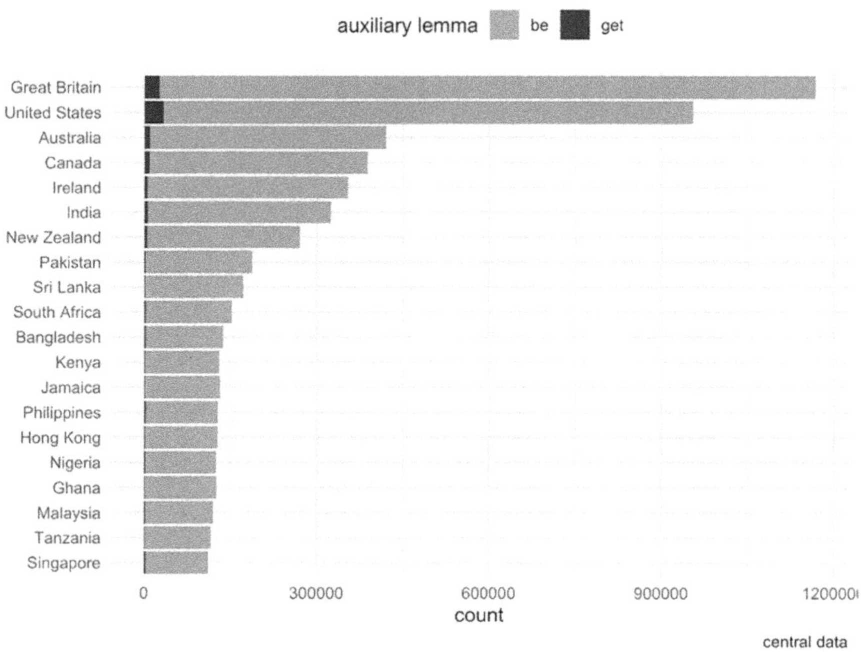

Figure 20 The raw frequency of BE- and GET-passives in different GloWbE countries (central data).

similar but not identical; the top five countries in both datasets are the United States, Singapore, Canada, Australia, and Great Britain. The position of India shows a discrepancy between the two figures. Based on the full data, it represents one of the countries with the most *get*, but in the central data, it falls to the middle of the ranking. Other mid-ranking countries in both datasets, with only minor differences in ordering, are the Philippines, Malaysia, New Zealand, Bangladesh, Nigeria, South Africa, and Ireland. Countries with the least relative use of *get* as a passive auxiliary in GloWbE are Kenya, Pakistan, Jamaica, Hong Kong, Sri Lanka, Tanzania, and Ghana (similarly with slight differences in order between the full and central datasets). The percentage of GET-passives among all passives in the central data ranges from 1.04 percent in the Ghanaian data to 3.48 percent in the US-American data. At the face of it, it initially seems that the L1 varieties are more favorable to the innovative GET-passive than L2 varieties, and Asian varieties are more favorable to it than African varieties of English. In order to make more reliable statements about differences between countries (aside from descriptive statistics), also considering other factors that influence the choice of the passive auxiliary, we will examine our two mixed-effects regression models fitted on the GloWbE data.

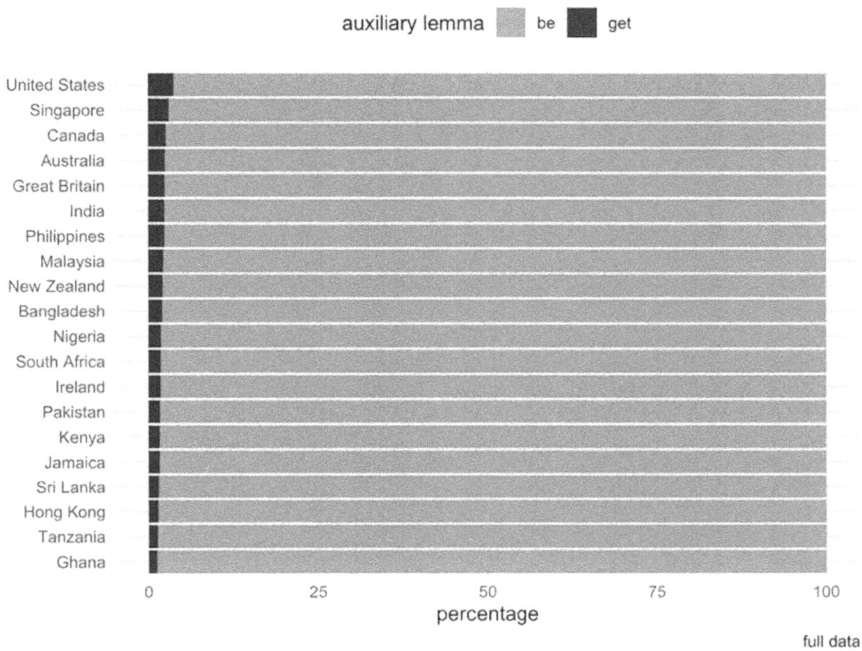

Figure 21 The proportion of BE- and GET-passives in different GloWbE countries (full data).

10.3 Model Fit and Output

We calculate the measures of model fit for the two GloWbE models analogously to the procedure described earlier in Section 9.2 for the two COHA models. The adjusted McFadden pseudo-R^2 for the central model is 0.1686 for the fixed effects only and 0.3382 for fixed and random effects together, while the corresponding measures for the model on the complete data are 0.1296 and 0.2877. Considerable differences between these measures imply that a great amount of variation between *be* and *get* is located in the individual verb participles and their preferences. Both pseudo-R^2 measures are slightly higher for the central than for the full model, which may be due to the tidier nature of the former. Overall, the adjusted McFadden pseudo-R^2 is slightly lower for the GloWbE models than it is for the COHA models when fixed and random effects are considered; the pseudo-R^2 in both GloWbE and COHA is similar when only fixed effects are considered. We attribute this to the complex random effects structure in those models and would additionally like to point out the inherently messy nature of large corpora generally and large collections of online data specifically, which certainly is

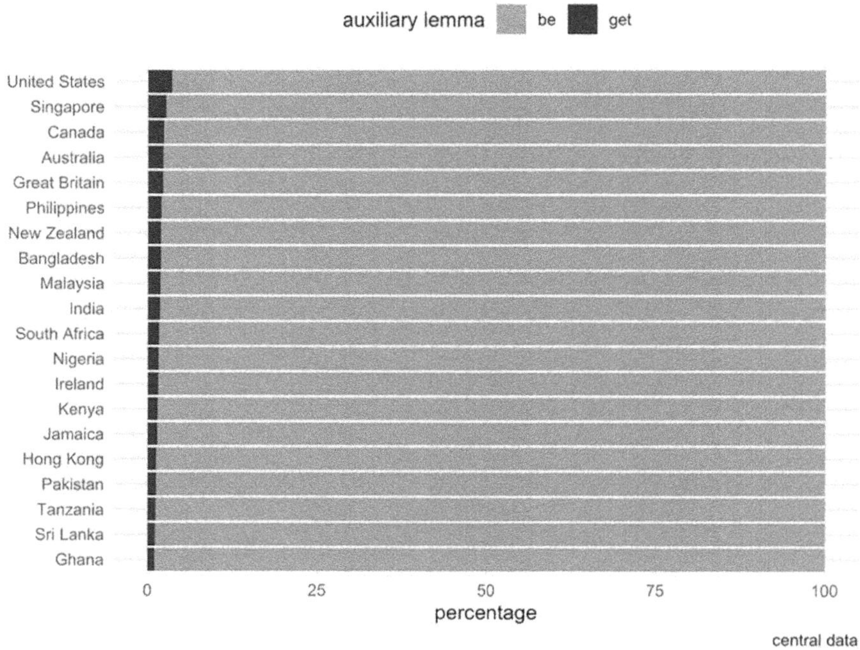

Figure 22 The proportion of BE- and GET-passives in different GloWbE countries (central data).

relevant to these results. As described in Section 9.2, a random intercept for each corpus text or, better yet, for each writer would be desirable to account for individual variation on the speaker level, but this procedure is currently too computationally expensive.

In Table 14, we can observe the entire model summary for the model fitted on the full GloWbE dataset. Table 15 shows the same information for the model based on the central data.

10.4 Model Predictions

Now, we will proceed to discuss the predictions of our model variable by variable. We will start with the general differences between countries and then move through formality, different semantic variables, morpho-syntactic variables, persistence, and centrality, in this order. For those variables that most immediately operationalize constraints on the passive alternation proposed in the literature, we will consider the interaction of the variable with the variable country, while with other factors, an interaction could not be included in the

Table 14 Output of Mixed-Effects Logistic Regression Model Predicting *Get* (vs. *Be*) based on the Independent Variables Described in Chapter 8, *N* = 9932636, GloWbE, Full Data

Term	Estimate	Std. error	*z*-Value	*p*-Value	Sig.
Intercept	−3.1882	0.0288	−110.8207	<0.0001	sig.
country: Tanzania	−0.0810	0.0493	−1.6439	0.100199	n.s.
country: Kenya	−0.1377	0.0467	−2.9495	0.003183	sig.
country: Hong Kong	−0.0350	0.0443	−0.7896	0.429756	n.s.
country: Bangladesh	0.2473	0.0419	5.9084	<0.0001	sig.
country: Ireland	−0.2094	0.0304	−6.8943	<0.0001	sig.
country: India	0.4291	0.0229	18.7629	<0.0001	sig.
country: Sri Lanka	0.0270	0.0358	0.7532	0.451349	n.s.
country: Ghana	−0.2155	0.0498	−4.3230	<0.0001	sig.
country: Malaysia	−0.0457	0.0386	−1.1840	0.236417	n.s.
country: Singapore	0.1680	0.0376	4.4645	<0.0001	sig.
country: Australia	−0.1421	0.0250	−5.6826	<0.0001	sig.
country: Jamaica	−0.1816	0.0489	−3.7121	0.000206	sig.
country: Nigeria	−0.0749	0.0422	−1.7770	0.075573	n.s.
country: Canada	0.1449	0.0243	5.9510	<0.0001	sig.
country: Philippines	0.1373	0.0373	3.6832	0.00023	sig.
country: New Zealand	−0.0745	0.0308	−2.4181	0.0156	sig.
country: South Africa	−0.0997	0.0423	−2.3572	0.018413	sig.
country: Pakistan	0.0249	0.0338	0.7364	0.461487	n.s.
country: Great Britain	−0.1051	0.0165	−6.3759	<0.0001	sig.
F-measure (z-scored)	−0.5421	0.0031	−176.3220	<0.0001	sig.
animacy: inanimate	−0.2686	0.0081	−32.9554	<0.0001	sig.
animacy: animate	0.3671	0.0081	45.3444	<0.0001	sig.
animacy: collective	−0.0681	0.0147	−4.6276	<0.0001	sig.
animacy: body part	−0.2136	0.0236	−9.0433	<0.0001	sig.
clause sentiment: negative	0.1407	0.0052	27.0045	<0.0001	sig.
clause sentiment: positive	0.1192	0.0063	18.8590	<0.0001	sig.
participle sentiment (z-scored)	0.0740	0.0045	16.3830	<0.0001	sig.
participle sentiment (squared)	0.3979	0.0244	16.2784	<0.0001	sig.
PP with by	−0.7542	0.0074	−102.2817	<0.0001	sig.

(Continued)

Table 14 (*Continued*)

Term	Estimate	Std. error	*z*-Value	*p*-Value	Sig.
cluster: interpersonal transaction and communication	−1.1611	0.0822	−14.1231	<0.0001	sig.
cluster: change of state (industrial and scientific)	2.2901	0.0717	31.9194	<0.0001	sig.
cluster: change of position and value	−0.2816	0.1061	−2.6551	0.007928	sig.
cluster: everyday actions with human agents	−1.1704	0.0794	−14.7348	<0.0001	sig.
cluster: change of state (household and workplace)	0.9910	0.0893	11.0931	<0.0001	sig.
cluster: physical interaction (minor impact)	0.2596	0.0711	3.6499	0.000262	sig.
cluster: administration	−0.6115	0.0737	−8.2950	<0.0001	sig.
cluster: legal	−0.7497	0.0722	−10.3852	<0.0001	sig.
cluster: disruptive impact	0.1924	0.0806	2.3858	0.017044	sig.
cluster: disruptive impact (lower frequency)	1.5633	0.0545	28.6963	<0.0001	sig.
previous auxiliary: GET	0.7018	0.0036	193.5878	<0.0001	sig.
PP with to	−0.2078	0.0045	−45.9607	<0.0001	sig.
polarity: negated	0.0814	0.0046	17.7698	<0.0001	sig.
tense/aspect: preterite	−0.3140	0.0079	−39.5731	<0.0001	sig.
tense/aspect: modal + infinitive	−0.1591	0.0088	−17.9991	<0.0001	sig.
tense/aspect: infinitive	0.6976	0.0078	89.9560	<0.0001	sig.
tense/aspect: present perfect	0.1705	0.0090	18.9674	<0.0001	sig.
tense/aspect: present progressive	0.5719	0.0132	43.3703	<0.0001	sig.
tense/aspect: past perfect	−1.7019	0.0332	−51.2982	<0.0001	sig.
tense/aspect: modal + perfect	−1.0698	0.0376	−28.4437	<0.0001	sig.
tense/aspect: gerund/ nonfinite –ing	0.6891	0.0088	77.9413	<0.0001	sig.
tense/aspect: past progressive	0.4429	0.0227	19.5131	<0.0001	sig.
adverb premodification	−0.0986	0.0049	−20.0638	<0.0001	sig.
subject person: third	−0.3070	0.0046	−66.0650	<0.0001	sig.
subject person: second	0.1889	0.0074	25.5353	<0.0001	sig.

(*Continued*)

Table 14 (*Continued*)

Term	Estimate	Std. error	*z*-Value	*p*-Value	Sig.
subject person: first	0.0825	0.0090	9.1760	<0.0001	sig.
probability of central passive (z-scored)	1.5159	0.0123	123.0869	<0.0001	sig.
country: Tanzania & F-measure (z-scored)	−0.0226	0.0177	−1.2821	0.199792	n.s.
country: Kenya & F-measure (z-scored)	0.0042	0.0148	0.2847	0.775885	n.s.
country: Hong Kong & F-measure (z-scored)	−0.0396	0.0165	−2.3992	0.016432	sig.
country: Bangladesh & F-measure (z-scored)	−0.0406	0.0137	−2.9726	0.002952	sig.
country: Ireland & F-measure (z-scored)	−0.0877	0.0102	−8.5892	<0.0001	sig.
country: India & F-measure (z-scored)	0.1197	0.0088	13.6128	<0.0001	sig.
country: Sri Lanka & F-measure (z-scored)	0.0142	0.0155	0.9176	0.358811	n.s.
country: Ghana & F-measure (z-scored)	0.0132	0.0168	0.7868	0.431418	n.s.
country: Malaysia & F-measure (z-scored)	−0.0339	0.0151	−2.2488	0.024524	sig.
country: Singapore & F-measure (z-scored)	0.0310	0.0134	2.3161	0.020553	sig.
country: Australia & F-measure (z-scored)	−0.0570	0.0087	−6.5794	<0.0001	sig.
country: Jamaica & F-measure (z-scored)	−0.0900	0.0156	−5.7789	<0.0001	sig.
country: Nigeria & F-measure (z-scored)	0.0680	0.0147	4.6361	<0.0001	sig.
country: Canada & F-measure (z-scored)	−0.0169	0.0083	−2.0491	0.040456	n.s.
country: Philippines & F-measure (z-scored)	0.0495	0.0129	3.8272	0.00013	sig.
country: New Zealand & F-measure (z-scored)	−0.0477	0.0113	−4.2068	<0.0001	sig.
country: South Africa & F-measure (z-scored)	−0.0492	0.0137	−3.5842	0.000338	sig.
country: Pakistan & F-measure (z-scored)	0.1043	0.0139	7.5159	<0.0001	sig.

(*Continued*)

Table 14 (*Continued*)

Term	Estimate	Std. error	*z*-Value	*p*-Value	Sig.
country: Great Britain & F-measure (z-scored)	−0.0073	0.0058	−1.2561	0.209066	n.s.
country: Tanzania & animacy: inanimate	−0.0114	0.0464	−0.2451	0.806398	n.s.
country: Kenya & animacy: inanimate	−0.0450	0.0455	−0.9880	0.323133	n.s.
country: Hong Kong & animacy: inanimate	−0.1131	0.0413	−2.7400	0.006143	sig.
country: Bangladesh & animacy: inanimate	−0.0035	0.0391	−0.0888	0.929247	n.s.
country: Ireland & animacy: inanimate	−0.0467	0.0277	−1.6814	0.092676	n.s.
country: India & animacy: inanimate	0.0852	0.0208	4.1030	<0.0001	sig.
country: Sri Lanka & animacy: inanimate	0.0579	0.0331	1.7477	0.080517	n.s.
country: Ghana & animacy: inanimate	−0.0243	0.0480	−0.5064	0.612566	n.s.
country: Malaysia & animacy: inanimate	−0.0711	0.0356	−1.9968	0.045844	n.s.
country: Singapore & animacy: inanimate	0.0078	0.0352	0.2208	0.825276	n.s.
country: Australia & animacy: inanimate	0.0768	0.0230	3.3372	0.000846	sig.
country: Jamaica & animacy: inanimate	−0.0429	0.0459	−0.9339	0.350371	n.s.
country: Nigeria & animacy: inanimate	−0.0557	0.0398	−1.3987	0.161917	n.s.
country: Canada & animacy: inanimate	0.0312	0.0224	1.3953	0.162931	n.s.
country: Philippines & animacy: inanimate	−0.0728	0.0352	−2.0696	0.038488	n.s.
country: New Zealand & animacy: inanimate	−0.0041	0.0278	−0.1475	0.882735	n.s.
country: South Africa & animacy: inanimate	0.0222	0.0398	0.5566	0.577812	n.s.
country: Pakistan & animacy: inanimate	0.0967	0.0319	3.0324	0.002426	sig.
country: Great Britain & animacy: inanimate	0.0309	0.0151	2.0434	0.041013	n.s.

(*Continued*)

Table 14 (*Continued*)

Term	Estimate	Std. error	*z*-Value	*p*-Value	Sig.
country: Tanzania & animacy: animate	−0.0187	0.0453	−0.4124	0.68004	n.s.
country: Kenya & animacy: animate	0.0388	0.0436	0.8901	0.373407	n.s.
country: Hong Kong & animacy: animate	0.0216	0.0410	0.5269	0.598269	n.s.
country: Bangladesh & animacy: animate	−0.0143	0.0393	−0.3645	0.715478	n.s.
country: Ireland & animacy: animate	0.0554	0.0270	2.0492	0.04044	n.s.
country: India & animacy: animate	−0.1925	0.0215	−8.9363	<0.0001	sig.
country: Sri Lanka & animacy: animate	−0.1039	0.0330	−3.1506	0.001629	sig.
country: Ghana & animacy: animate	−0.0323	0.0462	−0.6996	0.484182	n.s.
country: Malaysia & animacy: animate	−0.0180	0.0345	−0.5213	0.602138	n.s.
country: Singapore & animacy: animate	0.0615	0.0342	1.7993	0.071971	n.s.
country: Australia & animacy: animate	0.0909	0.0226	4.0252	<0.0001	sig.
country: Jamaica & animacy: animate	0.0567	0.0440	1.2885	0.197555	n.s.
country: Nigeria & animacy: animate	0.0008	0.0374	0.0212	0.98308	n.s.
country: Canada & animacy: animate	−0.0397	0.0220	−1.8022	0.071517	n.s.
country: Philippines & animacy: animate	0.0274	0.0340	0.8082	0.418957	n.s.
country: New Zealand & animacy: animate	0.0554	0.0275	2.0159	0.043808	n.s.
country: South Africa & animacy: animate	0.0099	0.0390	0.2532	0.800121	n.s.
country: Pakistan & animacy: animate	−0.0417	0.0314	−1.3263	0.184754	n.s.
country: Great Britain & animacy: animate	0.0372	0.0147	2.5264	0.011524	sig.
country: Tanzania & animacy: collective	−0.0048	0.0836	−0.0569	0.954642	n.s.

(*Continued*)

Table 14 (*Continued*)

Term	Estimate	Std. error	*z*-Value	*p*-Value	Sig.
country: Kenya & animacy: collective	0.0342	0.0731	0.4677	0.639979	n.s.
country: Hong Kong & animacy: collective	−0.0661	0.0823	−0.8038	0.421495	n.s.
country: Bangladesh & animacy: collective	0.0885	0.0665	1.3318	0.182936	n.s.
country: Ireland & animacy: collective	0.1025	0.0477	2.1479	0.031721	n.s.
country: India & animacy: collective	−0.0061	0.0403	−0.1525	0.878777	n.s.
country: Sri Lanka & animacy: collective	0.0618	0.0563	1.0969	0.272679	n.s.
country: Ghana & animacy: collective	−0.1260	0.0828	−1.5222	0.127959	n.s.
country: Malaysia & animacy: collective	−0.1458	0.0724	−2.0126	0.044162	n.s.
country: Singapore & animacy: collective	−0.1357	0.0743	−1.8263	0.067802	n.s.
country: Australia & animacy: collective	−0.0060	0.0426	−0.1413	0.88763	n.s.
country: Jamaica & animacy: collective	0.0220	0.0801	0.2744	0.783813	n.s.
country: Nigeria & animacy: collective	−0.1018	0.0708	−1.4376	0.150557	n.s.
country: Canada & animacy: collective	0.0794	0.0402	1.9748	0.048288	n.s.
country: Philippines & animacy: collective	−0.0463	0.0748	−0.6199	0.535309	n.s.
country: New Zealand & animacy: collective	−0.0716	0.0533	−1.3430	0.179277	n.s.
country: South Africa & animacy: collective	0.0517	0.0732	0.7061	0.480146	n.s.
country: Pakistan & animacy: collective	0.1243	0.0552	2.2510	0.024388	sig.
country: Great Britain & animacy: collective	0.0633	0.0263	2.4102	0.015942	sig.
country: Tanzania & animacy: body part	0.0789	0.1362	0.5790	0.562559	n.s.
country: Kenya & animacy: body part	−0.0731	0.1422	−0.5142	0.607095	n.s.

(*Continued*)

Table 14 (*Continued*)

Term	Estimate	Std. error	*z*-Value	*p*-Value	Sig.
country: Hong Kong & animacy: body part	0.1207	0.1127	1.0714	0.284007	n.s.
country: Bangladesh & animacy: body part	−0.0926	0.1227	−0.7554	0.45002	n.s.
country: Ireland & animacy: body part	−0.1388	0.0860	−1.6147	0.106382	n.s.
country: India & animacy: body part	0.2530	0.0584	4.3286	<0.0001	sig.
country: Sri Lanka & animacy: body part	0.0966	0.0937	1.0311	0.302484	n.s.
country: Ghana & animacy: body part	0.1064	0.1431	0.7437	0.457042	n.s.
country: Malaysia & animacy: body part	0.2387	0.0923	2.5854	0.009727	sig.
country: Singapore & animacy: body part	0.0874	0.0948	0.9218	0.356631	n.s.
country: Australia & animacy: body part	−0.2016	0.0709	−2.8431	0.004468	sig.
country: Jamaica & animacy: body part	−0.1039	0.1402	−0.7415	0.458409	n.s.
country: Nigeria & animacy: body part	0.1836	0.1125	1.6320	0.102676	n.s.
country: Canada & animacy: body part	−0.1091	0.0684	−1.5951	0.110683	n.s.
country: Philippines & animacy: body part	0.1717	0.0922	1.8631	0.062443	n.s.
country: New Zealand & animacy: body part	0.0278	0.0825	0.3370	0.736098	n.s.
country: South Africa & animacy: body part	−0.1011	0.1210	−0.8356	0.403367	n.s.
country: Pakistan & animacy: body part	−0.2065	0.0918	−2.2480	0.024576	sig.
country: Great Britain & animacy: body part	−0.1311	0.0464	−2.8225	0.004766	sig.
country: Tanzania & clause sentiment: negative	−0.0917	0.0298	−3.0775	0.002087	sig.
country: Kenya & clause sentiment: negative	−0.1054	0.0258	−4.0905	<0.0001	sig.
country: Hong Kong & clause sentiment: negative	0.0532	0.0279	1.9031	0.05703	n.s.

(*Continued*)

Table 14 (*Continued*)

Term	Estimate	Std. error	*z*-Value	*p*-Value	Sig.
country: Bangladesh & clause sentiment: negative	−0.1109	0.0251	−4.4146	<0.0001	sig.
country: Ireland & clause sentiment: negative	0.0046	0.0159	0.2914	0.770767	n.s.
country: India & clause sentiment: negative	0.0051	0.0151	0.3409	0.733177	n.s.
country: Sri Lanka & clause sentiment: negative	0.0116	0.0241	0.4809	0.630579	n.s.
country: Ghana & clause sentiment: negative	−0.0247	0.0291	−0.8467	0.397172	n.s.
country: Malaysia & clause sentiment: negative	0.0858	0.0242	3.5495	0.000386	sig.
country: Singapore & clause sentiment: negative	0.1027	0.0217	4.7368	<0.0001	sig.
country: Australia & clause sentiment: negative	0.0233	0.0128	1.8198	0.068797	n.s.
country: Jamaica & clause sentiment: negative	0.0040	0.0265	0.1499	0.880822	n.s.
country: Nigeria & clause sentiment: negative	−0.1290	0.0247	−5.2189	<0.0001	sig.
country: Canada & clause sentiment: negative	0.0324	0.0133	2.4443	0.014513	sig.
country: Philippines & clause sentiment: negative	0.0646	0.0227	2.8464	0.004421	sig.
country: New Zealand & clause sentiment: negative	0.0492	0.0167	2.9402	0.00328	sig.
country: South Africa & clause sentiment: negative	0.0144	0.0231	0.6251	0.531912	n.s.
country: Pakistan & clause sentiment: negative	−0.0409	0.0216	−1.8944	0.058173	n.s.
country: Great Britain & clause sentiment: negative	0.0051	0.0087	0.5911	0.554479	n.s.
country: Tanzania & clause sentiment: positive	0.0921	0.0346	2.6640	0.007723	sig.
country: Kenya & clause sentiment: positive	0.0476	0.0307	1.5496	0.121226	n.s.
country: Hong Kong & clause sentiment: positive	−0.0056	0.0337	−0.1666	0.867701	n.s.
country: Bangladesh & clause sentiment: positive	0.1185	0.0298	3.9715	<0.0001	sig.

(*Continued*)

Table 14 (*Continued*)

Term	Estimate	Std. error	*z*-Value	*p*-Value	Sig.
country: Ireland & clause sentiment: positive	0.0001	0.0199	0.0074	0.994069	n.s.
country: India & clause sentiment: positive	0.0184	0.0185	0.9906	0.321881	n.s.
country: Sri Lanka & clause sentiment: positive	0.0153	0.0314	0.4866	0.626565	n.s.
country: Ghana & clause sentiment: positive	−0.0014	0.0366	−0.0374	0.970151	n.s.
country: Malaysia & clause sentiment: positive	−0.0864	0.0305	−2.8302	0.004652	sig.
country: Singapore & clause sentiment: positive	−0.0790	0.0265	−2.9836	0.002848	sig.
country: Australia & clause sentiment: positive	−0.0546	0.0164	−3.3279	0.000875	sig.
country: Jamaica & clause sentiment: positive	−0.0317	0.0333	−0.9511	0.341545	n.s.
country: Nigeria & clause sentiment: positive	0.0466	0.0306	1.5242	0.127457	n.s.
country: Canada & clause sentiment: positive	−0.0225	0.0167	−1.3485	0.177494	n.s.
country: Philippines & clause sentiment: positive	−0.0263	0.0278	−0.9465	0.343894	n.s.
country: New Zealand & clause sentiment: positive	−0.0134	0.0212	−0.6316	0.527649	n.s.
country: South Africa & clause sentiment: positive	−0.0078	0.0288	−0.2695	0.787573	n.s.
country: Pakistan & clause sentiment: positive	0.0753	0.0280	2.6928	0.007085	sig.
country: Great Britain & clause sentiment: positive	−0.0234	0.0111	−2.1077	0.035054	n.s.
country: Tanzania & participle sentiment (z-scored)	0.0322	0.0171	1.8768	0.060547	n.s.
country: Kenya & participle sentiment (z-scored)	0.1107	0.0145	7.6158	<0.0001	sig.
country: Hong Kong & participle sentiment (z-scored)	0.0027	0.0174	0.1576	0.8748	n.s.
country: Bangladesh & participle sentiment (z-scored)	0.0303	0.0145	2.0813	0.037408	n.s.

(*Continued*)

Table 14 (*Continued*)

Term	Estimate	Std. error	*z*-Value	*p*-Value	Sig.
country: Ireland & participle sentiment (z-scored)	−0.0234	0.0103	−2.2682	0.023319	sig.
country: India & participle sentiment (z-scored)	0.0268	0.0089	3.0173	0.00255	sig.
country: Sri Lanka & participle sentiment (z-scored)	−0.0069	0.0141	−0.4896	0.624427	n.s.
country: Ghana & participle sentiment (z-scored)	−0.0158	0.0174	−0.9091	0.363303	n.s.
country: Malaysia & participle sentiment (z-scored)	−0.0015	0.0147	−0.1000	0.920307	n.s.
country: Singapore & participle sentiment (z-scored)	0.0113	0.0133	0.8502	0.395239	n.s.
country: Australia & participle sentiment (z-scored)	−0.0293	0.0083	−3.5240	0.000425	sig.
country: Jamaica & participle sentiment (z-scored)	0.0245	0.0159	1.5467	0.121936	n.s.
country: Nigeria & participle sentiment (z-scored)	0.0271	0.0142	1.9046	0.056836	n.s.
country: Canada & participle sentiment (z-scored)	−0.0451	0.0085	−5.3069	<0.0001	sig.
country: Philippines & participle sentiment (z-scored)	−0.0400	0.0143	−2.7963	0.005169	sig.
country: New Zealand & participle sentiment (z-scored)	−0.0445	0.0109	−4.0943	<0.0001	sig.
country: South Africa & participle sentiment (z-scored)	0.0096	0.0140	0.6861	0.492622	n.s.
country: Pakistan & participle sentiment (z-scored)	−0.0154	0.0126	−1.2230	0.221332	n.s.

(*Continued*)

Table 14 (*Continued*)

Term	Estimate	Std. error	*z*-Value	*p*-Value	Sig.
country: Great Britain & participle sentiment (z-scored)	−0.0146	0.0056	−2.6221	0.00874	sig.
country: Tanzania & participle sentiment (squared)	0.0399	0.0142	2.8103	0.004949	sig.
country: Kenya & participle sentiment (squared)	0.0667	0.0116	5.7434	<0.0001	sig.
country: Hong Kong & participle sentiment (squared)	−0.0092	0.0155	−0.5930	0.553185	n.s.
country: Bangladesh & participle sentiment (squared)	0.0044	0.0120	0.3685	0.712471	n.s.
country: Ireland & participle sentiment (squared)	−0.0414	0.0088	−4.7128	<0.0001	sig.
country: India & participle sentiment (squared)	0.0013	0.0075	0.1683	0.86636	n.s.
country: Sri Lanka & participle sentiment (squared)	0.0434	0.0098	4.4516	<0.0001	sig.
country: Ghana & participle sentiment (squared)	0.0515	0.0142	3.6173	0.000298	sig.
country: Malaysia & participle sentiment (squared)	0.0278	0.0121	2.2939	0.021797	sig.
country: Singapore & participle sentiment (squared)	0.0352	0.0115	3.0573	0.002233	sig.
country: Australia & participle sentiment (squared)	−0.0509	0.0070	−7.2792	<0.0001	sig.
country: Jamaica & participle sentiment (squared)	0.0144	0.0128	1.1277	0.259436	n.s.
country: Nigeria & participle sentiment (squared)	0.0119	0.0110	1.0738	0.282907	n.s.
country: Canada & participle sentiment (squared)	−0.0407	0.0070	−5.7823	<0.0001	sig.

(*Continued*)

Table 14 (*Continued*)

Term	Estimate	Std. error	*z*-Value	*p*-Value	Sig.
country: Philippines & participle sentiment (squared)	0.0004	0.0116	0.0377	0.969954	n.s.
country: New Zealand & participle sentiment (squared)	−0.0662	0.0093	−7.0831	<0.0001	sig.
country: South Africa & participle sentiment (squared)	−0.0136	0.0112	−1.2139	0.224804	n.s.
country: Pakistan & participle sentiment (squared)	0.0065	0.0088	0.7378	0.460666	n.s.
country: Great Britain & participle sentiment (squared)	−0.0271	0.0045	−5.9788	<0.0001	sig.
country: Tanzania & PP with by	−0.0177	0.0307	−0.5754	0.565033	n.s.
country: Kenya & PP with by	0.0275	0.0258	1.0675	0.285747	n.s.
country: Hong Kong & PP with by	−0.0021	0.0288	−0.0721	0.942499	n.s.
country: Bangladesh & PP with by	−0.0143	0.0247	−0.5787	0.562763	n.s.
country: Ireland & PP with by	−0.0635	0.0181	−3.5149	0.00044	sig.
country: India & PP with by	0.0014	0.0149	0.0916	0.927042	n.s.
country: Sri Lanka & PP with by	−0.0409	0.0235	−1.7411	0.081669	n.s.
country: Ghana & PP with by	0.0336	0.0296	1.1381	0.255091	n.s.
country: Malaysia & PP with by	0.0356	0.0243	1.4653	0.142852	n.s.
country: Singapore & PP with by	0.0619	0.0221	2.7971	0.005156	sig.
country: Australia & PP with by	−0.0376	0.0140	−2.6886	0.007174	sig.
country: Jamaica & PP with by	−0.0373	0.0286	−1.3030	0.192566	n.s.
country: Nigeria & PP with by	0.0804	0.0258	3.1192	0.001813	sig.

(*Continued*)

Table 14 (*Continued*)

Term	Estimate	Std. error	*z*-Value	*p*-Value	Sig.
country: Canada & PP with by	−0.0088	0.0144	−0.6156	0.538184	n.s.
country: Philippines & PP with by	0.0038	0.0232	0.1650	0.868983	n.s.
country: New Zealand & PP with by	−0.0594	0.0186	−3.1895	0.001425	sig.
country: South Africa & PP with by	0.0490	0.0241	2.0328	0.042073	n.s.
country: Pakistan & PP with by	0.0499	0.0208	2.4007	0.016364	sig.
country: Great Britain & PP with by	−0.0604	0.0096	−6.2897	<0.0001	sig.

model as that would have made it too complex. In those situations, we observe the overall tendencies in these synchronic data.

10.4.1 Countries

Figures 23 and 24 show the predictions for different countries. Smaller values on the x-axis indicate a higher likelihood for *be* to occur; higher values predict that more *get* occurs. Bigger confidence intervals suggest more variation. Countries that differ significantly from the baseline (United States) are marked with an asterisk.

Both models predict that *get* is more likely to be used in the data from India, Bangladesh, Singapore, and Canada compared to the United States (the reference level not displayed in the graph). This tendency is also visible for the Philippines in the full but not in the central model. Conversely, the two models align with one another in their predictions concerning Ireland, Ghana, Jamaica, and Australia with significantly lower probabilities for *get* than the US baseline. Apart from those countries, the slopes for Kenya, Great Britain, and South Africa are also significant at $p < 0.025$ in the full model (cf. Figure 24), where a lower probability of *get* is predicted for these countries compared to the United States.

Striving to interpret these findings in the light of established categories in World Englishes, we can identify some tendencies related to the status of English as well as regional patterns. In our models, African Englishes are most clearly predicted to disfavor the GET-passive, while different Asian Englishes seem to

Table 15 Output of Mixed-Effects Logistic Regression Model Predicting *Get* (vs. *Be*) based on the Independent Variables Described in Chapter 8, *N* = 5650629, GloWbE, Central Data

Term	Estimate	Std. error	Z-value	*P*-value	Sig.
Intercept	−4.0172	0.0492	−81.7195	<0.0001	sig.
country: Tanzania	−0.0311	0.0904	−0.3446	0.730367	n.s.
country: Kenya	−0.1152	0.0798	−1.4437	0.148816	n.s.
country: Hong Kong	−0.0839	0.0837	−1.0031	0.315794	n.s.
country: Bangladesh	0.3012	0.0756	3.9834	0.000068	sig.
country: Ireland	−0.3409	0.0580	−5.8774	<0.0001	sig.
country: India	0.3989	0.0422	9.4475	<0.0001	sig.
country: Sri Lanka	−0.0960	0.0668	−1.4362	0.150943	n.s.
country: Ghana	−0.2655	0.0869	−3.0564	0.00224	sig.
country: Malaysia	0.0991	0.0625	1.5870	0.112524	n.s.
country: Singapore	0.1640	0.0662	2.4764	0.013271	sig.
country: Australia	−0.1181	0.0447	−2.6386	0.008324	sig.
country: Jamaica	−0.2223	0.0941	−2.3614	0.018204	sig.
country: Nigeria	−0.0748	0.0717	−1.0444	0.296284	n.s.
country: Canada	0.2275	0.0414	5.4930	<0.0001	sig.
country: Philippines	0.0728	0.0669	1.0879	0.276634	n.s.
country: New Zealand	−0.0292	0.0543	−0.5373	0.591061	n.s.
country: South Africa	−0.0691	0.0759	−0.9108	0.362381	n.s.
country: Pakistan	−0.1439	0.0703	−2.0453	0.040823	n.s.
country: Great Britain	−0.0447	0.0280	−1.5941	0.110918	n.s.
F-measure (z-scored)	−0.7042	0.0052	−134.5222	<0.0001	sig.
animacy: inanimate	−0.3666	0.0155	−23.5856	<0.0001	sig.
animacy: animate	0.5114	0.0151	33.7632	<0.0001	sig.
animacy: collective	−0.0367	0.0271	−1.3524	0.17626	n.s.
animacy: body part	−0.3488	0.0480	−7.2733	<0.0001	sig.
clause sentiment: negative	0.1413	0.0088	16.0255	<0.0001	sig.
clause sentiment: positive	0.1707	0.0107	15.9454	<0.0001	sig.
participle sentiment (z-scored)	0.0521	0.0071	7.3243	<0.0001	sig.
participle sentiment (squared)	0.2308	0.0390	5.9176	<0.0001	sig.
PP with by	−0.4304	0.0090	−47.5967	<0.0001	sig.

(*Continued*)

Table 15 (*Continued*)

Term	**Estimate**	**Std. error**	**Z-value**	***P*-value**	**Sig.**
cluster: interpersonal transaction and communication	−0.4274	0.1202	−3.5569	0.000375	sig.
cluster: change of state (industrial and scientific)	0.4252	0.1473	2.8871	0.003888	sig.
cluster: change of position and value	−0.4870	0.1664	−2.9268	0.003425	sig.
cluster: everyday actions with human agents	−0.4526	0.1102	−4.1072	<0.0001	sig.
cluster: change of state (household and workplace)	0.5274	0.1558	3.3851	0.000711	sig.
cluster: physical interaction (minor impact)	0.3696	0.1123	3.2919	0.000995	sig.
cluster: administration	−0.1727	0.1100	−1.5694	0.116549	n.s.
cluster: legal	0.0061	0.1090	0.0562	0.955151	n.s.
cluster: disruptive impact	0.6134	0.1211	5.0637	<0.0001	sig.
cluster: disruptive impact (lower frequency)	0.6829	0.0900	7.5880	<0.0001	sig.
previous auxiliary: GET	0.8049	0.0054	148.1315	<0.0001	sig.
PP with to	−0.2664	0.0070	−37.9273	<0.0001	sig.
polarity: negated	0.1419	0.0071	20.0154	<0.0001	sig.
tense/aspect: preterite	−0.1943	0.0149	−13.0820	<0.0001	sig.
tense/aspect: modal + infinitive	−0.1326	0.0164	−8.1076	<0.0001	sig.
tense/aspect: infinitive	0.8525	0.0144	59.0943	<0.0001	sig.
tense/aspect: present perfect	0.2684	0.0165	16.2915	<0.0001	sig.
tense/aspect: present progressive	0.6045	0.0223	27.1035	<0.0001	sig.
tense/aspect: past perfect	−2.3349	0.0740	−31.5495	<0.0001	sig.
tense/aspect: modal + perfect	−1.5146	0.0744	−20.3704	<0.0001	sig.
tense/aspect: gerund/ nonfinite -ing	0.8654	0.0156	55.3487	<0.0001	sig.
tense/aspect: past progressive	0.4117	0.0363	11.3490	<0.0001	sig.
adverb premodification	−0.5607	0.0172	−32.6509	<0.0001	sig.
subject person: third	−0.3764	0.0073	−51.5153	<0.0001	sig.
subject person: second	0.2598	0.0114	22.7713	<0.0001	sig.
subject person: first	0.1397	0.0142	9.8075	<0.0001	sig.

(*Continued*)

Table 15 (*Continued*)

Term	Estimate	Std. error	Z-value	*P*-value	Sig.
country: Tanzania & F-measure (z-scored)	−0.0200	0.0298	−0.6729	0.500996	n.s.
country: Kenya & F-measure (z-scored)	−0.0023	0.0255	−0.0889	0.929155	n.s.
country: Hong Kong & F-measure (z-scored)	−0.0155	0.0278	−0.5569	0.577579	n.s.
country: Bangladesh & F-measure (z-scored)	−0.0521	0.0230	−2.2612	0.023748	sig.
country: Ireland & F-measure (z-scored)	−0.0890	0.0171	−5.1898	<0.0001	sig.
country: India & F-measure (z-scored)	0.1291	0.0152	8.4763	<0.0001	sig.
country: Sri Lanka & F-measure (z-scored)	−0.0677	0.0283	−2.3908	0.016812	sig.
country: Ghana & F-measure (z-scored)	−0.0229	0.0293	−0.7830	0.433622	n.s.
country: Malaysia & F-measure (z-scored)	−0.0191	0.0255	−0.7506	0.452907	n.s.
country: Singapore & F-measure (z-scored)	0.0206	0.0228	0.9060	0.364933	n.s.
country: Australia & F-measure (z-scored)	−0.0473	0.0142	−3.3315	0.000864	sig.
country: Jamaica & F-measure (z-scored)	−0.1319	0.0266	−4.9628	<0.0001	sig.
country: Nigeria & F-measure (z-scored)	0.0905	0.0258	3.5094	0.000449	sig.
country: Canada & F-measure (z-scored)	0.0081	0.0136	0.5949	0.551906	n.s.
country: Philippines & F-measure (z-scored)	0.0371	0.0221	1.6759	0.093765	n.s.
country: New Zealand & F-measure (z-scored)	−0.0528	0.0186	−2.8463	0.004422	sig.
country: South Africa & F-measure (z-scored)	−0.0490	0.0226	−2.1671	0.030227	n.s.
country: Pakistan & F-measure (z-scored)	0.1238	0.0250	4.9450	<0.0001	sig.
country: Great Britain & F-measure (z-scored)	0.0195	0.0095	2.0593	0.039465	n.s.
country: Tanzania & animacy: inanimate	−0.0571	0.0908	−0.6283	0.529835	n.s.

(*Continued*)

Table 15 (*Continued*)

Term	Estimate	Std. error	Z-value	*P*-value	Sig.
country: Kenya & animacy: inanimate	−0.1559	0.0813	−1.9177	0.055145	n.s.
country: Hong Kong & animacy: inanimate	−0.0892	0.0840	−1.0619	0.288291	n.s.
country: Bangladesh & animacy: inanimate	−0.0215	0.0753	−0.2850	0.775625	n.s.
country: Ireland & animacy: inanimate	0.0104	0.0562	0.1852	0.853109	n.s.
country: India & animacy: inanimate	0.1759	0.0417	4.2185	<0.0001	sig.
country: Sri Lanka & animacy: inanimate	0.0136	0.0676	0.2011	0.840643	n.s.
country: Ghana & animacy: inanimate	−0.0984	0.0883	−1.1144	0.265102	n.s.
country: Malaysia & animacy: inanimate	−0.2127	0.0626	−3.4001	0.000674	sig.
country: Singapore & animacy: inanimate	0.0577	0.0652	0.8847	0.376342	n.s.
country: Australia & animacy: inanimate	0.1089	0.0432	2.5197	0.011745	sig.
country: Jamaica & animacy: inanimate	−0.0053	0.0935	−0.0566	0.954841	n.s.
country: Nigeria & animacy: inanimate	−0.1467	0.0714	−2.0542	0.039955	n.s.
country: Canada & animacy: inanimate	0.0530	0.0402	1.3189	0.187205	n.s.
country: Philippines & animacy: inanimate	−0.1024	0.0671	−1.5260	0.127014	n.s.
country: New Zealand & animacy: inanimate	0.0401	0.0518	0.7741	0.438869	n.s.
country: South Africa & animacy: inanimate	0.0092	0.0749	0.1234	0.9018	n.s.
country: Pakistan & animacy: inanimate	0.2256	0.0716	3.1508	0.001628	sig.
country: Great Britain & animacy: inanimate	0.0342	0.0271	1.2610	0.207315	n.s.
country: Tanzania & animacy: animate	−0.0893	0.0877	−1.0180	0.308666	n.s.
country: Kenya & animacy: animate	−0.0700	0.0768	−0.9120	0.361743	n.s.

(*Continued*)

Table 15 (*Continued*)

Term	Estimate	Std. error	Z-value	*P*-value	Sig.
country: Hong Kong & animacy: animate	0.1470	0.0811	1.8127	0.069872	n.s.
country: Bangladesh & animacy: animate	0.0400	0.0742	0.5392	0.589726	n.s.
country: Ireland & animacy: animate	0.1459	0.0546	2.6743	0.007489	sig.
country: India & animacy: animate	−0.1831	0.0424	−4.3212	<0.0001	sig.
country: Sri Lanka & animacy: animate	−0.0893	0.0646	−1.3820	0.166977	n.s.
country: Ghana & animacy: animate	−0.1456	0.0839	−1.7361	0.082545	n.s.
country: Malaysia & animacy: animate	−0.0715	0.0587	−1.2186	0.223007	n.s.
country: Singapore & animacy: animate	0.1047	0.0624	1.6790	0.093149	n.s.
country: Australia & animacy: animate	0.1222	0.0422	2.8995	0.003738	sig.
country: Jamaica & animacy: animate	0.1213	0.0897	1.3516	0.176512	n.s.
country: Nigeria & animacy: animate	−0.0607	0.0657	−0.9245	0.355237	n.s.
country: Canada & animacy: animate	−0.1023	0.0392	−2.6076	0.009118	sig.
country: Philippines & animacy: animate	0.0685	0.0640	1.0710	0.284168	n.s.
country: New Zealand & animacy: animate	0.0836	0.0507	1.6481	0.09933	n.s.
country: South Africa & animacy: animate	0.0310	0.0728	0.4260	0.670104	n.s.
country: Pakistan & animacy: animate	0.0026	0.0696	0.0377	0.969895	n.s.
country: Great Britain & animacy: animate	0.0144	0.0262	0.5483	0.58346	n.s.
country: Tanzania & animacy: collective	0.1956	0.1441	1.3571	0.174763	n.s.
country: Kenya & animacy: collective	0.0735	0.1295	0.5675	0.570378	n.s.
country: Hong Kong & animacy: collective	0.0287	0.1504	0.1908	0.848677	n.s.

(*Continued*)

Table 15 (*Continued*)

Term	Estimate	Std. error	Z-value	*P*-value	Sig.
country: Bangladesh & animacy: collective	−0.0597	0.1315	−0.4538	0.649967	n.s.
country: Ireland & animacy: collective	0.1575	0.0887	1.7760	0.075738	n.s.
country: India & animacy: collective	0.0467	0.0761	0.6137	0.539422	n.s.
country: Sri Lanka & animacy: collective	−0.1750	0.1222	−1.4313	0.152352	n.s.
country: Ghana & animacy: collective	−0.2965	0.1625	−1.8244	0.06809	n.s.
country: Malaysia & animacy: collective	−0.2082	0.1261	−1.6507	0.098801	n.s.
country: Singapore & animacy: collective	−0.0100	0.1236	−0.0813	0.935208	n.s.
country: Australia & animacy: collective	0.0402	0.0747	0.5377	0.590755	n.s.
country: Jamaica & animacy: collective	0.0243	0.1556	0.1559	0.876105	n.s.
country: Nigeria & animacy: collective	−0.1209	0.1296	−0.9327	0.350996	n.s.
country: Canada & animacy: collective	0.0516	0.0704	0.7328	0.463691	n.s.
country: Philippines & animacy: collective	−0.0915	0.1383	−0.6619	0.508048	n.s.
country: New Zealand & animacy: collective	−0.0194	0.0918	−0.2109	0.832989	n.s.
country: South Africa & animacy: collective	0.1463	0.1274	1.1483	0.250829	n.s.
country: Pakistan & animacy: collective	0.1169	0.1143	1.0229	0.306372	n.s.
country: Great Britain & animacy: collective	0.0148	0.0457	0.3246	0.745495	n.s.
country: Tanzania & animacy: body part	0.0158	0.2928	0.0540	0.956972	n.s.
country: Kenya & animacy: body part	0.1776	0.2553	0.6956	0.486705	n.s.
country: Hong Kong & animacy: body part	−0.2012	0.2593	−0.7758	0.437842	n.s.
country: Bangladesh & animacy: body part	−0.0293	0.2452	−0.1195	0.904875	n.s.

(*Continued*)

Table 15 (*Continued*)

Term	Estimate	Std. error	Z-value	*P*-value	Sig.
country: Ireland & animacy: body part	−0.3504	0.1896	−1.8480	0.064603	n.s.
country: India & animacy: body part	0.0841	0.1293	0.6504	0.515431	n.s.
country: Sri Lanka & animacy: body part	0.3381	0.1940	1.7426	0.081408	n.s.
country: Ghana & animacy: body part	0.4168	0.2603	1.6012	0.109341	n.s.
country: Malaysia & animacy: body part	0.6285	0.1618	3.8834	0.000103	sig.
country: Singapore & animacy: body part	−0.1271	0.1949	−0.6519	0.514485	n.s.
country: Australia & animacy: body part	−0.3198	0.1423	−2.2468	0.024651	sig.
country: Jamaica & animacy: body part	−0.2941	0.3083	−0.9540	0.340077	n.s.
country: Nigeria & animacy: body part	0.4619	0.2007	2.3012	0.02138	sig.
country: Canada & animacy: body part	−0.0136	0.1283	−0.1063	0.915311	n.s.
country: Philippines & animacy: body part	0.1726	0.1896	0.9105	0.362538	n.s.
country: New Zealand & animacy: body part	−0.1039	0.1668	−0.6229	0.533335	n.s.
country: South Africa & animacy: body part	−0.1632	0.2442	−0.6680	0.50412	n.s.
country: Pakistan & animacy: body part	−0.5028	0.2320	−2.1670	0.030238	n.s.
country: Great Britain & animacy: body part	−0.0123	0.0870	−0.1409	0.887933	n.s.
country: Tanzania & clause sentiment:negative	−0.0256	0.0495	−0.5168	0.60527	n.s.
country: Kenya & clause sentiment: negative	−0.0380	0.0437	−0.8703	0.384156	n.s.
country: Hong Kong & clause sentiment: negative	0.0892	0.0464	1.9239	0.054368	n.s.
country: Bangladesh & clause sentiment: negative	−0.1706	0.0425	−4.0170	<0.0001	sig.

(*Continued*)

Table 15 (*Continued*)

Term	Estimate	Std. error	Z-value	*P*-value	Sig.
country: Ireland & clause sentiment: negative	0.0146	0.0261	0.5620	0.574124	n.s.
country: India & clause sentiment: negative	−0.0442	0.0262	−1.6858	0.091835	n.s.
country: Sri Lanka & clause sentiment: negative	0.0544	0.0448	1.2141	0.224719	n.s.
country: Ghana & clause sentiment: negative	−0.1162	0.0505	−2.2999	0.021454	sig.
country: Malaysia & clause sentiment: negative	0.0571	0.0402	1.4204	0.155492	n.s.
country: Singapore & clause sentiment: negative	0.0986	0.0357	2.7608	0.005766	sig.
country: Australia & clause sentiment: negative	0.0167	0.0207	0.8088	0.418617	n.s.
country: Jamaica & clause sentiment: negative	−0.0167	0.0441	−0.3793	0.704499	n.s.
country: Nigeria & clause sentiment: negative	−0.1240	0.0423	−2.9348	0.003338	sig.
country: Canada & clause sentiment: negative	0.0886	0.0216	4.1026	<0.0001	sig.
country: Philippines & clause sentiment: negative	0.0965	0.0388	2.4838	0.012998	sig.
country: New Zealand & clause sentiment: negative	0.0395	0.0267	1.4797	0.138957	n.s.
country: South Africa & clause sentiment: negative	0.0436	0.0379	1.1499	0.250168	n.s.
country: Pakistan & clause sentiment: negative	−0.1392	0.0391	−3.5611	0.000369	sig.
country: Great Britain & clause sentiment: negative	0.0152	0.0140	1.0846	0.278088	n.s.
country: Tanzania & clause sentiment: positive	0.0759	0.0580	1.3087	0.190623	n.s.
country: Kenya & clause sentiment: positive	−0.0261	0.0526	−0.4965	0.619545	n.s.
country: Hong Kong & clause sentiment: positive	−0.0468	0.0576	−0.8130	0.416204	n.s.
country: Bangladesh & clause sentiment: positive	0.1670	0.0490	3.4103	0.000649	sig.
country: Ireland & clause sentiment: positive	−0.0048	0.0331	−0.1461	0.88386	n.s.

(*Continued*)

Table 15 (*Continued*)

Term	Estimate	Std. error	Z-value	*P*-value	Sig.
country: India & clause sentiment: positive	0.0651	0.0318	2.0507	0.040298	n.s.
country: Sri Lanka & clause sentiment: positive	−0.0337	0.0605	−0.5580	0.576826	n.s.
country: Ghana & clause sentiment: positive	0.0719	0.0624	1.1528	0.248974	n.s.
country: Malaysia & clause sentiment: positive	−0.0390	0.0512	−0.7619	0.446121	n.s.
country: Singapore & clause sentiment: positive	−0.0831	0.0440	−1.8882	0.059005	n.s.
country: Australia & clause sentiment: positive	−0.0679	0.0266	−2.5561	0.010584	sig.
country: Jamaica & clause sentiment: positive	0.0478	0.0554	0.8638	0.387725	n.s.
country: Nigeria & clause sentiment: positive	0.0541	0.0523	1.0351	0.300639	n.s.
country: Canada & clause sentiment: positive	−0.0917	0.0277	−3.3142	0.000919	sig.
country: Philippines & clause sentiment: positive	−0.1185	0.0489	−2.4228	0.015399	sig.
country: New Zealand & clause sentiment: positive	0.0355	0.0335	1.0602	0.289072	n.s.
country: South Africa & clause sentiment: positive	−0.0639	0.0478	−1.3361	0.181522	n.s.
country: Pakistan & clause sentiment: positive	0.1685	0.0502	3.3591	0.000782	sig.
country: Great Britain & clause sentiment: positive	−0.0461	0.0180	−2.5620	0.010407	sig.
country: Tanzania & participle sentiment (z-scored)	0.0624	0.0269	2.3226	0.020201	sig.
country: Kenya & participle sentiment (z-scored)	0.1879	0.0230	8.1537	<0.0001	sig.
country: Hong Kong & participle sentiment (z-scored)	−0.0963	0.0298	−3.2302	0.001237	sig.
country: Bangladesh & participle sentiment (z-scored)	0.0307	0.0235	1.3084	0.190735	n.s.
country: Ireland & participle sentiment (z-scored)	−0.0714	0.0172	−4.1629	<0.0001	sig.

(*Continued*)

Table 15 (*Continued*)

Term	Estimate	Std. error	Z-value	*P*-value	Sig.
country: India & participle sentiment (z-scored)	0.0690	0.0144	4.8005	<0.0001	sig.
country: Sri Lanka & participle sentiment (z-scored)	−0.0049	0.0245	−0.2004	0.841198	n.s.
country: Ghana & participle sentiment (z-scored)	−0.0058	0.0287	−0.2033	0.838913	n.s.
country: Malaysia & participle sentiment (z-scored)	−0.0330	0.0245	−1.3507	0.176804	n.s.
country: Singapore & participle sentiment (z-scored)	0.0202	0.0204	0.9907	0.321852	n.s.
country: Australia & participle sentiment (z-scored)	−0.0443	0.0130	−3.4171	0.000633	sig.
country: Jamaica & participle sentiment (z-scored)	0.0608	0.0247	2.4667	0.013638	sig.
country: Nigeria & participle sentiment (z-scored)	0.0679	0.0232	2.9235	0.003462	sig.
country: Canada & participle sentiment (z-scored)	−0.0913	0.0136	−6.7018	<0.0001	sig.
country: Philippines & participle sentiment (z-scored)	−0.0421	0.0235	−1.7916	0.073203	n.s.
country: New Zealand & participle sentiment (z-scored)	−0.0582	0.0171	−3.4050	0.000662	sig.
country: South Africa & participle sentiment (z-scored)	0.0364	0.0215	1.6953	0.090024	n.s.
country: Pakistan & participle sentiment (z-scored)	−0.0108	0.0210	−0.5158	0.605962	n.s.
country: Great Britain & participle sentiment (z-scored)	−0.0166	0.0086	−1.9187	0.055023	n.s.
country: Tanzania & participle sentiment (squared)	0.0380	0.0218	1.7429	0.081355	n.s.
country: Kenya & participle sentiment (squared)	0.0844	0.0184	4.5879	<0.0001	sig.

(*Continued*)

Table 15 (*Continued*)

Term	Estimate	Std. error	Z-value	*P*-value	Sig.
country: Hong Kong & participle sentiment (squared)	−0.0772	0.0253	−3.0554	0.002248	sig.
country: Bangladesh & participle sentiment (squared)	−0.0125	0.0188	−0.6627	0.507528	n.s.
country: Ireland & participle sentiment (squared)	−0.0707	0.0149	−4.7576	<0.0001	sig.
country: India & participle sentiment (squared)	0.0107	0.0119	0.8985	0.368945	n.s.
country: Sri Lanka & participle sentiment (squared)	0.0826	0.0155	5.3232	<0.0001	sig.
country: Ghana & participle sentiment (squared)	0.0852	0.0229	3.7247	0.000196	sig.
country: Malaysia & participle sentiment (squared)	0.0093	0.0190	0.4876	0.625819	n.s.
country: Singapore & participle sentiment (squared)	0.0563	0.0169	3.3410	0.000835	sig.
country: Australia & participle sentiment (squared)	−0.0480	0.0107	−4.4741	<0.0001	sig.
country: Jamaica & participle sentiment (squared)	0.0437	0.0193	2.2678	0.023342	sig.
country: Nigeria & participle sentiment (squared)	0.0064	0.0177	0.3639	0.715921	n.s.
country: Canada & participle sentiment (squared)	−0.0569	0.0111	−5.1171	<0.0001	sig.
country: Philippines & participle sentiment (squared)	0.0132	0.0178	0.7392	0.459815	n.s.
country: New Zealand & participle sentiment (squared)	−0.0953	0.0148	−6.4288	<0.0001	sig.
country: South Africa & participle sentiment (squared)	−0.0177	0.0172	−1.0279	0.303985	n.s.
country: Pakistan & participle sentiment (squared)	0.0368	0.0140	2.6323	0.008482	sig.

(*Continued*)

Table 15 (*Continued*)

Term	**Estimate**	**Std. error**	**Z-value**	***P*-value**	**Sig.**
country: Great Britain & participle sentiment (squared)	−0.0388	0.0070	−5.5452	<0.0001	sig.
country: Tanzania & PP with by	−0.0326	0.0427	−0.7638	0.444966	n.s.
country: Kenya & PP with by	0.0187	0.0373	0.5014	0.616081	n.s.
country: Hong Kong & PP with by	0.0040	0.0399	0.0995	0.920739	n.s.
country: Bangladesh & PP with by	−0.0152	0.0337	−0.4518	0.651383	n.s.
country: Ireland & PP with by	−0.1185	0.0257	−4.6059	<0.0001	sig.
country: India & PP with by	0.0643	0.0208	3.0894	0.002006	sig.
country: Sri Lanka & PP with by	0.0057	0.0335	0.1694	0.865462	n.s.
country: Ghana & PP with by	0.0295	0.0433	0.6811	0.495839	n.s.
country: Malaysia & PP with by	0.1024	0.0323	3.1736	0.001506	sig.
country: Singapore & PP with by	0.0969	0.0300	3.2326	0.001227	sig.
country: Australia & PP with by	−0.0831	0.0193	−4.3077	<0.0001	sig.
country: Jamaica & PP with by	−0.0478	0.0401	−1.1922	0.233183	n.s.
country: Nigeria & PP with by	0.0681	0.0376	1.8119	0.069999	n.s.
country: Canada & PP with by	−0.0289	0.0195	−1.4842	0.137745	n.s.
country: Philippines & PP with by	0.0114	0.0316	0.3611	0.718048	n.s.
country: New Zealand & PP with by	−0.1121	0.0258	4.3373	<0.0001	sig.
country: South Africa & PP with by	0.0261	0.0336	0.7770	0.437177	n.s.
country: Pakistan & PP with by	0.1384	0.0292	4.7389	<0.0001	sig.
country: Great Britain & PP with by	−0.1057	0.0132	−8.0184	<0.0001	sig.

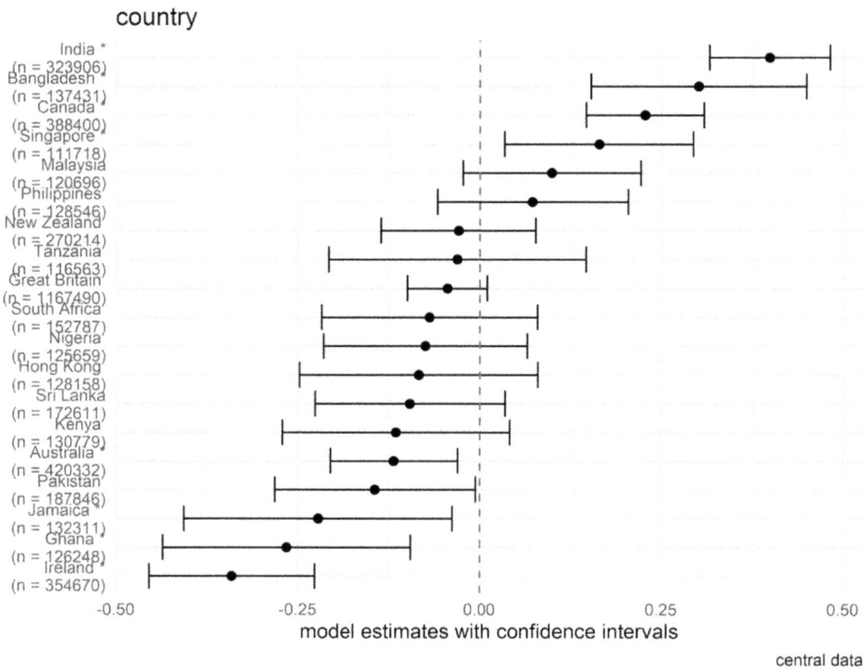

Figure 23 Predicted probability of GET-passives by country (central data).

be most favorable to this innovation. Moreover, most L1 varieties show a lower probability of *get*, with only Canada clearly departing from this trend. Canadian and Philippine English, both greatly influenced by AmE, favor *get* even more than AmE does. This does not apply to all varieties heavily influenced by AmE; speakers of JamE seem to particularly shy away from the GET-passive. This is particularly interesting in light of the fact that in the local English-based creole, *get* is used as a passive auxiliary (Winford 1993: 140–2). In JamC, *get* is followed by a base form of the main verb (Winford 1993: 140–2). We checked whether this structure occurs in GloWbE and found some instances of the JamC GET-passive in a clearly JamC context (see two examples in (142) and (143)), but the frequency is so low that we do not think that this could have an effect on the GET-passive in JamE.

(142) juss when yuh think you've heard &; seen it all suppen else get reveal (GloWbE/Jamaica/general)
"Just when you think you've heard and seen it all, something else gets revealed"

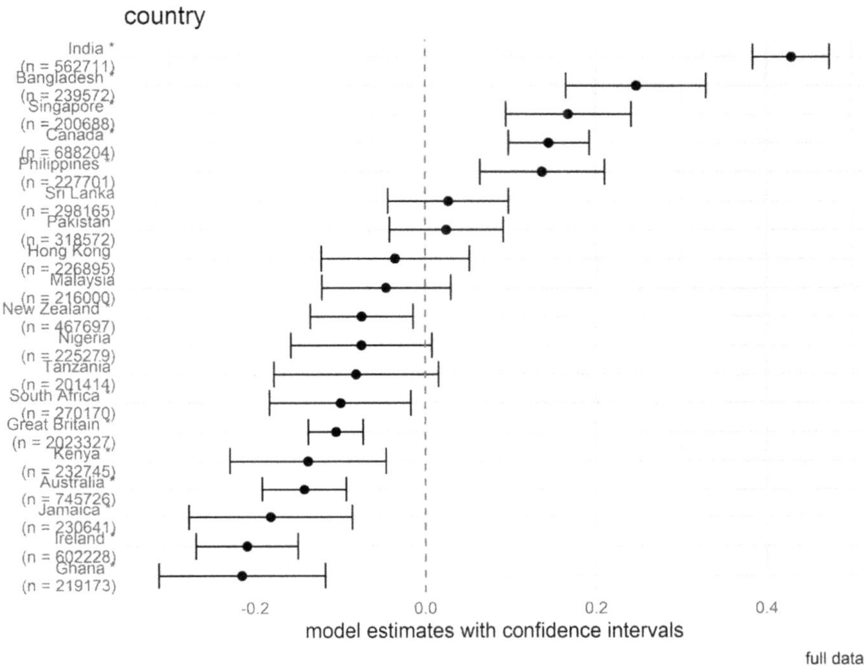

Figure 24 Predicted probability of GET-passives by country (full data).

(143) How much a dem new artiste yah woulda walk wid carton box wid dem records a sell inna sun-hot and nuh get discourage when pple throw piss pon u from dem gate? (GloWbE/Jamaica/general)
"How many of these new artists would have carried a carton box with their records and sold [them] in the heat and not get discouraged when people throw piss on them from their gates?"

In fact, Jamaicans may avoid the GET-passive because they associate it with JamC, a decidedly non-standardized variety with low overt prestige, and desire to use a more prestigious variant with *be* instead. A second explanation of the reduced use of *get* may be that its low frequency represents "some kind of a compromise" (Polinsky 2020: 141) between the different language systems that speakers of JamE use. In that sense, JamE speakers may "[minimize] less contrastive distinctions … in those instances where contrast is not important" (Polinsky 2020: 141) in the two language systems, quite similar to the heritage speakers reported in Polinsky (2020). Both hypotheses could be tested in future research.

In Chapter 7, we present an overview of the passive construction in the major languages spoken as L1s in the different GloWbE countries. It is interesting to observe whether this influence from substrate languages may explain some findings about country differences. The above observation about JamE and JamC may be one such case. Looking at others, the predicted higher probability of *get* in India and Bangladesh does not seem explainable through substrate influence from Hindi, Punjabi, or Bengali. These languages do not have a structure similar to the GET-passive; instead, their main passive is formed with an auxiliary verb corresponding to English *go* (Hoernlé 1880: 322; Beames 1891: 43–4; Tolstaya 1981: 47). If this was a strong factor, we would expect to observe the same tendency in Pakistan.

The substrate explanation is much more plausible for places in which one of the spoken languages features an adversative passive. In Singapore, for instance, the adversative KENA-passive, which relies on a Malay auxiliary, is commonly used in SingE (Bao & Wee 2003), and Singapore indeed is one of the countries where the probability of the GET-passive is predicted to be higher. Mandarin and Cantonese Chinese also have an adversative passive (Matthews & Yip 1994; Zhu & Huang 2023) that could promote the use of the GET-passive in Asian Englishes. This could also include HKE and MalE, but neither is statistically significantly different from the baseline United States. Similarly, Sinhala, spoken in Sri Lanka, has a passive construction using an equivalent of *get* as a passive auxiliary. However, this does not seem to promote the use of the GET-passive in SLE, perhaps because the passive construction is overall very rare in spoken Sinhala (Gunasekara [1891] 1999: 179).

Finally, in many African languages, especially in West Africa, as discussed in Section 7.8, passive meanings are not expressed through a separate verbal form but by utilizing an indefinite pronoun subject and an active verb. It seems plausible that the lack of parallels in their L1s makes African English speakers less prone to experimenting with the passive construction overall.

Our findings can be compared with previous statements about the relative preference of English varieties for the GET- versus BE-passive (cf. Section 2.3). Many scholars have suggested that the GET-passive is being accepted in the United States faster and more strongly than in Great Britain. Our findings rather support this, although the difference between the two countries is significant only in the full model ($\beta = -0.1051$, SE = 0.0165).

Previous studies find contrasting evidence with regard to the GET-passive in different varieties of English. Hundt, Dallas, and Nakanishi (2023), who fit a generalized mixed-model decision tree to passive data from ten ICE varieties of English, find that variety comes out as a statistically significant variable. However, the authors admit that the nodes of the decision tree cannot be interpreted in terms of known classifications into regions or Kachru's circles (Hundt, Dallas,

& Nakanishi 2023: 17). A look at the provided raw frequencies of GET-passives (Hundt, Dallas, & Nakanishi 2023: 12) suggests a very rough division into varieties with more GET-passive (NZE, IndE, CanE, and AusE, $N > 115$) and those with less GET-passive (HKE, BrE, SingE, PhE, IrE, and JamE, $N < 85$). Our model predictions show partly similar patterns but differ from these groupings in a number of prominent ways: we find SingE (and in the full model also PhE) to be among the top countries favoring *get*, while AusE (and in the full model also NZE) shows a lower probability of this innovative form. By contrast, while Hundt, Dallas, and Nakanishi (2023: 12) observe that JamE is among the varieties that use less GET-passives, Bruckmaier (2016: 132) claims, based on absolute token frequencies, that the GET-passive is more common in JamE than in BrE and SingE, which our model predictions plainly disagree with. Our study aligns, however, with Collins (1996), who found high numbers of the GET-passive in IndE (when compared to BrE, AmE, and AusE). Collins (1996: 54) explains this through IndE speakers' "striving for linguistic independence and identity."

Again, it is key to remember that our model predictions are calculated for all independent variables at the same time, and when observing any one variable, the effects of others are kept constant. Because of this, the predictions cannot be directly derived from or compared to any raw frequencies. This also explains the partly diverging results from the tendencies discussed in 10.2 based on descriptive counts that suggested that L1 varieties contain the most instances of the GET-passive. A likely factor driving this difference is the overall formality of a text, which we approximate with the F-measure (see Section 10.4.2). The predictions shown above for individual countries express probabilities for texts of the overall same level of formality. The fact that the model predicts such high probabilities of the GET-passive for India, for instance, while that country ranges in the middle in terms of proportions, as expressed in Figures 21 and 22, can probably be ascribed to the overall formality of IndE. Despite this formality, the GET-passive is well represented in the IndE component of GloWbE, leading to a very large positive coefficient associated with India.

After these general tendencies, which suggest some new directions for viewing regional variation in the passive alternation, it is time to look at the influence of other variables in GloWbE and their interplay with variety.

10.4.2 Formality: F-Measure

GloWbE does not contain a useful division into more or less formal genres, so we will use the F-measure (Heylighen & Dewaele 2002) alone as a measurement of text formality. An F-measure is calculated for each text (in GloWbE: web page) that contains a passive construction using the equation described in Chapter 8. The main effect of F-measure on the choice of passive auxiliary is significant at $p < 0.025$ in both models. The slopes are negative (β = -0.7042, SE = 0.0052 for the central, and β = -0.5421, SE = 0.0031 for the full model), which indicates lower log-odds for the GET-passive as the formality of a text increases. Through the interaction of the factor with country, we can observe how sensitive different varieties of English are to this condition. Figure 25 plots normalized F-values between -2 to 2. The stylistic range behind these numbers is illustrated in the following examples:

(144) A lawsuit aimed at busting the Jamaica Public Service's (JPS) monopoly on islandwide light and power distribution was filed Friday in the Supreme Court. (GloWbE/Jamaica/blog; F = 2.0)

(145) DON'T Draft, it ruins the race for everyone and you WILL get caught and DQ'd. (GloWbE/South Africa/blog; F = -2.0)

Starting with the central model, Figure 25 shows us a group of countries that differ from the baseline (United States) by containing fewer GET-passives across all levels of formality but significantly less so in more formal texts (on the right

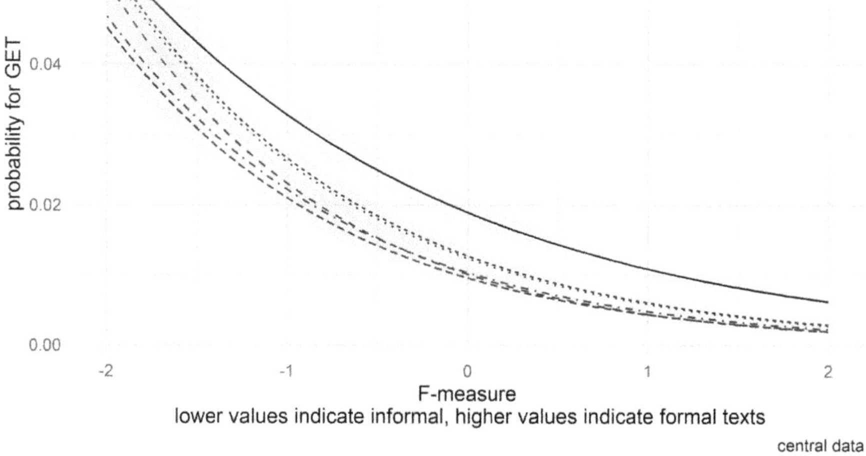

Figure 25 Predicted probability of GET-passives by country and F-measure (central data).

side of the graph). This is a group of L1 varieties plus Jamaica and Sri Lanka, where the GET-passive seems to be even more strongly than elsewhere a purely informal affair. It could be that JamE speakers are influenced by JamC, which also has a GET-passive (Winford 1993: 140–2), and may thus link it more to informality. Similarly, Sri Lankan-based speakers of Sinhala also have a passive relying on a translational equivalent of *get*, where the passive overall is only used in informal and spoken language (Gunasekara [1891] 1999: 179). In both cases, this might strengthen speakers' association of *get* with informality. This finding aligns with previous research on heritage speakers suggesting that bilingual speakers "tend to amplify properties that separate their two languages" (Polinsky 2020: 162). In the case of JamE and SLE, it may not be the mere existence of a similar GET-passive construction in the L1s JamC and Sinhala that prompts the stark contrast between informal and formal contexts in English, but the association of English *get* with informality that is amplified in both JamE and SLE.

Turning to the full model now, we see various tendencies in Figure 26. The first striking observation is that there is more variation between varieties in the informal end of the continuum (with a negative F-measure on the left), while formal texts (with a positive F-measure) more uniformly predict a low probability of *get*. Compared to the United States, the graph shows a higher predicted probability of *get* in informal texts for Bangladesh but then a steeper decline as formality increases for data points. India follows the same trajectory as the United States in terms of a decrease for formal texts but with an overall higher probability of *get*. Moreover, the model predicts that Hong Kong and Malaysia group together with a lower probability of *get* in informal texts and a comparable decrease in probability. Finally, Pakistan and Nigeria show the lowest predicted probabilities for *get* in informal texts, with a slightly attenuated decrease compared to the other countries shown here. These flatter lines suggest less distinction in the use of the GET-passive depending on register in Pakistan and Nigeria in the data analyzed here.

The remaining countries that significantly differ from the United States (Australia, Ireland, Jamaica, New Zealand, the Philippines, Singapore, and South Africa; see Figure 27) all show a similar pattern: for them, the model predicts an initially lower probability of *get* for informal texts and a slightly (Singapore, Philippines) or considerably (the rest) more pronounced decrease in probability with increasing formality. This is a similar patterning to what we see in Figure 25, with the same varieties showing relatively more avoidance for *get* in less informal texts. In the central model, the interaction between F-measure and country does not reach significance for Hong Kong, Malaysia, Singapore, Philippines, and South Africa.

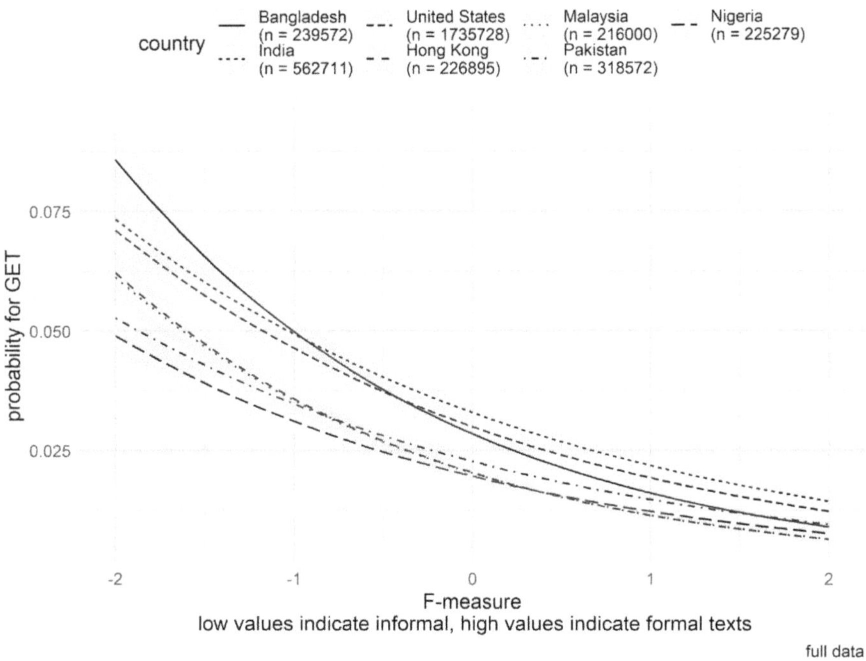

Figure 26 Predicted probability of GET-passives by country and F-measure (full data).

To sum up, all varieties show the general pattern that we already saw in COHA as well with more informal texts (i.e., with a lower F-score) favoring the GET-passive more. This functional distinction is less prominent than the baseline in a handful of L2 varieties: IndE, which has an above-average probability of *get*, and Nigeria and Pakistan (in the full model also Singapore and the Philippines), which have a below-average probability of *get*. In these varieties, there seems to be a somewhat weaker link between *get* and informality. On the other hand, there are a number of varieties—mostly L1 Englishes but also prominently BanglE—where the allocation of *get* to exclusively informal contexts is stronger than in the baseline AmE. Therefore, we can observe that register matters in the passive alternation in World Englishes as well, but this constraint is slightly less influential in the L2 varieties than the L1s. This idea aligns with the findings from COHA as well, where we saw a moderate weakening of the formality constraint in AmE over time.

10.4.3 Subject Responsibility

Analogous to the model fitted on passives found in COHA, we explore the effect of subject responsibility in GloWbE by evaluating the interaction between

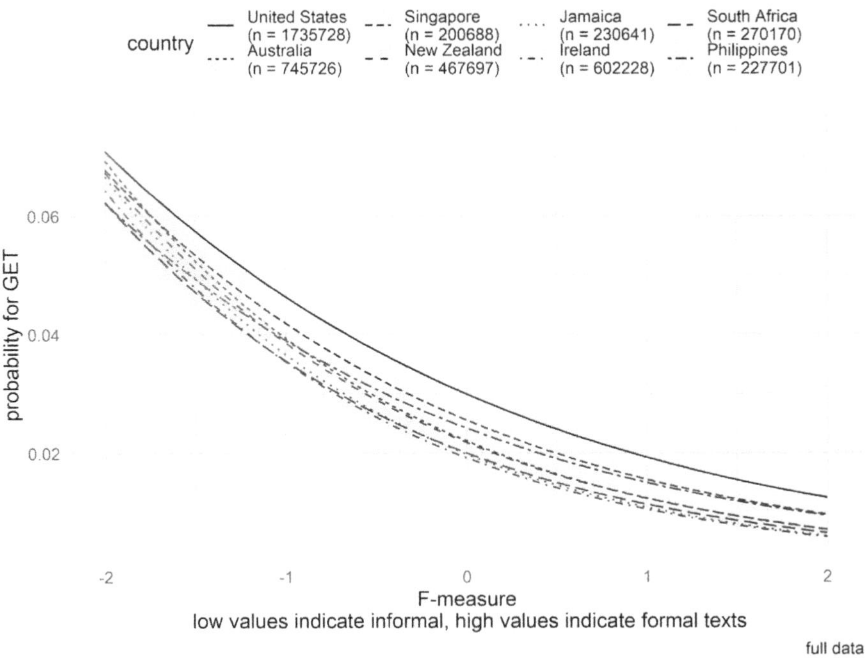

Figure 27 Predicted probability of GET-passives by country and F-measure (full data).

country and subject animacy as well as between country and the presence of a *by*-prepositional phrase.

10.4.3.1 Subject Animacy

Regarding subject animacy, the main effects of animate, inanimate, and body-part subjects compared to the baseline category unknown are significant at $p < 0.025$ in both models. Specifically, the negative slopes for inanimate ($\beta = -0.3666$, SE = 0.0155 for the central and $\beta = -0.2686$, SE = 0.0081 for the full model) and body-part referents ($\beta = -0.3488$, SE = 0.048 for the central and $\beta = -0.2136$, SE = 0.0236 for the full model) show a lower predicted probability of *get* for these categories, while the positive slope for animate referents ($\beta = 0.5114$, SE = 0.0151 for the central and $\beta = 0.3671$, SE = 0.0081 for the full model) implies higher log-odds for *get*. Additionally, the collective category is significant in the full model only with a negative slope, that is, with lower log-odds for *get* ($\beta = -0.0681$, SE = 0.0147). These general tendencies are very similar to the patterns detected in the model based on COHA. The finding of animate subjects favoring *get* and inanimates and body parts, along with collectives to a degree, preferring *be* seems robust across datasets. However, in the remainder of this

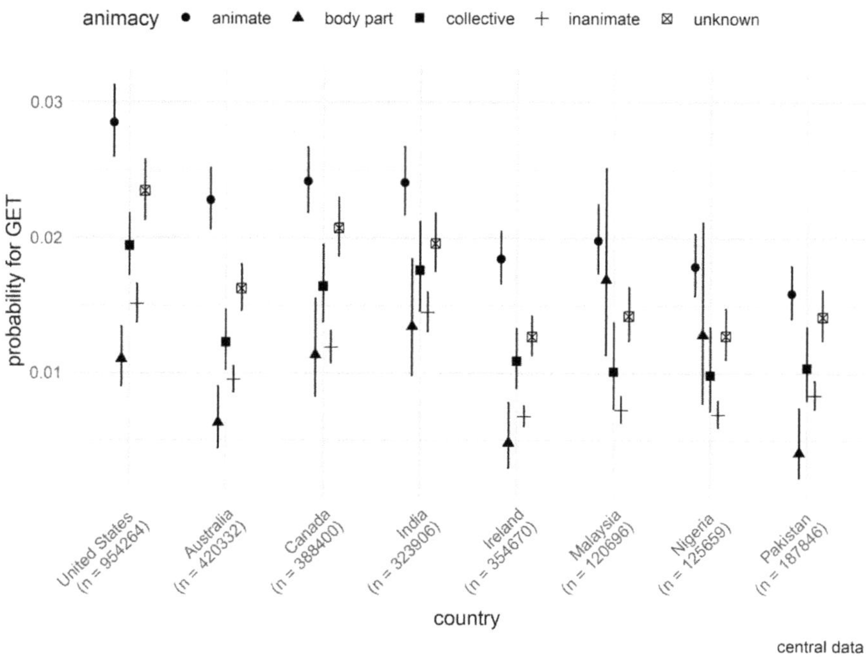

Figure 28 Predicted probability of GET-passives by country and animacy (central data).

section, we will observe whether some varieties of English do not follow these general trends and constraints or follow them to a more extreme degree than the average tendencies.

For the baseline country, the United States, all animacy categories are fairly clearly separated, with no overlap between their confidence intervals. In other varieties, animate referents are reliably associated with the highest predicted probability of *get*, while the differences between the other categories are often less pronounced. The overall order is similar for all countries, but the confidence intervals are larger for predictions for the minor categories of body parts and collectives, which often overlap with each other and inanimate, as well as for L2 varieties, due to fewer data points in these categories. Overall, of the many interactions considered, only a minority come out as statistically significantly different from the baseline.

Looking at some of these significant findings, India shows a unique lack of clear differentiation between animacy categories, especially in the full data (Figure 29). Inanimates and body parts show a heightened probability of *get*, and animate subjects show a lowered probability, which brings all the categories closer to one another. The Sri Lankan data show a similar pattern, but the predicted probability is lower across the board and only for animate subjects is

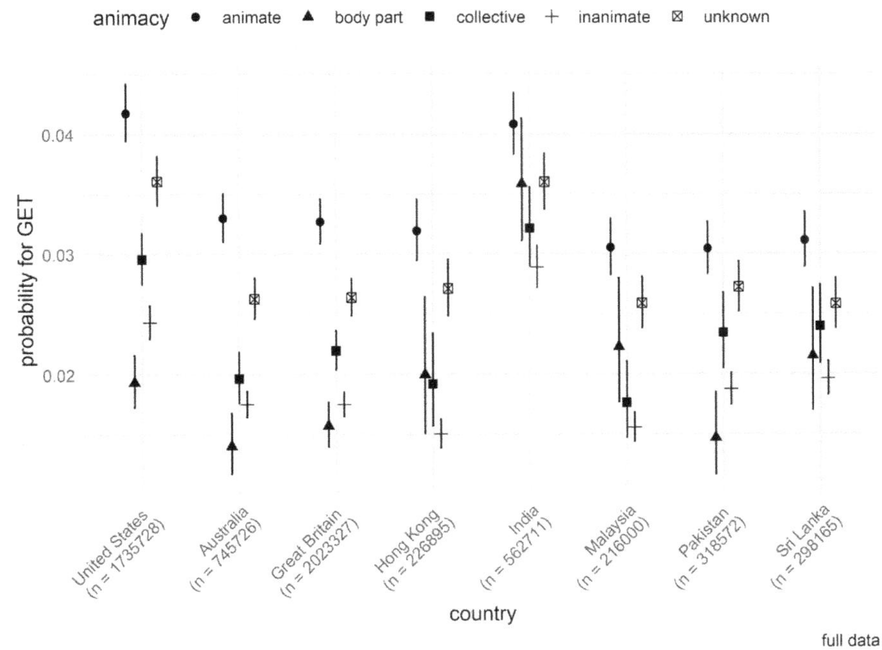

Figure 29 Predicted probability of GET-passives by country and animacy (full data).

$p < 0.025$. There seems to be something going on regarding animacy in the South Asian varieties: speakers of Pakistani English are less averse to choosing *get* as passive auxiliary with inanimate and collective subjects. The dislike of body-part subjects for *get*, which is very prominent in the COHA data (see Section 9.3.3.1), is particularly strong in the Australian, British, and Pakistani data (and absent in Indian and Malaysian data). Some L1 varieties (Australia and Great Britain in the full model and Australia and Ireland in the central model) show a strengthened tendency for the GET-passive to occur with primarily animate subjects.

In sum, the GloWbE data show the same overall tendencies for more *be* with inanimate and more *get* with animate subjects, in favor of the idea of subject responsibility being part of the semantic landscape of the GET-passive. This pattern is in some cases stronger in L1 varieties, whereas South Asian varieties display less sensitivity to this semantic constraint in the passive.

10.4.3.2 Prepositional Phrases with By

Overall, both models predict a lower probability of *get* when a prepositional phrase with *by* is present than when it is absent (β = -0.4304, SE = 0.009 for the central and β = -0.7542, SE = 0.0074 for the full model). This tendency is

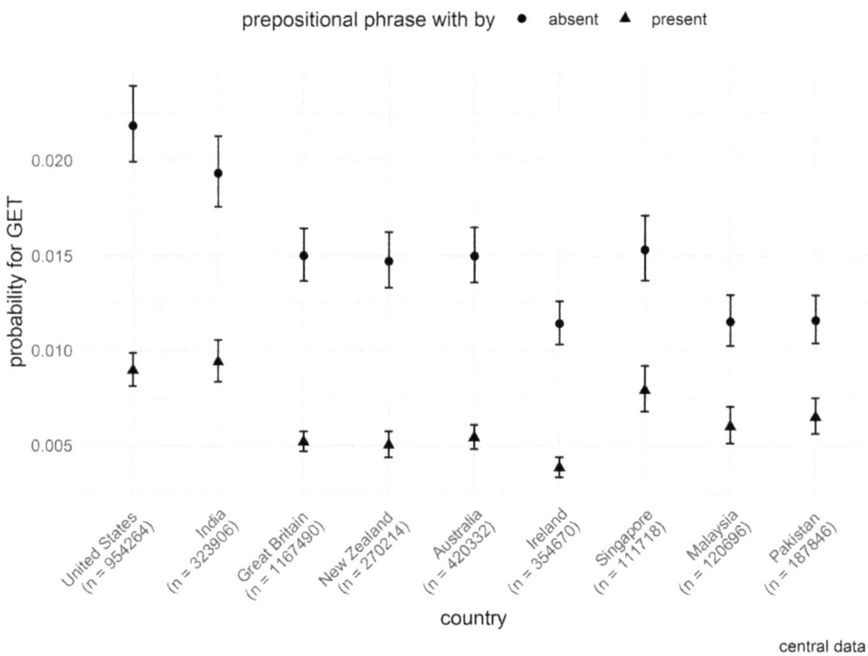

Figure 30 Predicted probability of GET-passives by country and *by*-PP (central data).

visible in all countries in the sample, so the significant interaction slopes only refer to differences in the magnitude of that difference. Overall, the differences between absent and present *by*-prepositional phrases are larger for the full data because the predicted probability of *get* is higher for sentences without a *by*-PP in the full data (Figure 31). While the difference in predicted probability of *get* depending on whether a *by*-prepositional phrase is absent versus present is the largest for the United States, it is considerably smaller especially for Singapore, Malaysia, and Pakistan in the central model (Figure 30). Like with the other variable connected to subject responsibility (animacy, discussed earlier), Asian L2 varieties seem to show a less strong adherence to the previously suggested and otherwise robust restrictions.

10.4.4 Adversativity versus Non-Neutrality

We will now test the hypothesis that the GET-passive is used for situations depicting adverse or non-neutral events by modeling sentiment scores for the main verb (non-neutrality from the point of view of the subject) and for the whole clause (non-neutrality from the point of view of the author). For more details on adversativity and the method of testing it, see Chapter 5. We will first

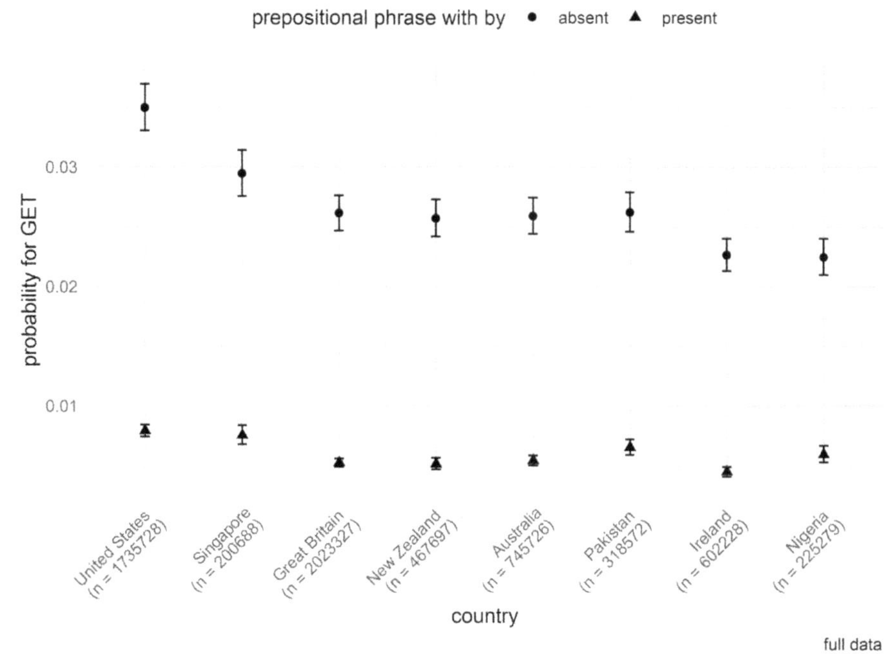

Figure 31 Predicted probability of GET-passives by country and *by*-PP (full data).

look at the narrower participle sentiments (10.4.4.1) and then the broader clause sentiments (10.4.4.2).

10.4.4.1 Participle Sentiment

In the central model, the baseline level (United States) is associated with a small negative effect of participle sentiment. In other words, the more positive the sentiment of the participle is, the lower the predicted probability of *get* is. The data points for Australia, New Zealand, and Ireland show a similar pattern. We see this in Figure 32, where observations on the left of the x-axis are participles expressing more negative sentiments, and those on the right are participles expressing more positive sentiments. However, the predicted probability of *get* is overall lower in these varieties than it is for the United States, especially in Ireland. Canada and Hong Kong both also show overall lower predicted probabilities for *get*, but their tendencies for participle sentiment are much more clearly negative, so for them, *get* is most likely with verbs expressing negative sentiments.

The remaining countries that emerge as significant in their interactions with participle sentiment all show positive tendencies (cf. Figure 33). While they all

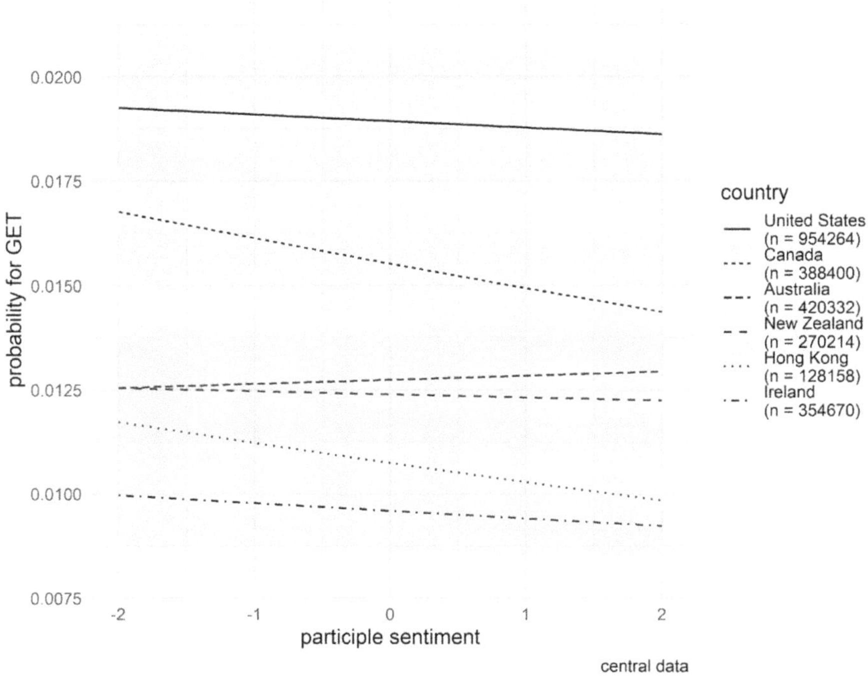

Figure 32 Predicted probability of GET-passives by country and participle sentiment (central data).

exhibit a lower predicted probability of *get* compared to the United States for negative sentiments, the positive tendency for India is so steep that the model predicts a higher probability of *get* for positive participles for India compared to the United States. The positive tendency for Kenya is similarly steep, but the initial probability of *get* for negative sentiments is the lowest in this group. The data points from Tanzania, Jamaica, and Nigeria cluster together and fall in between the predictions for India and Kenya, with less pronounced positive predictions.

In the full model, all significant interaction slopes with country and participle sentiment show an association between positive sentiments and a higher probability of *get* compared to negative sentiments (cf. Figure 34), so the model predicts that more positive sentiments are associated with a higher probability of *get* compared to negative sentiments. However, the steepness of these predicted trends differs: the predictions for Canada, the Philippines, New Zealand, Australia, Great Britain, and Ireland are almost parallel to those for the United States but are all lower overall. In contrast, Indian English is predicted to have a similar probability of *get* for negative participles when contrasted with

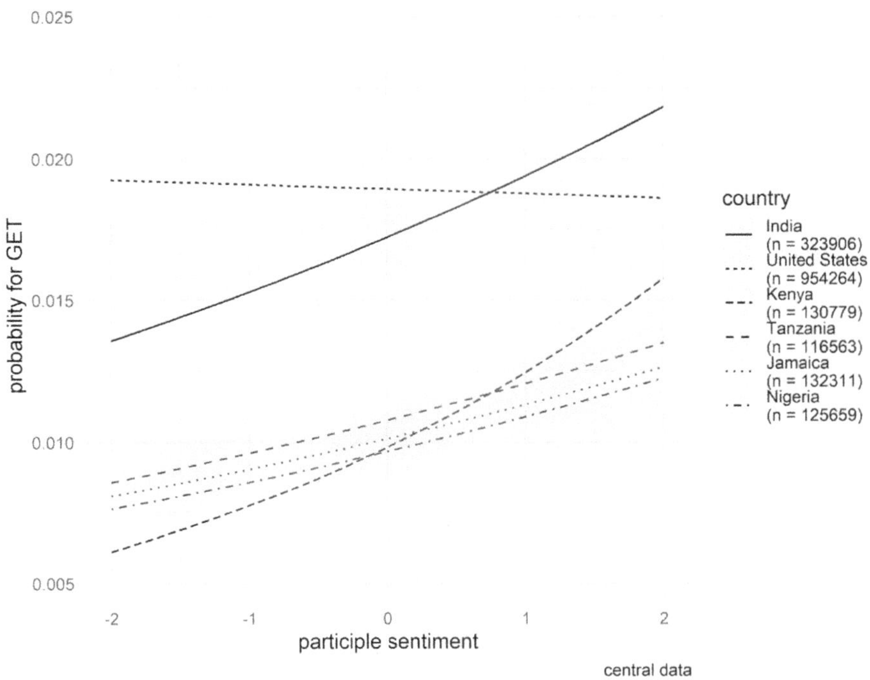

Figure 33 Predicted probability of GET-passives by country and participle sentiment (central data).

AmE, but the predicted increase for IndE is much steeper. The predictions for Kenya follow a similar trajectory, but the initial probability of *get* is the lowest among the significant countries.

We also included a quadratic term for participle sentiment in our models, under the assumption that—should non-neutrality be the decisive feature of the GET-passive (Coto Villalibre 2015)—a U-shaped effect would emerge with lowest predicted probabilities around zero and higher ones with an increasing distance from zero. While there is a significant effect for the quadratic term in both models, it only introduces slight curvature to the linear trends observed earlier. As such, we refrain from discussing it here any further and note that, from the perspective of the sentence subject, there is no strong evidence to suggest non-neutrality of the situation plays a role.

10.4.4.2 Clause Sentiment

Regarding the clause-level sentiment, *get* is always predicted to be least likely in neutral compared to positive or negative contexts in the central model (cf. Figure 35), but the magnitude and direction of the effect varies for some

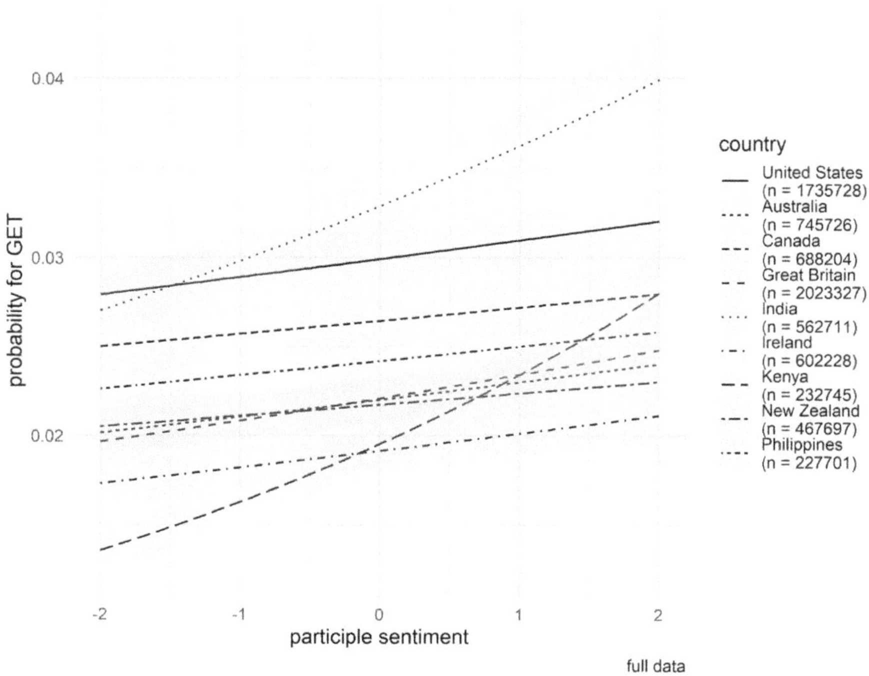

Figure 34 Predicted probability of GET-passives by country and participle sentiment (full data).

countries. For the United States, Canada, Singapore, and the Philippines, *get* is slightly more likely to be associated with negative compared to positive clause sentiment. For Bangladesh and Pakistan, this tendency is reversed, and the probability of *get* is much higher for positive compared to negative contexts. This is true to a lesser extent for Nigeria and Ghana, whereas the model predicts similar probabilities for *get* for positive and negative sentiments for Australia and Great Britain.

The model on the full data predicts a lower probability of *get* in neutral compared to negative or positive clauses for all countries with a significant interaction slope (cf. Figure 36). It predicts that negative clauses are associated more strongly with *get* than positive ones for the United States, Singapore, and Malaysia, and, to a lesser extent, for Canada, the Philippines, Australia, and New Zealand. The reverse prediction, that positive contexts favor *get*, is visible for Bangladesh and less strongly for Pakistan, Tanzania, Nigeria, and Kenya. Therefore, the GET-passive is predicted to be more likely to occur in negative over positive over neutral contexts for most of the countries discussed here, but the strongest finding is the non-neutrality of the GET-passive across all varieties.

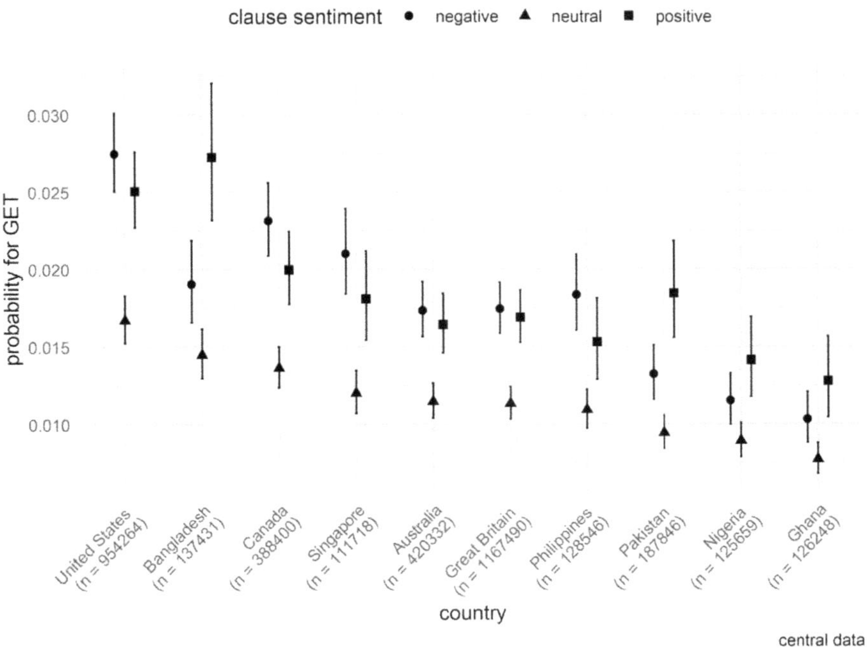

Figure 35 Predicted probability of GET-passives by country and clause sentiment (central data).

Additionally, some L2 varieties show the unexpected tendency of positive sentences having the highest probability of *get*.

10.4.5 Verb Semantics

This section will investigate whether different semantic groups of verbs display different preferences regarding the passive in the GloWbE, relying again on distributional semantic clustering as described in Chapter 6. The verbal groups are created anew for the GloWbE data, so the findings are not directly comparable to those based on COHA, discussed in Section 9.3.5. Our clustering divided the GloWbE data into eleven clusters, which we labeled based on their shared semantic properties (see Chapter 6 for all the clusters). The cluster containing most observations, verbs of TRANSFER AND PRODUCTION, such as *created*, *produced*, *transported*, and *carried*, is used as the baseline. The model estimates for different clusters are visualized in Figures 37 and 38. Positive values (on the right) indicate a higher probability of *get*, while negative values (on the left) signal a preference for *be*. Interactions with country are not considered for this variable because the model would be highly complex to run and interpret.

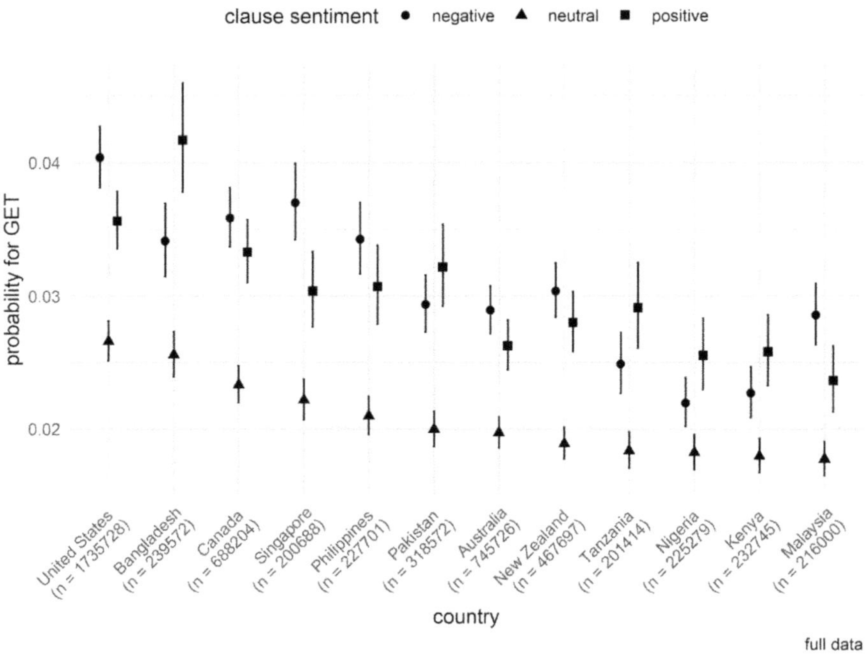

Figure 36 Predicted probability of GET-passives by country and clause sentiment (full data).

In the model run on the full data, five out of ten clusters show a probability of *get* that is higher than the baseline, while for the remaining five clusters, a stronger preference for *be* is predicted (cf. Figure 37). The clusters favoring *get* include the two CHANGE OF STATE clusters and the two depicting DISRUPTIVE IMPACT. Verbs depicting a CHANGE OF STATE (INDUSTRIAL OR SCIENTIFIC), such as *fixed*, *classified*, *inflated*, and *purified*, are associated with the highest positive estimate. This cluster is followed by the clusters DISRUPTIVE IMPACT (LOWER FREQUENCY), with verbs like *corrected*, *overwritten*, *pestered*, and *lynched*, and CHANGE OF STATE (HOUSEHOLD AND WORKPLACE), with verbs like *substituted*, *cooked*, *accepted*, and *hired*. The slopes for clusters PHYSICAL INTERACTION (MINOR IMPACT), containing verbs such as *crammed*, *cleaned*, *picked*, and *brushed*, and DISRUPTIVE IMPACT, with verbs such as *swallowed*, *diverted*, *tackled*, and *massacred*, are only weakly positive. These are the types of verbs that are more likely to occur in the GET-passive.

The five remaining clusters have negative slopes and predict a higher-than-average likelihood of *be*. One group with a slightly negative slope is the cluster CHANGE OF POSITION AND VALUE (e.g., *put*, *cut*, *increased*, and *shared*). The two more formal clusters, named ADMINISTRATION (with verbs like *issued*,

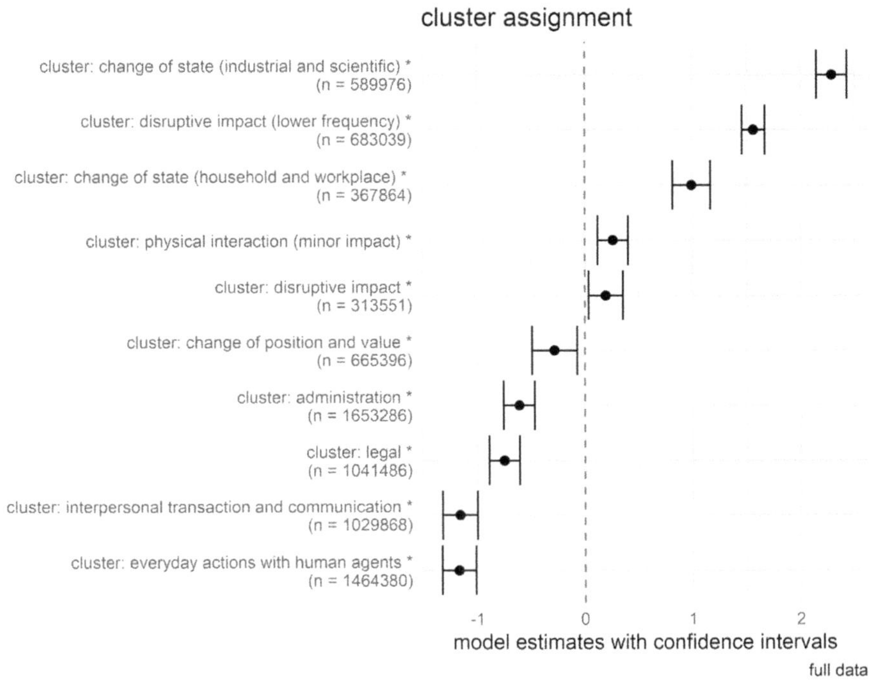

Figure 37 Model estimates for GET-passives by semantic verb clusters (full data).

stated, *named*, and *credited*) and LEGAL (including *saved*, *judged*, *documented*, and *denied*), have fairly similar negative slopes. The two final clusters, INTERPERSONAL TRANSACTION AND COMMUNICATION (such as *confirmed*, *sold*, *seized*, and *advertised*) and EVERYDAY ACTIONS WITH HUMAN AGENTS (including *met*, *asked*, *said*, *invited*), are predicted to have the strongest negative slopes and, therefore, the least association with *get*.

In the potentially tidier central model, the same five clusters are associated with positive slopes as in the central model; they are only ordered slightly differently (cf. Figure 38). Both clusters that relate to DISRUPTIVE IMPACT have similar model estimates and clearly favor *get* compared to the baseline. The slopes for the two CHANGE OF STATE clusters are also similar to one another. The final cluster to favor *get* is the cluster PHYSICAL INTERACTION (MINOR IMPACT).

Regarding the negative slopes, there are now only three clusters that are linked to a lower probability with *get*. These are the clusters of INTERPERSONAL TRANSACTION AND COMMUNICATION, EVERYDAY ACTIONS WITH HUMAN AGENTS, and CHANGE OF POSITION AND VALUE. Two clusters (LEGAL and ADMINISTRATION) no longer show a significant difference from the baseline.

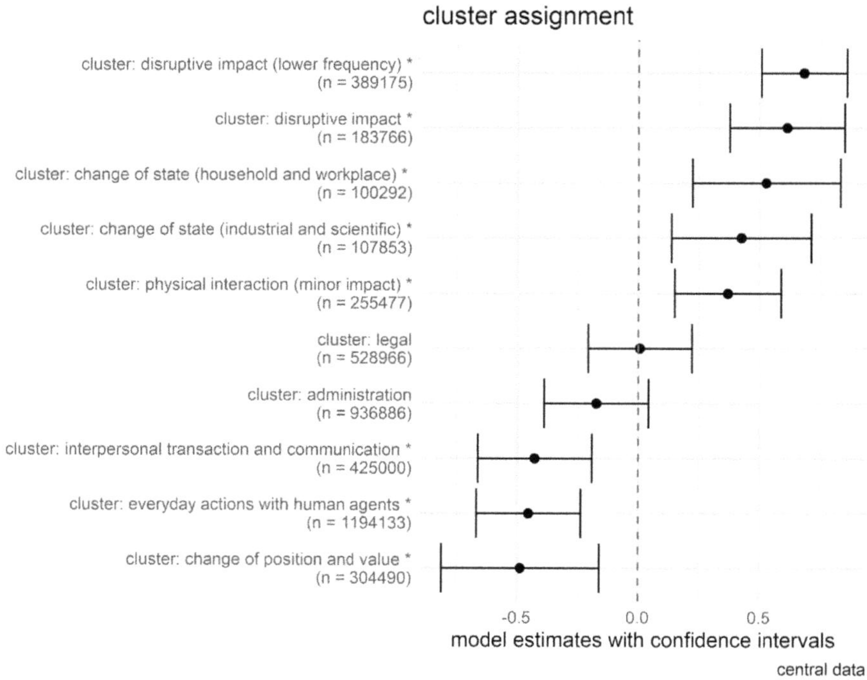

Figure 38 Model estimates for GET-passives by semantic verb clusters (central data).

Overall, the data from GloWbE show more potential than COHA did (cf. Section 9.3.5) for explaining the choice of the passive auxiliary in relation to semantic verb groups. This could be related to the larger size of the GloWbE dataset and the scarcity of GET-passives with different verbs in the older COHA data. In the central model based on GloWbE, eight out of ten clusters show a tendency that is significantly different from the baseline.

The passive with *get* occurs particularly with verbs of different kinds of change and disruption: situations where the passive subject is altered or attacked. The passive with *be* is chosen with everyday verbs and verbs of communication and position, and in the full dataset, also verbs of more technical and formal nature. In both datasets, ADMINISTRATION verbs tend to favor *be*, and HOUSEHOLD verbs favor *get*.

10.4.6 Morpho-syntax

In this section, we will test the potential influence of a number of morpho-syntactic factors on the choice of the passive auxiliary to see whether the GET-passive occurs in similarly syntactically varied and complex contexts as the BE-passive or whether we find structural constraints on the use of the newer variant. In most cases, there is no specific hypothesis to explore beyond the general idea of structural complexity favoring *be*, but we compare our findings to previous studies when relevant. We do not include an interaction between country and these morpho-syntactic variables in our model, so we will be observing the overall tendencies in these web-based synchronic data rather than looking for differences across varieties.

10.4.6.1 Negation

In both models, the slopes for polarity are positive and statistically significant, so both models agree on a higher predicted probability of *get* in negated sentences ($\beta = 0.1419$, SE = 0.0071 for the central and $\beta = 0.0814$, SE = 0.0046). This finding differs from our results based on the COHA dataset, where the interaction between year and polarity reached statistical significance only in the full model but not in the smaller tidier central model (Figure 12), and from Fehringer's (2022: 16) results, suggesting that negation does not play a role in choice of *be* versus *get* in the passive construction. Note, moreover, that the slope is tilted in the unexpected direction if we assume *get* to favor syntactic simplicity: sentences with an additional negator (see Examples (146) and (147)) have a higher probability of *get* in GloWbE.

(146) the idea that artists didn't get paid anything is a myth. artists DEFINITELY made more before than they are now. (GloWbE/Jamaica/blog)

(147) Fees for excess luggage cannot be paid online. (GloWbE/Ireland/general)

10.4.6.2 Tense, Aspect, and Modality

We investigate how the use of different tense and aspectual forms and modal auxiliaries affects the choice of passive auxiliary. The baseline is the simple present form. Positive values on the x-axis represent a higher likelihood for *get*, and negative values represent a higher likelihood for *be*. The relative ordering as well as the direction of slopes for all the considered more complex forms are the same in both the full and the central model based on GloWbE (cf. Figures 39 and 40), so these can be discussed together. The slopes for gerund or nonfinite *-ing* and the *to*-infinitive are very similar and suggest the strongest preference for the GET-passive, followed by present progressive and past progressive forms, and finally, present perfect forms, which weakly favor *get*. Modal + infinitive constructions and preterite forms, on the other hand, have small negative slopes, while modal + perfect constructions strongly and past perfect forms very strongly disfavor *get*.

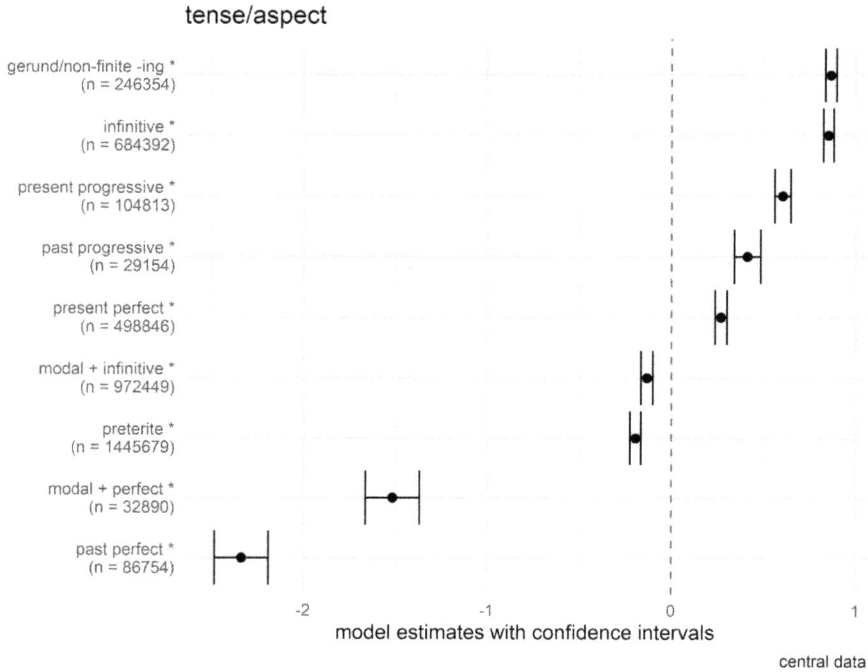

Figure 39 Model estimates for GET-passives by tense/aspect (central data).

These results are strikingly similar to the findings in COHA, further underlining the fact that what we find are stable tendencies independent of the specific data used. The most favorable contexts for *get* are nonfinite forms such as gerunds and *to*-infinitives, as well as the present progressive (even more so earlier than now). In contrast, and in line with previous studies (Schwarz 2017: 317; Fehringer 2022: 11), the past perfect is the most reluctant to take *get*, followed by combinations with modal verbs and the preterite.

10.4.6.3 Adverb

An intervening adverb between auxiliary and participle is thought to add complexity to a sentence and to disfavor *get* (Carter & McCarthy 1999: 53; Xiao, McEnery, & Qian 2006: 116). Moreover, the adverb may take the focus away from the subject or patient, which is thought to be a distinctive characteristic of GET-passives (Xiao, McEnery, & Qian 2006: 116).

Both models agree on negative slopes, that is, lower probabilities for *get* in sentences with an adverb than those without one. The slope is much larger for the central model (β = -0.5607, SE = 0.0172) compared to the full model (β = -0.0986,

SE = 0.0049). These results are in line with the findings from the COHA data. In that corpus, the absence of an intervening adverb is associated with a higher probability of *get* throughout, and this tendency strengthens over time.

10.4.6.4 Nonfinite Complement Phrases with To

As a final morpho-syntactic feature, nonfinite complement phrases with *to* have been suggested to only appear with *be* (Xiao, McEnery, & Qian 2006: 112). Verbs that can select nonfinite constructions and occur with such complements, such as *to pay* (*somebody to do something*), are more likely to be verbal, while verbs that do not select nonfinite complements and occur with such, for instance, *to paint*, are said to be more adjectival. Examples of the verbal type with each of the auxiliaries are presented below as (148) and (149).

(148) Would you like to get paid to WRITE? (GloWbE/Australia/general)

(149) Hey you Josh Rogin, the real question is how much you have been paid to write this utterly garbage piece! (GloWbE/US/general)

Both the full and the central models suggest a lower probability of *get* in sentences containing *to*-complement phrases (β = -0.2664, SE = 0.007 for the central and β = -0.2078, SE = 0.0045). This finding aligns with the COHA findings for both models and dovetails with previous assumptions that nonfinite complements are more likely to co-occur with *be* (Xiao, McEnery, & Qian 2006: 112).

10.4.7 Persistence

We additionally checked whether the model predicts a higher probability of *get* in the current sentence if this variant is used in the preceding sentence in the same text. This variable allows us to establish the role of persistence (Szmrecsanyi 2006), which can be described as a priming effect (as commonly investigated in cognitive linguistics research; see, e.g., Levelt & Kelter 1982; Bock 1986; Bock & Loebell 1990; Branigan, Pickering, & Cleland 2000; Tamminga 2016; Clark 2018). Here, however, we study this phenomenon in naturalistic production rather than experiments (as in, e.g., Sankoff & Laberge 1978; Poplack 1980; Gries 2005; Weiner & Labov 1983; Estival 1985).

In terms of the slopes for persistence, both models suggest large effects—the predicted probability of *get* is much higher when the previous token was also *get* (β = 0.8049, SE = 0.0054 for the central and β = 0.7018, SE = 0.0036). Language users, therefore, show behavior that Szmrecsanyi (2006: 1) would describe as "inertial." These effects are similar to the findings of our COHA model, where

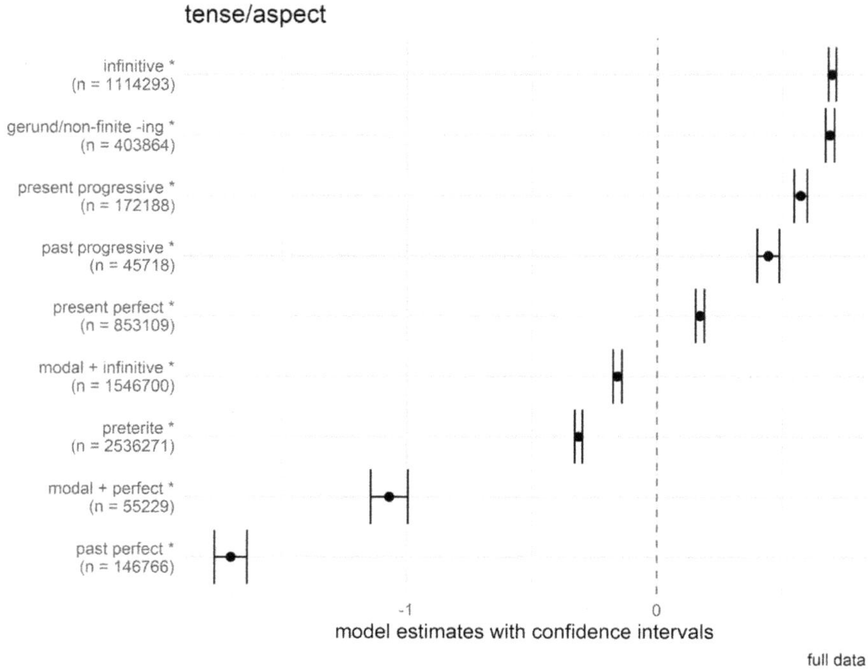

Figure 40 Model estimates for GET-passives by tense/aspect (full data).

the realization of the preceding passive with *get* is also associated with an increase in the predicted probability of *get* in the current token, even though this persistence effect weakens over time.

10.4.8 Probability of Central Passives

Finally, the full model suggests a large positive estimate for the effect of a token being a central passive ($\beta = 1.5159$, SE = 0.0123). In other words, the higher the probability of a token being a central passive, the higher the probability of *get*. These results are in line with the tendencies shown in the COHA data, where GET-passives were also predicted to be more likely with more central as opposed to more adjectival passives. Our interpretation is identical with the one presented in Section 9.3.8: it is the full, eventive passives that provide the most fertile ground for the *get* variant to be realized. Thus, delineating the variable context, while far from trivial in the case of the passive alternation, is worth the effort, and wherever the full and central models disagree, it is the latter whose output should be prioritized.

11

Discussion and Conclusion

The preceding chapters have laid out our method and statistical analysis in detail. At this point, it is time to take stock of what the analysis has yielded. What is the status of the passive alternation in Present-Day English? Is it "one of the most active grammatical changes taking place in English" (Weiner & Labov 1983: 43) or merely a "discourse phenomenon [not] involved in any direct grammatical changes in the past century" (Mair & Leech 2020: 268)? Of the many proposed and often contested restrictions that apply to the GET-passive, which ones stand up to large-scale empirical investigation? Can a study based on the kind of big corpus data we have developed in the preceding chapters shed new light on the dynamics of the alternation, including its spread across varieties of English?

In addition to addressing these questions in relation to the English passive, we take the opportunity in this chapter to reflect on our methodological choices and the promises, pitfalls, and intricacies of computational and machine-learning approaches in studying language variation. The efforts involved in extracting and delimiting the data, in operationalizing the predictor variables, and in statistical modeling have been considerable. It is worth considering which of these efforts were justified, how future research might draw on them, and also where problems for a fully automated approach remain.

11.1 Investigating the Passive Alternation

The linguistic phenomenon this book has engaged with is the English passive construction, particularly the choice between *be* and *get* as the auxiliary verb, that is, the passive alternation. There is a rich previous literature on the English passive, but most studies have tended to rely on small samples of handcoded data or, in the early days of scholarship, even on the researcher's native-speaker intuitions and invented examples only. In Chapter 2, we have argued that a central desideratum in research on the passive alternation is to make the claims proposed by various authors about constraints operationalizable to empirical testing. The present project now incorporates most of the suggested patterns and restrictions on the GET-passive in the same multivariate statistical model and runs it on a large set of automatically annotated data. Thus, we are able to examine the influence of these variables on the passive alternation simultaneously, in interaction, and on a robust quantitative basis in a way that has rarely been done before (see Fehringer 2022; Hundt, Dallas, & Nakanishi 2023 for two exceptions that employ a comparable method but on much smaller datasets). We have provided two case studies on the English passive alternation: one diachronic and one synchronic.

A complication that any study of the English passive must address is the difficulty of distinguishing passive constructions from formally similar structures that do not carry a passive meaning. A past participle following *be* or *get* can carry a more adjectival than verbal meaning, giving the clause a stative or inchoative reading. In between the fully verbal (passive) and fully adjectival (nonpassive) interpretations lies a gray area of sentences with some semantic nuances from both directions, which has inspired grammarians to posit that the passive is a continuum (Svartvik 1966: 156; Quirk et al. 1985: 167). Previous studies have relied on manual data sorting, with the researcher(s) choosing criteria and then applying those to separate "true" or "central" passives from other instances that show more or less commonality with the passive. In addition, there are a number of common, idiomatic constructions with the same form as the GET-passive but some idiosyncratic, nonpassive meaning (e.g., *get started*, *get involved*, *get stuck*, etc.) that must be excluded from a study of the passive alternation.

This issue and our solution were tackled in Chapter 3. As a first step, we excluded manually and categorically this handful of frequent verbs that show idiomatic active meanings with *get*. Subsequently, we chose a two-pronged approach. We argued that the remaining participles form a continuum without an absolute cut-off point between passives and nonpassives, so we modeled all these participles in our "full" models. However, we also wanted to establish a tidier dataset with fewer marginal members of the class "passive," constituting our "central" data. Our automated approach for distinguishing participles between central and noncentral relied on training a logistic regression model based on a sample of manually coded sentences, with predictor variables both at the type level of the participle (such as how frequently it occurs in coordination with adjectives or is premodified by adverbs in the corpus on the whole) and at the level of the individual clause (such as the presence or absence of adverbial premodification and a *by*-prepositional phrase).

Our rationale for working with the centrality measure was twofold. First, the extent to which the full and the central model for each corpus agree serves as an indicator of how much the full data are affected by noise. We generally place greater trust in the central model, as this one adopts a stricter definition of the variable context. Any divergences between the full and the central model would indicate a potentially problematic level of instability in the statistical analysis. Here, our findings are encouraging. For both COHA and GloWbE, there are very few differences in terms of significance and direction of effects. Of the ones that we do find, most can be attributed to greater statistical power of the full data and the loss of entire participle clusters in the central data. Taken together, however, the full and central model for each corpus tell very much the same story of linguistic variation.

The second way in which we draw on the centrality measure is by using it (or, to be precise, the probability of an observation being a true passive) as a predictor in the full model itself. Doing so has provided an important insight, especially in the diachronic perspective. As Section 9.3.8 has shown, there is a clear difference in productivity of the GET-passive between central and less central clauses. It is in the former in particular, that is, in those cases where there is true competition with *be*, that the change toward the GET-passive is at its most virulent. This finding both adds justification to our choice of modeling centrality and highlights the need to carefully define the variable context so as to get a reliable picture of developments in the English passive. The better pseudo-R^2 statistics of model fit for the central data in both studies corroborate this impression.

Before contextualizing findings relating to individual constraints and their operationalizations, it is also worth pointing out that the results from the two case studies together inspire confidence in the modeling procedure. All predictors that were included in the COHA and the GloWbE analysis, from agency to sentiment to grammatical constraints, are shown to have highly similar effects in both studies. It should be noted that there is no overlap between the material included in the two corpora, and, as such, there is no inherent reason the models should be in agreement to this extent. That they are, we propose, should be interpreted as evidence that the findings generalize beyond each individual corpus to the wider population of English speakers and writers.

With our confidence in the model output thus established, we now discuss the effect of individual predictors. In the following section, we aim to provide the joint perspective that emerges from both case studies and to organize the discussion around hypothesized characteristics of the passive alternation rather than strictly by individual predictor.

11.2 Our Findings: A Bird-Eye View

Our studies provide additional support to a number of claims about the GET-passive that have been made repeatedly in previous literature. These include particularly its increasing frequency over time and its association with informal language and with the semantic properties of subject responsibility and non-neutrality. In addition to that, we also explore verb semantics, syntactic constraints, and what role persistence and probability for central passives play in the adoption of *be* versus *get*, as well as differences between varieties of English.

First of all, the rise of the GET-passive and the concurrent dramatic decline of the BE-passive is a widely documented phenomenon that our data unambiguously support. Irrespective of which conditioning variable we observe in interaction with year in COHA, we see the probabilities of *get* ascend in the course of time in all our models. The BE-passive still represents the overwhelming majority of all observed instances in both corpora, but the GET-passive is more than a marginal variant. It appears implausible to treat the significant increase of the GET-passive, especially in the twentieth century, as merely an epiphenomenon of the colloquialization of written English (Mair & Leech 2020: 268). The models for COHA show an increase in even the most informal texts, and almost all interactions between year and other predictors reach significance, demonstrating that the passive alternation is itself undergoing change over time rather than simply spreading from one type of genre to another. In the following, we will discuss our findings concerning which conditions particularly favor the spread of the GET-passive and which resist it.

Formality has always played and continues to play a role: informal texts are much more likely to contain a GET-passive than formal ones. However, over time, the influence of formality has slightly decreased. Whereas in the oldest data from the early and mid-nineteenth century, the GET-passive practically only occurred in informal texts, this is no longer the case. Some varieties of English (five in the central model and seven in the full model, including both Australasian L1 Englishes) still seem to show an aversion toward the GET-passive in more formal texts. The opposite tendency of less register differentiation is found in three L2 varieties: Nigeria and Pakistan show an overall lower probability for *get*, while India shows a higher probability. When comparing specific genres in American English, it is journalistic writing in magazines and newspapers that shows the most increase in the use of *get* in the past decades. This fits with the idea that press texts adapt to changes in the surrounding speech community more readily (cf. Hundt & Mair 1999) and journalistic writing is undergoing a process of colloquialization (Leech et al. 2009: 239). The fact that, while controlling for the formality of the individual text, these two genres of journalistic writing overtake the fiction and movie data with regard to likelihood of *get* is certainly an interesting finding that attests to the increasing acceptance of the GET-passive even in contexts that are subject to editorial oversight and revision. In order to operationalize the formality of any individual text, we relied on the F-measure (Heylighen & Dewaele 2002), which is easily applicable to any large PoS-tagged dataset as it is based on proportions of different word classes in a text. Judging from our findings, this method seems to function well as a proxy for formality, even in diachronic data and diverse varieties of English with different contexts of acquisition and use.

Furthermore, the GET-passive has been associated in the literature with the concept of subject responsibility: the idea that the passive subject may bear some responsibility for what happens to them in the passive sentence. We operationalized this concept via two testable variables—subject animacy and the presence of a *by*-PP—and both of them in both corpora point in the direction of subject responsibility playing a role in the selection of a passive auxiliary. If the subject referent is capable of carrying some of the responsibility, by virtue of being animate, *get* is favored as a passive auxiliary. However, this semantic constraint has been slightly weakening over time. The different varieties of English examined show the same overall preference for *get* with animate subjects and *be* with inanimate subjects and aversion to *get* in passive constructions that contain *by*-PPs. But the number of GET-passives is rising, even and particularly with inanimate subjects. So in summary, our findings support the idea of the GET-passive indicating subject responsibility, but by no means is this semantic feature present in all passive sentences with *get*. South Asian varieties show these patterns less strongly, and there seems to be less differentiation and fewer semantic constraints in the use of the passive there, while some L1 varieties display a strengthened preference for the GET-passive to pair with animate subjects. Both datasets also concur in the tendencies they show for the minor subject categories: body parts show the highest probability for the BE-passive, and human collectives place themselves in between animate and inanimate categories but still rather favor *be*. These findings invite further studies with finer subdivisions of animacy categories. A qualitative investigation could reveal if body parts as passive subjects are used, for instance, metaphorically in place of inanimates or meronymically in place of animates. Also the need for publicly available animacy dictionaries became obvious in the course of the project, although type-level classifications are convoluted by polysemy and figurative language use.

Another oft-cited semantic feature of the GET-passive is its usage in sentences depicting non-neutral or often adverse events. This constraint is one of the more hotly debated ones in the literature, with two competing hypotheses: the traditional notion of adversativity—that the event in the passive clause is negative—and the idea of non-neutrality (Coto Villalibre 2015). Previous efforts to tease apart these two hypotheses have been hamstrung by their methodological approaches: usually small datasets of a few hundred observations coded impressionistically, and often without a clear differentiation made between emotional involvement of the sentence producer versus the clause subject.

Our approach was able to shed new light on formerly proposed restrictions. This was done by using two different methods for gauging sentiment: a traditional dictionary-based approach for detecting sentiment at the level of the verbal participle and supervised machine-learning for measuring sentiment in the larger syntactic unit. We suppose that the clause sentiment reflects the point of view of the speaker or writer rather than the grammatical subject if the two differ in stance. Our results suggest that the GET-passive is indeed associated with more emotional sentences, but this includes both positive and negative sentiments. Therefore, it is more accurate to call the GET-passive non-neutral than adversative. The model for COHA, further, does not provide support for the notion that this constraint is leveling out. Only the interaction between year and negative clauses emerges as significant and with a positive sign. While this means that, over time, negative sentences are predicted to be even more likely environments for *get*, the size of the coefficient is quite small and should not be accorded too much importance.

The non-neutral flavor of GET-passive becomes apparent when exploring the different varieties of English. In AmE, a link between *get* and adverse sentiment could hardly be found when examining the lexical verb alone but was clearly present when considering sentiment in the whole surrounding clause. The described patterns are quite stable over time and largely also across varieties of English. Regarding verb-level sentiment, a number of varieties of English (most significantly IndE and KenE) show a significantly higher probability for *get* with positive verbal participles. At the clause level, three other L2 varieties (BanglE, PakE, and TanzE) predict positive contexts to favor *get*, while most varieties rather associate it with negative clauses. In several Outer Circle varieties of English, the GET-passive has a positive prosody of indicating beneficial events.

For all varieties considered, however, it is the neutral clauses that are predicted to have the lowest probabilities of *get*, and this difference reaches statistical significance for all varieties.

In addition to these interesting findings, our study opens new theoretical and methodological ground in the adversativity question, being the first to try to tease apart participle versus clause sentiment and applying machine-learning methods to combine sentiment analysis with sociolinguistics. We resist the temptation to interpret the better predictive power of clause-level sentiment over participle-level sentiment to mean that it is really the sentence producer's sentiment that matters for the passive alternation. The problem with this interpretation is that the two methods are not equal in terms of sophistication and information to draw on, and the clause-level predictor has an a priori better chance of being attuned to fine-grained linguistic context. At this stage, we consider our attempt to disentangle subject sentiment from speaker or writer sentiment as a promising first step that warrants further attention. In more general terms, using sentiment scores as predictor variables to model the behavior of a linguistic dependent variable is an approach that can and, we argue, should be replicated in analyses of other sociolinguistic phenomena as well.

In our synchronic study, we compared the passive across twenty varieties of English worldwide. In discussing the findings, one may consider regional patterns, type of variety (L1 vs. L2), and potential substrate influence as possible explaining factors. Regarding the question of which varieties use the GET-passive the most, the literature has not provided clear answers so far. Findings have been inconclusive or sometimes even contradictory—with the exception of the consistent finding that American English is more open to the GET-passive than British English is. This claim is somewhat supported by our data, although only the model based on the full dataset and not the central data shows a significantly higher probability of *get* in AmE than in BrE. In frequency counts (normalized to take corpus size into consideration), there are more GET-passives in the US data. However, when other influencing factors are accounted for in the mixed-effects model, the effect is not unambiguously there. Tendencies such as an overall more informal character of the US subcorpus may account for this lack of significant differentiation, as may the overall skew of GloWbE toward linguistic uniformity (Loureiro-Porto 2017). At any rate, the analysis strongly suggests that the passive alternation is a shared phenomenon of the English-speaking world.

Considering other countries as well, the broad tendency is that Asian (particularly South Asian) varieties have the highest probability for *get*, followed by L1 varieties that have a lower probability and African Englishes that have the lowest probability for *get*. So regarding the passive, the distinction between L1 and L2, or Inner and Outer Circle of Englishes, seems to be less important than regional differences, possibly due to different substrate influences. We discuss how the lack of a formal passive in West African languages may make these speakers less prone to taking up new passive forms, while Singaporean and Jamaican English have local forms more comparable to the GET-passive. In the case of SingE, the local adversative passive may boost the use of the GET-passive as well, whereas in Jamaica, the association of the GET-passive with the local creole language and informality may curb its usage in English as well. Some findings, however, cannot be explained through substrate features, such as the high probability of the GET-passive in IndE and BanglE, particularly in informal writing.

Yet, regarding interactions of other variables with the variable "country," there are some differences between Inner and Outer Circle countries. We can summarize the findings outlined in the previous paragraphs with the statement that many L2 varieties seem to follow less strictly the preferences in the use of the GET-passive that have been suggested in the literature and supported by our diachronic case study on AmE. This is the case for formality as well as both features connected to subject responsibility. For the final feature for which we have an interaction with country (sentiment), there are unique tendencies found for a number of L2 varieties, with observations containing more positive sentiments showing an even higher probability for *get* than negative instances.

In addition to testing many previous claims about the English passive alternation, we added a new variable motivated by the concept of lexical grammar (Hunston & Francis 2000; Sinclair 2000) to explore whether specific semantic groups of verbs favor a certain variant of the passive auxiliary (cf. Rühlemann 2007). We created this grouping of verbs into semantic clusters for each corpus separately. The results of this endeavor based on COHA are modest. Three out of ten clusters need to be disregarded, and we are left with two clusters significantly associated with *get*, three clusters associated with *be* in the full model, and only one cluster significantly associated with each auxiliary in the tidier central model.

The procedure seems to work better on the larger dataset of contemporary web-based writing from GloWbE, where there are more instances of *get* with different main verbs. Our clustering method finds eleven clusters in this corpus, and our models predict for five of these a higher probability of *get* (in comparison to the baseline) and for five a higher probability of *be* in the full model, while five and three clusters significantly favor *get* and *be*, respectively, in the central model. Verbs favoring *get* fall mainly in the semantic realms of change and disruption: the passive subject is altered or attacked. Verbs of communication and position, on the other hand, favor *be*.

The relative lack of success of our distributional approach should, however, not be taken as evidence against participle-specific effects along the lines of lexical—or, more generally, construction—grammar. The importance of individual participles can be gleaned from the large contribution of the random effects to the models' pseudo-R^2 statistics. Thus, individual participles do show idiosyncratic preferences for *be* or *get*. What our participle clusters were meant to achieve was to add a mid-layer of shared verb semantics to the fully item-specific preferences. This indeed proved difficult.

To explore another less trekked terrain of conditioning the passive alternation, we included in our models a number of morpho-syntactic features as well. The aim was to test the claim that *get* is not yet fully grammaticalized into a substitute of *be* across all passive contexts but that the GET-passive occurs relatively less in structurally complex sentences. The results from both corpora are very similar but do not answer the posed questions unambiguously. Polarity, that is, whether the verb phrase contains a negative particle, does not seem to condition the passive alternation; it definitely does not support the idea that complex forms disfavor *get*. Two other possible additions to the clause—an adverb within the VP or a *to*-infinitive complement after it—however, do strongly favor *be*. This could be interpreted to mean that more complex sentences prefer *be*, but other explanations have been suggested in previous literature as well, such as an adverb being semantically incompatible with the GET-passive because the prior puts focus on the verb, while the latter focuses on the sentence subject (Xiao, McEnery, & Qian 2006: 116).

Our most interesting findings regarding morpho-syntax concern the use of different TAM (tense, aspect, modality) forms in the passive. The influence of TAM has become somewhat weaker over time, but it is still possible to identify forms that have a preference or dislike for *get*. In both datasets, it is *to*-infinitives and nonfinite *-ing* forms that are most likely to be realized with *get*. Also progressive forms favor *get*, possibly in avoidance of double *be*. On the other hand, clauses in the past tense and with modal verbs are more likely to be realized with *be* as the passive auxiliary. Ours is the first study of the passive alternation to model TAM at this level of detail and is thus able to critically reassess claims made in the previous literature (Fehringer 2022).

We also investigated what role "persistence" (or "priming" in cognitive linguistics; Szmrecsanyi 2006) plays in the adoption of the GET-passive. While the majority of previous studies explores such effects in controlled experiments or sociolinguistic interviews (e.g., Sankoff & Laberge 1978; Poplack 1980; Weiner & Labov 1983; Estival 1985; Gries 2005), we assess it in naturalistic production in historical and in online data. Our findings indicate that the predicted probability for *get* is always higher when the previous auxiliary used in the text was also *get*. This is true for both models in both corpora and is likely not an effect specific to the particular linguistic variable but rather a "universal of language use and processing" (Scherre & Naro 1991: 30).

It is noteworthy that the priming effect seems to have weakened over time. Here, we may observe a potential interaction between the variant's overall frequency and its susceptibility to priming; previous research suggests that less frequent items are more prone to priming effects (Wei et al. 2016: 1). In other words, the priming effects may have weakened over time prompted by the increased use of *get*.

11.3 Evaluating the Method

At the level of method, our case studies have marked a departure from previous research in a number of ways, most notably in terms of size and the attendant need to automate the operationalization of constraints. The corpora we draw on are well-established resources for the study of English: COHA (Davies 2010), covering 200 years of American English in 456 million words, and GloWbE (Davies 2013), comprising 1.84 billion words of web-based texts from twenty different English-speaking countries. Both these data sets entail challenges for automated tools in natural language processing in that they do not always fully adhere to the norms of written standardized English, for different reasons. The older segments in COHA are stylistically and sometimes orthographically different from twenty-first-century published texts, and they contain artifacts of automatic OCR processing. GloWbE includes the whole gamut of language found on the internet, ranging from highly standardized, monolingual texts to ones whose relationship to normative grammar and orthography is rather loose and which include languages other than English.

In short, COHA and GloWbE represent rather "large and messy" (Mair 2006: 355) corpora compared to the smaller but tidier resources typically found in sociolinguistic and earlier corpus-based research. As a consequence, we have found it necessary to adapt NLP tools to the specific data sets. We discuss these operationalizations and their advantages and drawbacks later.

Extracting instances of *get* or *be* + past participle proved to be a relatively straightforward, if time-consuming, task. It was necessary to draw on the automatically lemmatized and PoS-tagged versions of the data, which inevitably include a margin of error, but we have found these to not fundamentally affect the extraction process.

A much trickier question has been how to draw the line between true passives and nonpassive instances that should be excluded from the analysis. We approached this issue as a supervised learning task. Specifically, we trained a classifier on over 16,000 manually annotated examples and drawing on automatically extracted information at the levels of both the participle type and the individual example. Doing so was labor-intensive, but we feel the effort has been entirely justified. Centrality operationalized this way predicts the choice of the passive auxiliary in the full model and helps to reduce the data to a subset of only the central observations, for which model quality improves.

An issue that remains is that this procedure is inherently probabilistic rather than clear-cut. Some true passives may have been excluded in the process, and some more marginal instances are likely to remain even in the central dataset. We would like to submit, however, that this issue is not inherently new in the automated approach. As we discuss, different authors take different stances on what does and does not count as a passive, and they only make their inclusion criteria explicit to various degrees. Even drawing on the exemplary manual coding criteria provided by Schwarz (2015: 158), involving a number of replacement and modification tests, our two raters for the training data only agree in 88.61 percent of all cases. While the nature of the passive gradient makes it unlikely that any clear cut-off point for full agreement can be reached, then, what our automated approach achieves is to make the decision process fully transparent and reproducible, in addition to being able to upscale it to amounts of data that exceed prior studies by several orders of magnitude.

In addition to circumscribing the dependent variable in a probabilistic approach, we also automated predictors for a number of proposed constraints. As far as subject responsibility is concerned, the two main challenges were reliably identifying the head of the subject NP and then supplying animacy information for all such subject heads.

The former task was achieved with dependency parsing as implemented in Honnibal and Johnson's (2015) non-monotonic arc-eager transition system in spaCy (Honnibal & Montani 2017), combined with a simple look-up algorithm. We consider an accuracy of 88.7 percent for identifying the subject head, including resolving anaphoric reference of relative pronouns, to be a success, even while recognizing the margin of error that remains.

The much more difficult task consisted of automatically assigning an animacy category to each subject head. Our efforts to identify existing tools—either animacy dictionaries or even classifiers—were frustrated. This has led to extensive manual coding of over 43,000 types. In addition to the time and effort necessary to achieve this, there is an obvious limitation to approaching animacy at the type level. Polysemous items, metaphorical and metonymic extensions, and so on are all not accounted for in this procedure. With all these caveats, however, we were still able to report an accuracy of approximately 94 percent, which we consider robust enough for statistical modeling.

Still, future research stands to benefit tremendously from the availability of resources for automatic animacy detection. Animacy is a fundamental category involved in many phenomena of linguistic variation, such as the genitive (Hinrichs & Szmrecsanyi 2007) or the dative alternation (Paolini et al. 2023). We make our animacy dictionary available as a first step in this direction.

The claims about the passive alternation that have perhaps proved least amenable to empirical testing in the past have to do with the supposed adversativity or non-neutrality of the GET-passive. All previous research has essentially evaluated individual examples impressionistically, with consequences both for the amount of data considered and the replicability of the coding procedure. Unlike in the case of animacy, there exists a rich landscape of tools for automatic detection of sentiment in text, and we argue that linguistic research stands to benefit from incorporating these tools more actively.

We evaluated several dictionaries for identifying the participle-level sentiment and decided to work with VADER (Hutto & Gilbert 2014). In addition, we trained a task-aware representation of sentences (TARS) classifier (Halder et al. 2020) to predict the sentiment of the whole clause. In drawing this distinction between participle and clause, we attempted to disentangle the potentially multiple levels of sentiment present in a passive clause: from the perspective of the utterance producer versus the sentence subject. The results indicate a number of things that are worth considering here.

First, the clause-level sentiment was shown to be a more useful predictor than participle-level sentiment. An important question here is whether this fact reflects a genuinely greater relevance of utterance-producer sentiment or whether it is an artifact of the different sentiment scoring procedures. The TARS classifier we trained for clause-level sentiment scoring is simply able to draw on more and richer information than the simple dictionary look-up for participle sentiment. If the dictionary itself does not contain an entry for a particular participle, it defaults to zero. We experimented with imputing the sentiment of out-of-dictionary items by averaging over the sentiment scores of their nearest neighbors in word-embedding space but ultimately found this procedure to yield mixed results. This may be in large part because the relations among items in embedding space are only hazily defined. It would be a productive task for future research on the passive alternation to address sentiment from the subject and speaker perspectives separately and to develop tools to further test the importance of each perspective.

Second, in order to train the TARS classifier, we had to manually code examples for their sentiment (positive, negative, neutral). The two coders achieved only moderate agreement on this task, highlighting the highly subjective nature of sentiment evaluation. The classifier achieves similar levels of agreement with the tagged test data (which excludes cases where the two raters disagreed), giving overall support to the method.

As a third point, it should also be highlighted that the accuracy of sentiment analysis is significantly affected by discourse domain. Many available tools come from applied contexts where real-life detection of consumer or voter sentiment is of key importance. The primary data for training and analysis are social media posts, often from the United States. We have found it necessary to train our own classifiers specifically on the diachronic and global web-based data we are dealing with in our study. The same will apply, we expect, for much future linguistic research interested in modeling sentiment.

With these caveats in mind, we hasten to highlight that operationalizing sentiment in an automated way was a central element of the study and one that has allowed us to illuminate the trickiest hypothesized constraint on the GET-passive: adversativity or non-neutrality. Our results based on this method are unambiguous and robust. In all corpora, and across all varieties considered, it is both positive and negative sentiment scores at the clause level that significantly prefer *get* compared to neutral clauses.

The automated predictor that has turned out to be least useful was the clustering of different verbs in word-embedding space. The notion of automatically identifying related verbs with the distributional method based on the corpus data themselves is an attractive one, and the available algorithms for constructing word embeddings are powerful and well-tested. It is also theoretically plausible to expect different behavior for related verbs from a usage-based perspective on language variation, so it is worth reflecting on what held back verb clusters from playing a greater role in the statistical models in the present study.

The first aspect that deserves critical reflection has to do with the degrees of freedom in the methodological pipeline leading up to the cluster solution. For constructing the embedding space, these include choosing an algorithm (in our case, the CBOW implementation of Word2Vec; Mikolov et al. 2013), deciding which data this algorithm draws on (we opted for the same corpora that the observations for the study are extracted from), setting a range of hyper-parameters (such as the dimensionality of the embedding space and the minimum frequency of occurrence for words to be represented in the space), deciding whether to include all surface forms or only lexical words, whether to learn representations at the surface or the lemma level. A further set of choices is required when the embeddings themselves are created. The relations in high-dimensional space can be projected into lower-dimensional representations in a number of ways (our study drew on *t*-SNE van der Maaten & Hinton 2008), and different clustering techniques can be chosen (in our case, model-based clustering with Gaussian mixtures; Fraley & Raftery 1998). Both of these steps yet again involve further specific hyper-parameters, like the perplexity value of *t*-SNE and the number of clusters to consider. The combined effect of all these choices is that the space of possibilities to explore quickly becomes intractable.

This issue is exacerbated by a more fundamental concern and one that distinguishes the predictor verb cluster from the other ones in an important way. Whereas all other predictors operationalized a well-defined and theoretically motivated constraint on the passive alternation, verb cluster membership was included in the study in a much more exploratory fashion. We neither had a firm expectation of how many clusters should be constructed nor what the semantic contrasts should be that distinguish among them. There is a certain allure in the idea that the data themselves can be used to answer all these questions. Indeed, this is a major reason why we considered word embeddings a promising addition in the first place. However, there is ultimately an almost infinite number of ways in which groups of verbs can be established in this unsupervised approach, and while we put considerable effort into finding clusters that have some theoretical plausibility, we cannot claim with certainty that these are the best, certainly not the only possible solution.

The consequence for the models reported in Chapters 9 and 10 has been a relatively subordinate role of the predictor "verb cluster." But beyond these models, one has to ask questions about replicability of research findings. Our approaches to passive centrality and to sentiment were implemented as supervised learning in a way that can be reproduced in future studies. This is much less so the case for the unsupervised identification of verb clusters. Any future study would have to develop its own clusters (or simply take over ones reported in previous research, which in large parts defeats the point), and there is no reason to assume that those will be identical in number and composition to the ones reported here. Upon reflection of these issues, our conclusion is that distributional models continue to provide an attractive perspective on linguistic data, but we feel they are much better suited for exploratory investigations, such as tracing the development of schematicity of constructional slots (Perek 2018) than for strict hypothesis testing.

11.4 Relevance

Beyond findings on the individual linguistic variable our study has focused on, we have made the case at the level of method for a data-science approach to language variation. The study thus makes a contribution to the ongoing development of the field of computational sociolinguistics (Nguyen et al. 2016), on which we reflect here in more general terms.

A major motivation for drawing on machine-learning tools was the size of the data. We have argued that many of the hypothesized constraints on the passive alternation cannot be adequately studied on the limited quantitative basis entailed by handcoding individual examples. Paradoxically, upscaling the data through automated approaches to circumscribing the variable context and defining predictor variables initially leads to a requirement of even more data. This is due to the probabilistic nature of these automated procedures, each of which entails a certain margin of error. For instance, with an overall accuracy of 94 percent for subject animacy detection, one expects the randomness of the 6 percent of remaining erroneously categorized subjects to play less of a role the more robust the overall data are. Moreover, if automated approaches are to be extensively trained and evaluated, as we believe they have to be, there is non-negligible upfront effort that is only justified by being able to scale the analyses themselves to large amounts of data. As a consequence, we believe the approach to automate several aspects of the analysis constitutes a conceptual shift rather than just individual methodological adjustments: a move to much bigger data but at the expense of researcher control over individual tokens. This shift naturally may inspire feelings of unease, which deserve attention here.

The speed and success with which computational models, including large language models, have risen to prominence is well attested. One of the chief concerns related to many of these models is their black-box nature. Unlike inferential statistical approaches typically used in linguistic research, the purpose of these models is not to quantify the influence of individual predictors but simply to maximize prediction accuracy, usually through complex procedures in hidden layers that are not easily accessible. It is often clear that machine-learning models learn to achieve a certain task with success, but not how they do so, what information they draw on, in what way, and so on. Yet, it is the task of scientific research to answer precisely these latter questions. Therefore, it is essential to take steps to ameliorate these concerns.

It would be entirely misguided to believe a study of the passive alternation—or any linguistic variable—could be framed as a simple machine-learning task, with the linguistic particulars playing a minor role. On the contrary, it is absolutely essential that the nature of the variable itself and the hypothesized constraints on variation be understood from a theoretically informed perspective. Chapters 3 to 5 each give a detailed account of what previous research on the passive alternation has had to say on centrality, subject responsibility, and adversativity or non-neutrality before outlining the machine-learning approaches adopted to operationalize these constraints. It is perhaps telling that the only variable that is included in a more exploratory way, the verb clusters described in Chapter 6, turns out to be least relevant in the statistical analyses in Chapters 9 and 10. The models we report in these two chapters, overall, are successful both in corroborating prior statements about the passive (e.g., in terms of formality and subject responsibility), in adjudicating between competing hypotheses (e.g., in showing that non-neutrality really is the relevant constraint), and in showing new patterns (e.g., the differential profiles of genres in COHA and varieties in GloWbE). They are able to do so because the automated modeling of predictor variables was directly informed by a linguistically grounded understanding of the variable in question.

In this regard, our findings may also be taken as an indication that the convergence of linguistics and machine learning is not a one-way street, with linguists simply drawing on computational models. The incorporation of machine learning into linguistic analysis is certainly the direction that has been most central to our analysis, yet at the same time we believe that natural language processing stands to benefit from incorporating sociolinguistic insights. This concerns both theoretical insights—for instance, about how linguistic variation is connected to social meaning—as well as methodological choices such as the careful delineation of the variable context and the detailed modeling of constraints on variation this affords.

The approximation of predictors through probabilistic methods does impose potential issues of noise and error propagation. Limited success in precisely operationalizing one predictor may introduce confounds into the analysis that might even affect the coefficient estimates for other predictors as well as the overall model fit. The assumption that large amounts of data even out some inevitable noise is borne out in many cases, but if the operationalization of the predictors is affected not just by random inaccuracies but skewed, this skew will be equally prominent no matter the size of the data. It is therefore important to consider not just the accuracy with which constraints are approximated but also the nature of the erroneously categorized cases, such as instrumental and locative *by*-PPs or coordinated clause subjects (see Chapter 4).

In addition to interpretable and theoretically plausible output of the statistical models, we have found it important to provide examples from the corpus data in generous quantities to tie the various measures—such as the F-measure (Heylighen & Dewaele 2002) or sentiment scores—back to the specific kinds of phenomena they express. We consider it a key desideratum in corpus-based research that any statistical finding should be able to be illustrated with specific examples from the data. In the interpretation of findings, one important direction that should always be considered is "back to the concordance line."

Finally, we hasten to emphasize that we do not propose that all research into linguistic variation should follow the large-scale, computational approach we developed here. The case of the passive alternation is such that our method was necessary in order to address hypotheses from the literature that had proven recalcitrant to empirical testing and also to provide a robust quantitative basis in the first place. We were only able to achieve this, however, based on the rich, contextualized analyses of smaller data sets that laid the groundwork for our operationalizations. The ideal scenario is thus not a replacement of traditional variation studies with large-scale computational ones but a mutual cross-pollination between these approaches, always with a solid, theoretically grounded understanding of the linguistic phenomena under analysis.

11.5 Future Directions

To answer the question set forth at the beginning of this chapter—whether the passive alternation is an active grammatical change in English or largely a discourse phenomenon—we find plenty of areas of active development. It is, in our view, therefore, justified to treat the English passive as a vibrant sociolinguistic variable. The increase of the GET-passive is one of the biggest success stories over the past century of English, yet at the same time, the BE-passive is witnessing a drastic decline. Its decrease in frequency cannot simply be accounted for with reference to the competing variant, since even at present, the GET-passive comprises barely 2.5 percent of all passives. These shifts are indeed part of larger trends in written English, particularly its increasing colloquialization (Leech et al. 2009), but they also involve restructuring some of the constraints on the passive alternation. While most of these, such as informality, subject responsibility, and non-neutrality, are robust diachronically, they are also weakening as a function of time. In the synchronic view, different varieties show different levels of sensitivity and sometimes even different directions of effect, especially in regard to sentiment. Variation in the English passive, therefore, should be treated as an active development warranting continued attention.

An interesting speculative question concerns the long-term outcome of the competition. Three scenarios are conceivable: first, continued existence of both variants in active competition, being distinguished primarily along axes of style and semantic nuance as is presently the case; second, an entire ousting of the BE-passive at the hands of the GET-passive; and third, a functional differentiation between BE-passives categorically expressing statal and GET-passives categorically dynamic meanings, as is the case for instance with *sein* and *werden* in German. For the time being, the first scenario appears to be the most likely. If the GET-passive is to stand a real chance of replacing the BE-passive entirely (scenario two), it still has a long way to go, both in terms of overall frequency and shedding its constraints, which appear to be weakening only slightly. The third scenario is appealing for its form-function mapping, but at present, we are not aware of any empirical findings that actively lend support to it. The fact that our diachronic study shows central (i.e., dynamic) passives to be the environment where the variant with *get* is particularly virulent may inspire speculation in this direction, even if the long-term development remains impossible to predict with certainty.

One area that deserves more attention is the careful modeling of sentiment, for which we have argued that a separation of perspectives—sentence subject versus sentence producer—is important. In general, research into how affect and sentiment interact with linguistic variation is scarce at present, but there is good reason to hypothesize a connection between the two. Many linguistic descriptions, for instance, of the *always*-progressive (Carter & McCarthy 2006: 47) or positive *anymore* (Murray 1993), mention affect as a salient feature, but with the notable exceptions of Viola (2023) and Strelluf and Hills (2021), these have not been put to the large-scale quantitative test.

Returning to the English passive in particular, while the number of English varieties investigated in our synchronic study is high, it does not cover all of the English-speaking world. What is presently not represented at all is the Expanding Circle—countries where English plays no official role and competences vary broadly. Future studies could observe, for example, whether the use of the GET-passive correlates with competence levels and whether these speakers adhere to the same constraints of usage found in native and second language use.

Our studies rely on written data only. Considering that the GET-passive seems to be more frequent in speech, this is an unfortunate limitation. However, the type of complex statistical models that we have built require an amount of data that does not currently exist in a spoken, publicly available form. The largest corpora of today consist of written web-based data (such as GloWbE); we can hope that through future technological developments—such as improvements in automatic speech recognition eliminating the tedious step of transcription—we will overcome the practical and ethical challenges in the way of collecting mega corpora of speech.

We see potential for many components of our methodological toolkit to be applied, with appropriate adjustments, to other sociolinguistic questions. Automated circumscription of the variable context and modeling of sentiment are probably the most readily adaptable aspects of our study. Distributional modeling of word relationships in vector space will also play a role in future research, but as we have pointed out earlier, it may be more suited for exploratory than inferential analyses. While we very much hope that future research can take some inspiration from our project, we do not claim to have established new baselines or standards. Computational sociolinguistics is a young field undergoing rapid development, and we expect that future research will be in a position to learn from and improve on the modeling attempts we have outlined in this book.

Notes

1 Introduction

1 This example sentence is from the Corpus of Historical American English (COHA, Davies 2010) from 1975 and the newspaper subsection of the corpus. The source of each example is given in brackets in a similar manner. We also underline passive verb phrases.

2 This example sentence is from the Corpus of Global Web-Based English (GloWbE, Davies 2013). The country and corpus component (blogs vs. other, general websites) is indicated in brackets.

3 [Insert link to companion website here.]

2 The English Passive Voice: Be and Get

1 See Brus (1992) for a "typology of voice."

2 Some of these were per-million-words (pmw) frequencies in the original studies that have been converted back to raw figures for this table.

3 These claims are made based on 100 instances in ICE-JA, 74 in ICE-SIN, and 63 in ICE-GB (Bruckmaier 2017: 102).

4 The eight corpora investigated in Collins (1996) comprise written data from LOB (for BrE), Brown (for AmE), the Australian Corpus of English (Smith & Peters 2023), and the Kolhapur Corpus of Indian English (Shastri 1988), and spoken data from the London-Lund Corpus (Svartvik & Quirk 1959–90) and the British ICE corpus (Greenbaum & Nelson 1996) for BrE, and luncheon and dinner party conversations (Collins 1996: 44) and selected dialogue texts from the Australian ICE corpus (Greenbaum & Nelson 1996) for AusE.

5 The Philadelphia Neighborhood Corpus (Labov, Rosenfelder, & Fruehwald 2013) is based on sociolinguistic interviews; Sneller and Fischer (2015) use data from 162 speakers.

6 We would like to point out that in numerous previous studies on the GET-passive, the provided example sentences describe male violence on women and feed into the narrative that women share responsibility when, for example, being raped, killed, or shot. Linguistic examples should be carefully selected, contextualized, and their

relevance justified. As a result, in such cases, we chose names that are not tied to a single gender and thus do not feed into highly problematic stereotypical narratives.

7 Banks' (1986: 129) analysis is, on the whole, somewhat off the beaten track. He also suggests, for instance, that the common noun in the *by*-PP in Example (26) should not be analyzed as an agent but as an "animate instrument" or a "locative."

8 The percentage points do not add up to 100 because of 4.7 percent of "indeterminate" cases (Downing 1996: 196).

9 Phoocharoensil (2020: 129–30) is able to generalize over a larger number of observations by only looking at the thirty most common lexical verbs that occur in the GET-passive and staying on the type-level. The sentence context is not considered but only the lexical verb.

10 The "other" category encompasses future, conditional, past perfect, conditional perfect, and infinitive forms.

3 Centrality and the Passive Gradient

1 For instance, several studies use the (possibility of adding a) *by*-PP as a diagnostic for centrality, but Quirk et al. (1985: 169) reject its pertinence.

2 Central passives do not allow for this without a change in the semantic pattern.

4 Operationalizing Subject Responsibility

1 This estimate is based on a manual checking of a sample of 1,000 observations.

2 Vehicles may be treated as living beings in pronoun selection (Zaenen et al. 2004: 121).

3 See later for how we treat these "borderline cases" (Dahl & Fraurud 1996: 63) in our analysis.

4 [insert link here]

5 Operationalizing Adversativity and Non-Neutrality

1 Using punctuation as a proxy for clause boundaries is convenient but not fully accurate. If commas are not systematically used in the text in question, this process will yield sentences rather than clauses.

2 A score of 1.0 would represent absolute agreement between the coders; 0 would represent none.

6 Distributional Verb Semantics

1 Data were extracted from https://www.english-corpora.org/coha/ on October 19, 2024.
2 Note that the number of participles per clusters changes when the data are reduced to true passives for the statistical analysis.

7 Varieties of English and Substrate Influence

1 These are the emic ethnoracial labels used in South African society, for example, in the official censuses (Statista 2024).
2 See Abrefa and Ansah (2021) for a discussion on complications.
3 Native Americans form a very small portion of the American population and speak a wide variety of languages that belong to several different language families, that is, that are structurally very different from one another. In census data from 2018 to 2022, 1.3 percent choose the label "American Indian or Alaska native alone," and 3.0 percent report "two or more races" (US Census Bureau 2024).

References

Aarts, Bas. 2007. *Syntactic Gradience: The Nature of Grammatical Indeterminacy*. Oxford: Oxford University Press.

Abrefa, Kofi, & Juliet Ansah. 2021. Akan Grammatical Relations Revisited. *Drumspeak* 5(3). 108–32.

Agirre, Eneko, & Philip Edmonds (eds.). 2007. *Word Sense Disambiguation: Algorithms and Applications* (Text, Speech and Language Technology 33). Dordrecht: Springer.

Akbik, Alan, Tanja Bergmann, Duncan 1, Kashif Rasul, Stefan Schweter, & Roland Vollgraf. 2019. FLAIR: An Easy-to-Use Framework for State-of-the-Art NLP. In *Proceedings of the 2019 Conference of the North*, 54–9. Minneapolis, MN: Association for Computational Linguistics. https://doi.org/10.18653/v1/N19-4010.

Alday, Phillip, Dave Kleinschmidt, & Alexander Arslan. 2024. beacon-biosignals/Effects.jl: Effects Prediction for Regression Models. Julia. Beacon Biosignals. https://github.com/beacon-biosignals/Effects.jl (accessed September 26, 2024).

Alday, Phillip, & Tristan-Siegfried. 2020. JellyMe4.jl. Julia. https://doi.org/10.5281/zenodo.12609564.

Alexiadou, Artemis, & Florian Schäfer (eds.). 2013. *Non-Canonical Passives* (Linguistik Aktuell/Linguistics Today). Vol. 205. Amsterdam: John Benjamins. https://doi.org/10.1075/la.205.

Amadi, Scholastica Chinyere. 2018. Learning the English Passive Voice: Difficulties, Learning Strategies of Igbo ESL Learners and Pedagogical Implications. *International Journal of English and Literature* 9(5). 50–62. https://doi.org/10.5897/IJEL2018.1146.

Anderwald, Lieselotte. 2018. Language Change and Cultural Change: The Grammaticalizatioin of the Get-Passive in Context. *Language and Communication* 62(2018). 1–14.

Anesa, Patrizia. 2019. *Lexical Innovations in World Englishes: Cross-Fertilization and Evolving Paradigms*. London: Routledge.

Arce-Arenales, Manuel, Melissa Axelrod, & Barbara Fox. 1994. Active Voice and Middle Diathesis: A Cross-Linguistic Perspective. In Barbara Fox & Paul Hopper (eds.), *Voice: Form and Function* (Typological Studies in Language 27), 1–22. Amsterdam: John Benjamins.

Ashiwaju, Michael. 1968. *Lehrbuch der Yoruba-Sprache*. Vol. 13. Leipzig: VEB Verlag Enzyklopädie.

Atteveldt, Wouter van, Mariken A. C. G. van der Velden, & Mark Boukes. 2021. The Validity of Sentiment Analysis: Comparing Manual Annotation, Crowd-Coding, Dictionary Approaches, and Machine Learning Algorithms. *Communication*

Methods and Measures 15(2). 121–40. https://doi.org/10.1080/19312458.2020.1869198.

Australian Bureau of Statistics. 2022. Australia: Language Used at Home. https://www.abs.gov.au/statistics/people/people-and-communities/cultural-diversity-census/latest-release#data-downloads (July 30, 2024).

Baccianella, Stefano, Andrea Esuli, & Fabrizio Sebastiani. 2010. SENTIWORDNET 3.0: An Enhanced Lexical Resource for Sentiment Analysis and Opinion Mining. In *International Conference on Language Resources and Evaluation*, 2200–4. Valetta: University of Malta.

Bailey, Guy, Tom Wikle, Jan Tillery, & Lori Sand. 1991. The Apparent Time Construct. *Language Variation and Change* 3(3). 241–64. https://doi.org/10.1017/S0954394500000569.

Bamman, David, Chris Dyer, & Noah A. Smith. 2014. Distributed Representations of Geographically Situated Language. In Kristina Toutanova & Hua Wu (eds.), *Proceedings of the 52nd Annual Meeting of the Association for Computational Linguistics (Volume 2: Short Papers)*, 828–34. Baltimore, MD: Association for Computational Linguistics. https://doi.org/10.3115/v1/P14-2134.

Banks, David. 1986. Getting by with Get. *La Linguistique* 22(1). 125–30.

Bao, Zhiming, & Lionel Wee. 2003. The Passive in Singapore English. *World Englishes* 18(1). 1–11. https://doi.org/10.1111/1467-971X.00117.

Baroni, Marco, Georgiana Dinu, & Germán Kruszewski. 2014. Don't Count, Predict! A Systematic Comparison of Context-Counting vs. Context-Predicting Semantic Vectors. In *Proceedings of the 52nd Annual Meeting of the Association for Computational Linguistics (Volume 1: Long Papers)*, 238–47. Baltimore, MD: Association for Computational Linguistics. https://doi.org/10.3115/v1/P14-1023.

Baroni, Marco, & Alessandro Lenci. 2010. Distributional Memory: A General Framework for Corpus-Based Semantics. *Computational Linguistics* 36(4). 673–721. https://doi.org/10.1162/coli_a_00016.

Bates, Douglas, Phillip Alday, Dave Kleinschmidt, José Bayoán Santiago Calderón, Likan Zhan, Andreas Noack, Milan Bouchet-Valat, Alex Arslan, Tony Kelman, Antoine Baldassari, Benedikt Ehinger, Daniel Karrasch, Elliot Saba, Jacob Quinn, Michael Hatherly, Morten Piibeleht, Patrick Kofod Mogensen, Simon Babayan, Tim Holy, Yakir Luc Gagnon, and Yoni Nazarathy. 2013. JuliaStats/MixedModels.jl. Julia. Julia Statistics. https://github.com/JuliaStats/MixedModels.jl (accessed September 26, 2024).

Beames, John. 1891. *Grammar of the Bengali Language Literary and Colloquial.* Oxford: Clarendon Press.

Bellman, Richard. 1957. *Dynamic Programming.* Princeton: Princeton University Press.

Benson, Phil. 2000. Hong Kong Words: Variation and Context. *World Englishes* 19(3). 373–80. https://doi.org/10.1111/1467-971X.00185.

Bernaisch, Tobias. 2015. *The Lexis and Lexicogrammar of Sri Lankan English* (Varieties of English around the World). Vol. G54. Amsterdam: John Benjamins. https://doi.org/10.1075/veaw.g54.

Bernolet, Sarah, & Robert J. Hartsuiker. 2010. Does Verb Bias Modulate Syntactic Priming? *Cognition* 114(3). 455–61. https://doi.org/10.1016/j.cognition.2009.11.005.

Bezanson, Jeff, Alan Edelman, Stefan Karpinski, & Viral B. Shah. 2017. Julia: A Fresh Approach to Numerical Computing. *SIAM Review*. Society for Industrial and Applied Mathematics 59(1). 65–98. https://doi.org/10.1137/141000671.

Biagioni, Raoul. 2016. *The SenticNet Sentiment Lexicon: Exploring Semantic Richness in Multi-Word Concepts* (SpringerBriefs in Cognitive Computation). Vol. 4. Cham: Springer. https://doi.org/10.1007/978-3-319-38971-4_3.

Biber, Douglas. 1988. *Variation across Speech and Writing*. Cambridge: Cambridge University Press.

Biber, Douglas, Susan Conrad, & Geoffrey Leech. 1999. *Student Grammar of Spoken and Written English*. Harlow: Longman.

Biber, Douglas, Susan Conrad, & Geoffrey Leech. 2003. *Student Grammar of Spoken and Written English*. 2nd edn. Harlow: Longman.

Biewer, Carolin. 2009. Passive Constructions in Fiji English: A Corpus-Based Study. In Andreas H. Jucker, Daniel Schreier, & Marianne Hundt (eds.), *Corpora: Pragmatics and Discourse: Papers from the 29th International Conference on English Language Research on Computerized Corpora (ICAME 29). Ascona, Switzerland, 14–18 May 2008*, 361–77. Amsterdam: Brill. https://doi.org/10.1163/9789042029101.

Blake, Renée. 1997. Defining the Envelope of Linguistic Variation: The Case of "Don't Count" Forms in the Copula Analysis of African American Vernacular English. *Language Variation and Change* 9(1). 57–79.https://doi.org/10.1017/S0954394500001794.

Bleaman, Isaac L., & Rhea Kommerell. 2024. A Computational Approach to Detecting the Envelope of Variation. *Linguistics Vanguard* 10(1). 385–95. https://doi.org/10.1515/lingvan-2023-0157.

Blei, David, Andrew Y. Ng, & Michael I. Jordan. 2003. Latent Dirichlet Allocation. *Journal of Machine Learning Research* 3. 993–1022.

BNC Consortium. 2007. British National Corpus, XML edition. Oxford Text Archive. http://hdl.handle.net/20.500.14106/255. (6 December, 2024).

Boateng, Ernest Amano, John D. Fage, Oliver Davies, & Donna J. Maier. 2024. Ghana. History, Flag, Map, Population, Language, Currency, & Facts. Britannica. https://www.britannica.com/place/Ghana. (1 August, 2024).

Bobicev, Victoria, & Marina Sokolova. 2017. Inter-Annotator Agreement in Sentiment Analysis: Machine Learning Perspective. In *RANLP 2017 – Recent Advances in Natural Language Processing Meet Deep Learning*, 97–102. Shoumen: Incoma. https://doi.org/10.26615/978-954-452-049-6_015.

Bock, J. Kathryn. 1986. Syntactic Persistence in Language Production. *Cognitive Psychology* 18(3). 355–87. https://doi.org/10.1016/0010-0285(86)90004-6.

Bock, Kathryn, & Helga Loebell. 1990. Framing Sentences. *Cognition* 35(1). 1–39. https://doi.org/10.1016/0010-0277(90)90035-I.

Bohmann, Axel. 2019. *Variation in English Worldwide: Registers and Global Varieties* (Studies in English Language). Cambridge: Cambridge University Press.

Bohmann, Axel. 2023. Contrastive Usage Profiling: A Word Vector Perspective on World Englishes. In Beatrix Busse, Nina Dumrukcic, & Ingo Kleiber (eds.), *Language and Linguistics in a Complex World*, 11–30. Berlin: De Gruyter. https://doi.org/10.1515/9783111017433-002.

Bohmann, Axel. 2024. Towards "Large and Tidy" Establishing Internal Structure in Mega-Corpora. In Steven Coats & Veronika Laippala (eds.), *Linguistics across Disciplinary Borders: The March of Data* (Language, Data Science and Digital Humanities), 157–84. London: Bloomsbury Academic.

Bohmann, Axel, Julia Müller, Mirka Honkanen, & Miriam Neuhausen. 2023. A Large-Scale Diachronic Analysis of the English Passive Alternation. In Beatrix Busse, Nina Dumrukcic, & Ingo Kleiber (eds.), *Language and Linguistics in a Complex World*, 31–56. Berlin: De Gruyter. https://doi.org/10.1515/9783111017433-003.

Bojanowski, Piotr, Edouard Grave, Armand Joulin, & Tomas Mikolov. 2017. Enriching Word Vectors with Subword Information. *Transactions of the Association for Computational Linguistics* 5. 135–46. https://doi.org/10.1162/tacl_a_00051.

Bowerman, Sean. 2020. White South African English. In Bernd Kortmann, Kerstin Lunkenheimer, & Katharina Ehret (eds.), *The Electronic World Atlas of Varieties of English*. Zenodo. http://ewave-atlas.org/languages/51. (December 18, 2024).

Branigan, Holly P., Martin J. Pickering, & Alexandra A. Cleland. 2000. Syntactic Co-Ordination in Dialogue. *Cognition* 75(2). B13–25. https://doi.org/10.1016/S0010-0277(99)00081-5.

Bruckmaier, Elisabeth. 2016. Dialect Contact Influences on the Use of GET and the GET-Passive. In Olga Timofeeva, Anne-Christine Gardner, Alpo Honkapohja, & Sarah Chevalier (eds.), *Studies in Language Companion Series*, vol. 177, 117–40. Amsterdam: John Benjamins. https://doi.org/10.1075/slcs.177.05bru.

Bruckmaier, Elisabeth. 2017. *Getting at GET in World Englishes: A Corpus-Based Semasiological-Syntactic Analysis*. Berlin: De Gruyter. https://doi.org/10.1515/9783110497311.

Brunila, Mikael, & Jack LaViolette. 2022. What Company Do Words Keep? Revisiting the Distributional Semantics of J.R. Firth & Zellig Harris. In *Proceedings of the 2022 Conference of the North American Chapter of the Association for Computational Linguistics: Human Language Technologies*, 4403–17. Seattle: Association for Computational Linguistics. https://doi.org/10.18653/v1/2022.naacl-main.327.

Brus, Ineke. 1992. Towards a Typology of Voice. In Michael Kefer & Johan van der Auwera (eds.), *Meaning and Grammar: Cross-Lingustic Perspectives* (Empirical Approaches to Language Typology 10), 45–76. BerlinMouton de Gruyter.

Buschfeld, Sarah, & Alexander Kautzsch. 2017. Towards an Integrated Approach to Postcolonial and Non-Postcolonial Englishes. *World Englishes* 36(1). 104–26. https://doi.org/10.1111/weng.12203.

Bybee, Joan. 2010. *Language, Usage and Cognition*. 1st ed. Cambridge: Cambridge University Press. https://doi.org/10.1017/CBO9780511750526.

Carter, Ronald, & Michael McCarthy. 1999. The English Get-Passive in Spoken Discourse: Description and Implications for an Interpersonal Grammar. *English Language and Linguistics* 3(1). 41–58.

Carter, Ronald, & Michael McCarthy. 2006. *Cambridge Grammar of English*. Cambridge: Cambridge University Press.

Census and Statistics Department. 2012. Hong Kong 2011 Population Census—Main Report: Vol I. *Census and Statistics Department. The Government of the Hong Kong Special Administrative Region*. https://www.censtatd.gov.hk/en/EIndexbySubject.html?pcode=B1120059&scode=170. (July 30, 2024).

Census of India. 2011. *Language: India, States and Union Territories*. New Delhi: Office of the Registrar General, India. file:///C:/Users/honkanen.ENGSEM/Downloads/C-16_25062018-1.pdf.

Central Statistics Office. 2023. Census 2022 Profile 8—the Irish Language and Education. Irish Language and the Gaeltacht. https://www.cso.ie/en/releasesandpublications/ep/p-cpp8/census2022profile8-theirishlanguageandeducation/irishlanguageandthegaeltacht/. (July 30, 2024).

Chafe, Wallace L. 1982. Integration and Involvement in Speaking, Writing, and Oral Literature. In Deborah Tannen (ed.), *Spoken and Written Language: Exploring Orality and Literacy* (Advances in Discourse Processes IX), 35–53. Norwood: Ablex.

Chappell, Hilary. 1980. Is the Get-Passive Adversative? *Papers in Linguistics* 13(3). 411–52.

Cheshire, Jenny. 2005. Syntactic Variation and Spoken Language. In Cornips Leonie & Karen Corrigan (eds.), *Syntax and Variation. Reconciling the Biological and the Social* (Current Issues in Linguistic Theory), vol. 265, 81–106. Amsterdam: John Benjamins.

Cheshire, Jenny, Paul Kerswill, & Anne Williams. 2005. Phonology, Grammar, and Discourse in Dialect Convergence. In Peter Auer, Frans Hinskens, & Paul Kerswill (eds.), *Dialect Change: Convergence and Divergence in European Languages*, 135–67. Cambridge: Cambridge University Press.

Cho, Eun Jung, & Byeongkil Ahn. 2017. A Corpus-Based Study of the Auxiliary-Like Get, the Copular Get, and the Causative Get. *Journal of Mirae English Language and Literature* 22(1). 293–317.

Chomsky, Noam. 1957. *Syntactic Structures*. The Hague: Mouton.

Clark, Lynn. 2018. Priming as a Motivating Factor in Sociophonetic Variation and Change. *Topics in Cognitive Science* 10(4). 729–44. https://doi.org/10.1111/tops.12338.

Cohen, Jacob. 1960. A Coefficient of Agreement for Nominal Scales. *Educational and Psychological Measurement* 20(1). 37–46.

Collins, Peter. 2016. Grammatical Change in the Verb Phrase in Contemporary Philippine English. *Asiatic: IIUM Journal of English Language and Literature* 10(2). 50–67. https://doi.org/10.31436/asiatic.v10i2.894.

Collins, Peter. 2021. Hypercorrection in English: An Intervarietal Corpus-Based Study. *English Language and Linguistics* 26(2). 279–305.

Collins, Peter C. 1996. Get-Passives in English. *World Englishes* 15(1). 43–56.

Collins, Peter, & Xinyue Yao. 2013. Colloquial Features in Word Englishes. *International Journal of Corpus Linguistics* 18(4). 479–505. https://doi.org/10.1075/ijcl.18.4.02col.

Comrie, Bernard. 1981. *Language Universals and Linguistic Typology*. 2nd ed. Oxford: Basil Blackwell.

Coto Villalibre, Eduardo. 2015. Is the Get-Passive Really that Adversative? *Miscelánea: A Journal of English and American Studies* 51. 13–30.

Coupland, Nikolas. 1983. Patterns of Encounter Management: Further Arguments for Discourse Variables. *Language in Society* 12(4). 459–76.

Cowan, Ron. 2008. *The Teacher's Grammar of English*. Cambridge: Cambridge University Press.

Croft, William. 1991. *Syntactic Categories and Grammatical Relations: The Cognitive Organization of Information*. Chicago: Chicago Press.

Croft, William. 2000. *Explaining Language Change: An Evolutionary Approach* (Longman Linguistics Library). Harlow: Longman.

Crowther, Samuel. 1852. *A Grammar and Vocabulary of the Yoruba Language*. London: Seeley. https://dds.crl.edu/crldelivery/1035.

Dahl, Östen, & Kari Fraurud. 1996. Animacy in Grammar and Discourse. In Thorstein Fretheim & Jeanette K. Gundel (eds.), *Reference and Referent Accessibility*, 47–64. Amsterdam: John Benjamins.

Davies, Mark. 2007. *TIME Magazine Corpus*. https://www.english-corpora.org/coha/.

Davies, Mark. 2008. *The Corpus of Contemporary American English (COCA)*. https://www.english-corpora.org/coca/.

Davies, Mark. 2010. *The Corpus of Historical American English*. https://www.english-corpora.org/coha/.

Davies, Mark. 2013. *Corpus of Global Web-Based English*. https://www.english-corpora.org/glowbe/.

Davies, Mark. 2019. *Corpus of Historical American English (COHA)*. https://www.english-corpora.org/coha/.

Davies, Mark, & Robert Fuchs. 2015. Expanding Horizons in the Study of World Englishes with the 1.9 Billion Word Global Web-Based English Corpus (GloWbE). *English World-Wide. A Journal of Varieties of English* 36(1). 1–28. https://doi.org/10.1075/eww.36.1.01dav.

Denecke, Kerstin, & Daniel Reichenpfader. 2023. Sentiment Analysis of Clinical Narratives: A Scoping Review. *Journal of Biomedical Informatics* 140. 1–13. https://doi.org/10.1016/j.jbi.2023.104336.

Deng, Yuan. 2017. On the Syntactic Structure of English Get-Passive. *Overseas English* 20. 217–18, 226.

Denison, David. 1998. Syntax. In Suzanne Romaine (ed.), *The Cambridge History of the English Language*, vol. IV, 92–329. Cambridge: Cambridge University Press.

Devonish, Hubert, & Otelemate G. Harry. 2008. Jamaican Creole and Jamaican English: Phonology. In Bernd Kortmann & Edgar W. Schneider (eds.), *The Americas and the Caribbean*, 256–89. Berlin: Mouton de Gruyter. https://doi.org/10.1515/9783110208405.1.256.

Dines, Elizabeth R. 1980. Variation in Discourse—"And Stuff Like That." *Language in Society* 9(1). 13–33.

Dinu, Georgiana, & Mirella Lapata. 2010. Measuring Distributional Similarity in Context. In Hang Li & Luís Màrquez (eds.), *Proceedings of the 2010 Conference on Empirical Methods in Natural Language Processing*, 1162–72. Cambridge, MA: Association for Computational Linguistics.

Dixon, Robert M. W. 2005. *A Semantic Approach to English Grammar* (Oxford Textbooks in Linguistics). 2nd ed. Oxford: Oxford University Press.

Donaldson, Bruce. 1993. *A Grammar of Afrikaans*. Berlin: Mouton de Gruyter.

Downing, Angela. 1996. The Semantics of Get-Passives. In Ruqaiya Hasan, Carmel Cloran, & David Butt (eds.), *Functional Descriptions: Theory in Practice*, 179–206. Amsterdam: John Benjamins. https://www.jbe-platform.com/content/books/9789027276308-cilt.121.07dow.

Eisenstein, Jacob. 2013. What to Do about Bad Language on the Internet. In Lucy Vanderwende, Hal Daumé III, & Katrin Kirchhoff (eds.), *Proceedings of the 2013 Conference of the North American Chapter of the Association for Computational Linguistics: Human Language Technologies*, 359–69. Atlanta: Association for Computational Linguistics. https://aclanthology.org/N13-1037.

Erk, Katrin. 2012. Vector Space Models of Word Meaning and Phrase Meaning: A Survey. *Language and Linguistics Compass* 6(10). 635–53. https://doi.org/10.1002/lnco.362.

Erk, Katrin, & Gabriella Chronis. 2023. Word Embeddings Are Word Story Embeddings (and That's Fine). In Shalom Lappin & Jean-Philippe Bernardy (eds.), *Algebraic Structures in Natural Language*, 189–218. 1st ed. Boca Raton: CRC Press.

Erk, Katrin, Sebastian Padó, & Ulrike Padó. 2010. A Flexible, Corpus-Driven Model of Regular and Inverse Selectional Preferences. *Computational Linguistics* 36(4). 723–63. https://doi.org/10.1162/coli_a_00017.

Estival, Dominique. 1985. Syntactic Priming of the Passive in English. *Text—Interdisciplinary Journal for the Study of Discourse* 5(1–2). 7–21. https://doi.org/10.1515/text.1.1985.5.1-2.7.

Evans, Stephen. 2015. Modelling the Development of English in Hong Kong. *World Englishes* 34(3). 389–410. https://doi.org/10.1111/weng.12154.

Everaert, Christine. 2017. *Essential Hindi Grammar*. Honololu: University of Hawai'i Press.

Faraclas, Nicholas. 1996. *Nigerian Pidgin* (Descriptive Grammars). London: Routledge.

Farquharson, Joseph T. 2013. Jamaican. In Susanne Maria Michaelis, Philippe Maurer, Martin Haspelmath, & Magnus Huber (eds.), *The Survey of Pidgin and Creole Languages* (English-Based and Dutch-Based Languages), vol. I, 81–91. Oxford: Oxford University Press.

Feagin, Crawford. 1979. *Variation and Change in Alabama English: A Sociolinguistic Study of a White Community*. Washington, DC: Georgetown University Press.

Fehringer, Carol. 2022. The *Get*-Passive in Tyneside English: A Highly Frequent yet Constrained Variant. *English World-Wide* 43(43). 330–56. https://doi.org/10.1075/eww.21039.feh.

Ferreira, Victor S., & Kathryn Bock. 2006. The Functions of Structural Priming. *Language and Cognitive Processes* 21(7–8). 1011–29. https://doi.org/10.1080/01690960600824609.

Firth, John R. 1957. *Studies in Linguistic Analysis* (Special Volume of the Philological Society). Oxford: Blackwell.

Fleisher, Nicholas. 2006. The Origin of Passive Get. *English Language and Linguistics* 10(2). 225–52.

Flood, Josephine. 2019. *The Original Australians: The Story of the Aboriginal People*. 2nd ed. Sydney: Allen & Unwin.

Foley, Joseph. 2001. Is English a First or Second Language in Singapore? In Beng Yeow Vincent Ooi (ed.), *Evolving Identities: The English Language in Singapore and Malaysia*, 12–32. Singapore: Times Academic Press. https://scholarbank.nus.edu.sg/handle/10635/79555.

Fonteyn, Lauren, & Enrique Manjavacas. 2021. Adjusting Scope: A Computational Approach to Case-Driven Research on Semantic Change. In Maud Ehrmann & Karsdorp (eds.), *Proceedings of the Conference on Computational Humanities Research 2021*, 280–98. Amsterdam: CEUR Workshop Proceedings.

Fraley, Chris, & Adrian E. Raftery. 1998. How Many Clusters? Which Clustering Method? Answers via Model-Based Cluster Analysis. *Computer Journal* 41(8). 578–88.

Francis, W. N., & H. Kučera. 1963. *The Standard Corpus of Present-Day Edited American English (the Brown Corpus)*. https://varieng.helsinki.fi/CoRD/corpora/BROWN/.

Fryd, Marc. 2009. Change and Continuity in the English Passive: From Weorthan to Get. *Groninger Arbeiten zur Germanistischen Linguistik* 49. 274–300.

Garside, R. G., Geoffrey N. Leech, & Geoffrey Sampson (eds.). 1987. The CLAWS Word-Tagging System. In *The Computational Analysis of English: A Corpus-Based Approach*, 30–41. London: Longman.

Givón, Talmy. 1993. *English Grammar: A Function-Based Introduction*. Vol. I. Amsterdam: John Benjamins. https://doi.org/10.1075/z.engram1.

Givón, Thomas, & Phil Yang. 1994. The Rise of the English GET-Passive. In Barbara Fox & Paul J. Hopper (eds.), *Voice: Form and Function*, 119–50. Amsterdam: John Benjamins.

Granger, Sylviane. 1983. *The Be + Past Participle Construction in Spoken English* (North-Holland Linguistic Series 49). Amsterdam: North Holland.

Greenbaum, Sidney, & Gerald Nelson. 1996. The International Corpus of English (ICE) Project. *World Englishes* 15(1). 3–15.

Gries, Stefan Th. 2005. Syntactic Priming: A Corpus-Based Approach. *Journal of Psycholinguistic Research* 34(4). 365–99. https://doi.org/10.1007/s10936-005-6139-3.

Grieve, Jack, Andrea Nini, & Diansheng Guo. 2017. Analyzing Lexical Emergence in Modern American English Online. *English Language & Linguistics*. 21(1). 99–127. https://doi.org/10.1017/S1360674316000113.

Gronemeyer, Claire. 1999. On Deriving Complex Polysemy: The Grammaticalization of Get. *English Language and Linguistics* 3(1). 1–39.

Gunasekara, Abraham Mendis. 1999. *A Comprehensive Grammar of the Sinhalese Language*. New Delhi: Colombo, reprint by Asian Educational Services.

Haegeman, Liliane. 1985. The Get-Passive and Burzio's Generalization. *Lingua* 66(1). 53–77.

Halder, Kishaloy, Alan Akbik, Josip Krapac, & Roland Vollgraf. 2020. Task-Aware Representation of Sentences for Generic Text Classification. In *Proceedings of the 28th International Conference on Computational Linguistics*, 3202–13. Barcelona, Spain (Online): International Committee on Computational Linguistics. https://doi.org/10.18653/v1/2020.coling-main.285.

Halliday, Michael A. K. 1994. *An Introduction to Functional Grammar*. 2nd ed. London: Arnold.

Hansen, Beke. 2018. *Corpus Linguistics and Sociolinguistics: A Study of Variation and Change in the Modal Systems of World Englishes* (Language and Computer 82). Leiden: Brill.

Harris, Harlan, EPRI, Chris DuBois, John Myles White, Milan Bouchet-Valat, & Bogumił Kamiński. 2012. JuliaData/DataFrames.jl. Julia. JuliaData. https://github.com/JuliaData/DataFrames.jl (accessed September 26, 2024).

Harris, Zellig S. 1954. Distributional Structure. *WORD* 10(2–3). 146–62. https://doi.org/10.1080/00437956.1954.11659520.

Hartigan, J. A., & M. A. Wong. 1979. Algorithm AS 136: A K-Means Clustering Algorithm. *Applied Statistics* 28(1). 100. https://doi.org/10.2307/2346830.

Hashim, Azirah, & Gerhard Leitner. 2011. Contact Expressions in Contemporary Malaysian English. *World Englishes* 30(4). 551–68.

Haspelmath, Martin. 2013. Passive Constructions. In Susanne Michaelis, Philippe Maurer, Martin Haspelmath, & Magnus Huber (eds.), *The Atlas of Pidgin & Creole Language Structures*, 358–61. Oxford: Oxford University Press.

Hatcher, Anna G. 1949. To Get/Be Invited. *Modern Language Notes* 64(7). 433–46.

Heine, Bernd. 1993. *Auxiliaries: Cognitive Forces and Grammaticalization.* New York: Oxford University Press. https://doi.org/10.1093/oso/9780195083873.001.0001.

Heller, Benedikt, & Melanie Röthlisberger. 2015. Big Data on Trial: Researching Syntactic Alternations in GloWbE and ICE. Presented at the D2E, Helsinki. https://www.academia.edu/17202811/Big_data_on_trial_Researching_syntactic_alternations_in_GloWbE_and_ICE.

Herold, Ruth. 1986. A Quantitative Study of the Alternation between the BE- and GET-Passives. *Proceedings of the XVth NWAV Conference.* Stanford: Stanford University.

Heylighen, Francis, & Jean-Marc Dewaele. 2002. Variation in the Contextuality of Language: An Empirical Measure. *Foundations of Science* 7. 293–340.

Hilpert, Martin. 2012. Diachronic Collostructional Analysis Meets the Noun Phrase: Studying Many a Noun in Coha. In Terttu Nevalainen & Elizabeth Closs Traugott (eds.), *The Oxford Handbook of the History of English* (Oxford Handbooks), 233–44. New York: Oxford University Press. https://doi.org/10.1093/oxfordhb/9780199922765.013.0022.

Hinkel, Eli. 2002. Why English Passive Is Difficult to Teach (and Learn). In Eli Hinkel & Sandra Fotos (eds.), *New Perspectives on Grammar Teaching in Second Language Classrooms*, 233–59. Mahwah, NJ: Routledge.

Hinrichs, Lars. 2006. *Codeswitching on the Web: English and Jamaican Creole in E-Mail Communication.* Amsterdam: John Benjamins.

Hinrichs, Lars, & Benedikt Szmrecsanyi. 2007. Recent Changes in the Function and Frequency of Standard English Genitive Constructions: A Multivariate Analysis of Tagged Corpora. *English Language & Linguistics* 11(3). 437–74. https://doi.org/10.1017/S1360674307002341.

Hocking, Toby Dylan. 2024. Directlabels: Direct Labels for Multicolor Plots. https://cran.r-project.org/web/packages/directlabels/index.html (accessed September 26, 2024).

Hoernlé, A. F. Rudolf. 1880. *A Grammar of the Eastern Hindi Compared with the Other Gaudian Languages.* London: Trübner. https://archive.org/details/agrammareastern00hoergoog/page/n5/mode/2up.

Honda, Shoko. 2012. On the Origin and Development of the Get-Passive: With Special Reference to Grammaticalization. *English Linguistics* 29(1). 69–87.

Honnibal, Matthew, & Mark Johnson. 2015. An Improved Non-Monotonic Transition System for Dependency Parsing. In *Proceedings of the 2015 Conference on Empirical Methods in Natural Language Processing*, 1373–8. Lisbon, Portugal: Association for Computational Linguistics. https://doi.org/10.18653/v1/D15-1162.

Honnibal, Matthew, & Ines Montani. 2017. spaCy 2: Natural Language Understanding with Bloom Embeddings, Convolutional Neural Networks and Incremental Parsing.

Hopper, Paul J., & Elizabeth Closs Traugott. 2003. *Grammaticalization*. 2nd edn. Cambridge: Cambridge University Press. https://doi.org/10.1017/CBO9781139165525.

Horch, Stephanie. 2016. *Conversion in Asian Englishes: A Usage-based Account of the Emergence of New Local Norms*. Freiburg: FreiDok plus. https://freidok.uni-freiburg.de/data/12910.

Hovy, Dirk, & Christoph Purschke. 2018. Capturing Regional Variation with Distributed Place Representations and Geographic Retrofitting. In *Proceedings of the 2018 Conference on Empirical Methods in Natural Language Processing*, 4383–94. Brussels, Belgium: Association for Computational Linguistics. https://doi.org/10.18653/v1/D18-1469.

Huddleston, Rodney. 1976. *An Introduction to English Transformational Syntax* (English Language Series 10). London: Longman.

Huddleston, Rodney, & Geoffrey K. Pullum. 2002. *The Cambridge Grammar of the English Language*. 1st ed. Cambridge: Cambridge University Press. https://doi.org/10.1017/9781316423530.

Hundt, Marianne. 2001a. What Corpora Tell Us about the Grammaticalisation of Voice in Get-Constructions. *Studies in Language* 25(1). 49–88. https://doi.org/10.1075/sl.25.1.03hun.

Hundt, Marianne. 2001b. Grammatical Variation in National Varieties of English—the Corpus-Based Approach. *Revue Belge de Philologie et d'Histoire* 79(3). 737–56. https://doi.org/10.3406/rbph.2001.4545.

Hundt, Marianne. 2004. The Passival and the Progressive Passive: A Case Study of Layering in the English Aspect and Voice Systems. In Hans Lindquist & Christian Mair (eds.), *Studies in Corpus Linguistics*, vol. 13, 79–120. Amsterdam: John Benjamins. https://doi.org/10.1075/scl.13.06hun.

Hundt, Marianne, Bethany Dallas, & Shimon Nakanishi. 2023. The *Be*- Versus *Get*-Passive Alternation in World Englishes. *World Englishes* 43(1). 86–108. https://doi.org/10.1111/weng.12633.

Hundt, Marianne, & Christian Mair. 1999. "Agile" and "Uptight" Genres: The Corpus-Based Approach to Language Change in Progress. *International Journal of Corpus Linguistics* 4(2). 221–42. https://doi.org/10.1075/ijcl.4.2.02hun.

Hunston, Susan, & Gill Francis. 2000. *Pattern Grammar: A Corpus-Driven Approach to the Lexical Grammar of English* (Studies in Corpus Linguistics Volume 4). Amsterdam: John Benjamins. https://doi.org/10.1075/scl.4.

Hunt, Matthew, Colleen Cotter, Hazel Pearson, & Linnaea Stockall. 2023. Swear(ING) Ain't Play(ING): The Interaction of Taboo Language and the Sociolinguistic Variable. *Journal of Sociolinguistics* 27(2). 136–58. https://doi.org/10.1111/josl.12588.

Hutto, C., & Eric Gilbert. 2014. VADER: A Parsimonious Rule-Based Model for Sentiment Analysis of Social Media Text. *Proceedings of the International AAAI Conference on Web and Social Media* 8(1). 216–25. https://doi.org/10.1609/icwsm.v8i1.14550.

Israel, Michael, Christopher Johnson, & Patricia J. Brooks. 2001. From States to Events: The Acquisition of English Passive Participles. 11(1–2). 103–29. https://doi.org/10.1515/cogl.2001.005.

I Wanna Learn Malay. 2020. *LEARN MALAY—How to Create Sentences in a Passive Voice (Part 1)*. https://www.youtube.com/watch?v=Vgrf05TPBhg. (August 1, 2024).

Jaeger, Florian T., & Neal Snider. 2007. Implicit Learning and Syntactic Persistence: Surprisal and Cumulativity. *University of Rochester Working Papers in the Language Sciences* 3(1). 26–44.

Jenset, Gard B. 2013. Mapping Meaning with Distributional Methods: A Diachronic Corpus-Based Study of Existential *There*. *Journal of Historical Linguistics* 3(2). 272–306. https://doi.org/10.1075/jhl.3.2.04jen.

Johansson, Stig, & Signe Oksefjell. 1996. Towards a Unified Account of the Syntax and Semantics of Get. In Jenny Thomas & Mick Short (eds.), *Using Corpora for Language Research*, 57–75. London: Longman.

Jowitt, David. 2019. *Nigerian English* (Dialects of English 18). Boston: De Gruyter.

Jucker, Andreas H. 2018. Apologies in the History of English: Evidence from the Corpus of Historical American English (COHA). *Corpus Pragmatics: International Journal of Corpus Linguistics and Pragmatics* 2(4). 375–98. https://doi.org/10.1007/s41701-018-0038-y.

Kachru, Braj B. 1985. Standards, Codification and Sociolinguistic Realism: The English Language in the Outer Circle. In Randolph Quirk & Henry G. Widdowson (eds.), *English in the World: Teaching and Learning the Language and Literatures*, 11–30. Cambridge: Cambridge University Press.

Kant Agnihotri, Rama. 2023. *Hindi: An Essential Grammar* (Routledge Essential Grammars). 2nd ed. London: Routledge.

Kaufman, Leonard, & Peter J. Rousseeuw. 1990. *Finding Groups in Data: An Introduction to Cluster Analysis* (Wiley Series in Probability and Statistics). 1st ed. Hoboken, NJ: Wiley. https://doi.org/10.1002/9780470316801.

Kemmer, Suzanne. 1993. *The Middle Voice* (Typological Studies in Language 23). Amsterdam: John Benjamins.

Kim, Chonghyuck, & Yosuke Sato. 2013. More on Kena-Passives in Singapore English. *World Englishes* 32(3). 297–307.

Koch, Peter, & Wulff Oesterreicher. 1985. Sprache der Nähe—Sprache der Distanz. Mündlichkeit und Schriftlichkeit um Spannungsfeld von Sprachtheorie und Sprachgeschichte. *Romanistisches Jahrbuch* 36(85). 15–43.

Korkontzelos, Ioannis, Azadeh Nikfarjam, Matthew Shardlow, Abeed Sarker, Sophia Ananiadou, & Graciela H. Gonzalez. 2016. Analysis of the Effect of Sentiment Analysis on Extracting Adverse Drug Reactions from Tweets and Forum Posts. *Journal of Biomedical Informatics* 62. 148–58. https://doi.org/10.1016/j.jbi.2016.06.007.

Kortmann, Bernd, Kerstin Lunkenheimer, & Katharina Ehret (eds.). 2020. *The Electronic World Atlas of Varieties of English*. Zenodo. http://ewave-atlas.org.

Krijthe, Jesse. 2014. Rtsne: T-Distributed Stochastic Neighbor Embedding Using a Barnes-Hut Implementation. https://doi.org/10.32614/CRAN.package.Rtsne.

Krippendorff, Klaus. 2004. *Content Analysis: An Introduction to Its Methodology*. 2nd ed. Thousand Oaks, CA: Sage.

Kuya, Aimi. 2021. A Corpus-Based Variationist Approach to the Use of It Is I and It Is Me: A Real-Time Observation of a Syntactic Change Nearing Completion in COHA. *Gengo Kenkyū: Journal of the Linguistic Society of Japan* 159. 7–35.

La Heij, Wido, M. Carmen Puerta-Melguizo, Mark Van Oostrum, & Peter A. Starreveld. 1999. Picture Naming: Identical Priming and Word Frequency Interact. *Acta Psychologica* 102(1). 77–95. https://doi.org/10.1016/S0001-6918(99)00020-7.

Labov, William. 1963. The Social Motivation of a Sound Change. *WORD* 19(3). 273–309. https://doi.org/10.1080/00437956.1963.11659799.

Labov, William. 1982. Building on Empirical Foundations. In Winfred P. Lehmann & Yakov Malkiel (eds.), *Current Issues in Linguistic Theory*, vol. 24, 17–92. Amsterdam: John Benjamins. https://doi.org/10.1075/cilt.24.06lab.

Labov, William. 1990. The Intersection of Sex and Social Class in the Course of Linguistic Change. *Language Variation and Change* 2(2). 205–54. https://doi.org/10.1017/S0954394500000338.

Labov, William. 1994. *Principles of Linguistic Change* (Language in Society 20). Vol. 1: Internal Factors. Oxford: Blackwell.

Labov, William. 2007. Transmission and Diffusion. *Language* 83(2). 344–87. https://doi.org/10.1353/lan.2007.0082.

Labov, William, Paul Cohen, Clarence Robins, & John Lewis. 1968. *A Study of the Non-Standard English of Negro and Puerto Rican Speakers in New York City: Phonological and Grammatical Analysis*. New York: Columbia University.

Labov, William, Ingrid Rosenfelder, & Josef Fruehwald. 2013. One Hundred Years of Sound Change in Philadelphia: Linear Incrementation, Reversal, and Reanalysis. *Language* 89(1). 30–65. https://doi.org/10.1353/lan.2013.0015.

Lai, Randy, Simon Byrne, Douglas Bates, Phillip Alday, Viral B. Shah, Milan Bouchet-Valat, Dave Kleinschmidt, Dilum Aluthge, Changcheng Li, Ranjan Anantharaman, Antoine Baldassari, Steven G. Johnson, Robert Feldt, Páll Haraldsson, Pietro Monticone, Michael Hatherly, Lukas Elmiger, Iain Dunning, Gerhard Aigner, Frankie Robertson, Diego Javier Zea, Avik Sengupta, Alex Arslan, Kevin Squire, Mark Kittisopikul, Morten Piibeleht, and Patrick Kofod Mogensen. 2015. JuliaInterop/RCall.jl. Julia. JuliaInterop. https://github.com/JuliaInterop/RCall.jl (accessed September 26, 2024).

Lakoff, Robin. 1971. Passive Resistance. In Douglas Adams, Mary Ann Campbell, Victor Cohen, Julie Lovins, Edward Maxwell, Carolyn Nygren, & John Reighard (eds.), *Papers from the 7th Regional Meeting of the Chicago Linguistic Society*, 149–62. Chicago: University of Chicago, Chicago Linguistic Society.

Landis, J. Richard, & Gary G. Koch. 1977. The Measurement of Observer Agreement for Categorical Data. *Biometrics* 33(1). 159. https://doi.org/10.2307/2529310.

Langacker, Ronald. 1991. *Foundations of Cognitive Grammar*. Vol. II: Descriptive Application. Stanford: Stanford University Press.

Leech, Geoffrey, Marianne Hundt, Christian Mair, & Nicholas Smith. 2009. *Change in Contemporary English: A Grammatical Study*. 1st ed. Cambridge: Cambridge University Press. https://doi.org/10.1017/CBO9780511642210.

Leech, Geoffrey, Stig Johansson, & Knut Hofland. 1970. *The Lancaster-Oslo/Bergen Corpus (LOB Corpus)*. https://varieng.helsinki.fi/CoRD/corpora/LOB/.

Leech, Geoffrey, & Jan Svartvik. 2002. *A Communicative Grammar of English*. 3rd edn. London: Routledge. https://doi.org/10.4324/9781315836041.

Levelt, Willem J. M, & Stephanie Kelter. 1982. Surface Form and Memory in Question Answering. *Cognitive Psychology* 14(1). 78–106. https://doi.org/10.1016/0010-0285(82)90005-6.

Levin, Beth. 1993. *English Verb Classes and Alternations: A Preliminary Investigation*. Chicago: University of Chicago.

Levin, Beth, & Malka Rappaport. 1986. The Formation of Adjectival Passives. *Linguistic Inquiry* 17(4). 623–61.

Loureiro-Porto, Lucía. 2017. ICE vs GloWbE: Big Data and Corpus Compilation. *World Englishes* 36(3). 448–70. https://doi.org/10.1111/weng.12281.

Lowenberg, Peter H. 1986. Sociolinguistic Context and Second-Language Acquisition: Acculturation and Creativity in Malaysian English. *World Englishes* 5(1). 71–83. https://doi.org/10.1111/j.1467-971X.1986.tb00641.x.

Maaten, Laurens van der, & Geoffrey Hinton. 2008. Visualizing Data Using *t*-SNE. *Journal of Machine Learning Research* 9. 2579–605.

Macaulay, Ronald K. S. 1991. *Locating Dialect in Discourse: The Language of Honest Men and Bonnie Lassies in Ayr*. Oxford: Oxford University Press.

Mair, Christian. 1991. *The Freiburg–LOB Corpus of British English (F-LOB)*. https://varieng.helsinki.fi/CoRD/corpora/FLOB/index.html.

Mair, Christian. 1992. *The Freiburg-Brown Corpus of American English (FROWN)*. https://varieng.helsinki.fi/CoRD/corpora/FROWN/.

Mair, Christian. 1997. The Spread of the Going-to-Future in Written English: A Corpus-Based Investigation into Language Change in Progress. In Raymond Hickey & Stanislaw Puppel (eds.), *Language History and Linguistic Modelling. A Festschrift for Jacek Fisiak*, 1537–43. Berlin: Mouton de Gruyter.

Mair, Christian. 2006. Tracking Ongoing Grammatical Change and Recent Diversification in Present-Day Standard English: The Complementary Role of Small and Large Corpora. In Antoinette Renouf & Andrew Kehoe (eds.), *The Changing Face of Corpus Linguistics* (Language and Computers 55), 355–76. Amsterdam: Brill.

Mair, Christian, & Geoffrey Leech. 2020. Current Changes in English Syntax. In Bas Aarts, April McMahon, & Lars Hinrichs (eds.), *The Handbook of English Linguistics*, 249–76. 2nd ed. Hoboken: Wiley. https://doi.org/10.1002/9781119540618.fmatter.

Mair, Christian, & Andrea Sand. n.d. The English Language in Jamaica. *Professor Mair | Projects*. https://www.anglistik.uni-freiburg.de/sections/linguistics/lsmair/projects/index. (March 20, 2024).

Manning, Christopher D., Prabhakar Raghavan, & Hinrich Schütze. 2008. *Introduction to Information Retrieval*. New York: Cambridge University Press.

Marchman, Virginia A., Elizabeth Bates, Antionette Burkardt, & Amy B. Good. 1991. Functional Constraints of the Acquisition of the Passive: Toward a Model of the Competence to Perform. *First Language* 11(31). 65–92. https://doi.org/10.1177/014272379101103104.

Matthews, Stephen, & Virginia Yip. 1994. *Cantonese: A Comprehensive Grammar*. London: Routledge.

Matzel, Klaus. 1966. *Einführung in die Singhalesische Sprache*. Wiesbaden: Harrassowitz.

McFadden, Daniel. 1974. Conditional Logit Analysis of Qualitative Choice Behavior. In Paul Zarembka (ed.), *Frontiers in Econometrics*, 104–42. New York: Academic Press.

McIntyre, Andrew. 2013. Adjectival Passives and Adjectival Participles in English. In Artemis Alexiadou & Florian Schäfer (eds.), *Linguistik Aktuell/Linguistics Today*, vol. 205, 21–42. Amsterdam: John Benjamins. https://doi.org/10.1075/la.205.02mci.

Mesthrie, Rajend. 2002. South Africa: A Sociolinguistic Overview. In Rajend Mesthrie (ed.), *Language in South Africa*, 11–26. 1st ed. Cambridge: Cambridge University Press. https://doi.org/10.1017/CBO9780511486692.

Mesthrie, Rajend. 2020a. Black South African English. In Bernd Kortmann, Kerstin Lunkenheimer, & Katharina Ehret (eds.), *The Electronic World Atlas of Varieties of English*. http://ewave-atlas.org/languages/49. (December 18, 2024).

Mesthrie, Rajend. 2020b. Indian South African English. In Bernd Kortmann, Kerstin Lunkenheimer, & Katharina Ehret (eds.), *The Electronic World Atlas of Varieties of English*. http://ewave-atlas.org/languages/50. (December 18, 2024).

Mike. 2020. Learning to Speak isiXhosa: Revisiting Its Level of Difficulty. *Mike's Xhosa Challenge*. https://mikesxhosachallenge.wordpress.com/2020/03/15/learning-to-speak-isixhosa-revisiting-its-level-of-difficulty/. (August 1, 2024).

Mikolov, Tomas, Kai Chen, Greg Corrado, & Jeffrey Dean. 2013. Efficient Estimation of Word Representations in Vector Space. In *ICLR Workshop*.

Mikolov, Tomas, Iya Sutskever, Kai Chen, Greg Corrado, & Jeffrey Dean. 2013. Distributed Representations of Words and Phrases and their Compositionality. In *Proceedings of NIPS*, 3111–19. Lake Tahoe.

Mindt, Dieter. 2000. *An Empirical Grammar of the English Verb System*. Berlin: Cornelsen.

Ministry for Ethnic Communities. 2024. Languages Spoken in New Zealand. https://www.ethniccommunities.govt.nz/resources/our-languages-o-tatou-reo/languages-in-new-zealand/.

Mitchell, Jeff, & Mirella Lapata. 2010. Composition in Distributional Models of Semantics. *Cognitive Science* 34(8). 1388–429. https://doi.org/10.1111/j.1551-6709.2010.01106.x.

Mitkovska, Liljana, & Eleni Bužarovska. 2012. An Alternative Analysis of the English *Get*-Past Participle Constructions: Is *Get* All That Passive? *Journal of English Linguistics* 40(2). 196–215. https://doi.org/10.1177/0075424211418978.

Mrkšić, Nikola, Ivan Vulić, Diarmuid Ó Séaghdha, Ira Leviant, Roi Reichart, Milica Gašić, Anna Korhonen, & Steve Young. 2017. Semantic Specialization of Distributional Word Vector Spaces Using Monolingual and Cross-Lingual Constraints. *Transactions of the Association for Computational Linguistics* 5. 309–24. https://doi.org/10.1162/tacl_a_00063.

Murray, Thomas E. 1993. Positive Anymore in the Midwest. In Timothy C. Frazer (ed.), *Heartland English: Variation and Transition in the American Midwest* (Centennial Series of the American Dialect Society), 173–86. Tuscaloosa: University of Alabama Press.

Newman, Paul. 2000. *The Hausa Language: An Encyclopedic Reference Grammar*. New Haven: Yale University Press.

Nguyen, Dong, A. Seza Doğruöz, Carolyn P. Rosé, & Franciska De Jong. 2016. Computational Sociolinguistics: A Survey. *Computational Linguistics* 42(3). 537–93. https://doi.org/10.1162/COLI_a_00258.

Nickel, Maximillian, & Douwe Kiela. 2017. Poincaré Embeddings for Learning Hierarchical Representations. In I. Guyon, U. Von Luxburg, S. Bengio, H. Wallach, R. Fergus, S. Vishwanathan, & R. Garnett (eds.), *Advances in Neural Information Processing Systems*, vol. 30. Curran Associates. https://proceedings.neurips.cc/paper_files/paper/2017/file/59dfa2df42d9e3d41f5b02bfc32229dd-Paper.pdf.

Nielsen, Finn Årup. 2011. A New ANEW: Evaluation of a Word List for Sentiment Analysis in Microblogs. arXiv. http://arxiv.org/abs/1103.2903. (November 7, 2024).

Nthoba, Maria Busisiwe. 1995. *The Passive and Contactive Extensions of IsiZulu* Johannesburg: University of Johannesburg. https://ujcontent.uj.ac.za/esploro/outputs/9912069007691#file-0. (August 1, 2024).

Núñez Pertejo, Paloma. 2017. Terrific-Looking Creatures and Terrific, Funny Guys: On the Historical Development of English Terrific. *Miscelánea: A Journal of English and American Studies* 55. 65–85. https://doi.org/10.26754/ojs_misc/mj.20176815.

Obi-Okoye, A. 2008. *An Introduction to Applied English Linguistics*. Enugu: Frefabag.

Ojiambo, Peter. 2022. Kiswahili Darasa la Kwanza. University of Kansas Open Resource Publications. https://kiswahili.ku.edu/sites/kiswahili/files/documents/lessons/lesson_58.pdf.

Oliphant, Margaret. 1877. *The Makers of Florence: Dante, Giotto, Savonarola; and their City*. London: Macmillan.

Ostergaard, Arne L. 1998. The Effects on Priming of Word Frequency, Number of Repetitions, and Delay Depend on the Magnitude of Priming. *Memory & Cognition* 26(1). 40–60. https://doi.org/10.3758/BF03211369.

Paolini, Chiara, Benedikt Szmrecsanyi, Mariana Montes, Hubert Cuyckens, & KU Leuven. 2023. Distributional Semantics and the English Dative

Alternation: Recipient and Theme Slots Matter (to Some Extent). *Paper of the Linguistic Society of Belgium* 17. https://doi.org/10.61430/CSGM7397.

Parliament of Australia. 2022. Parliament Explained: Federation. *Parliament of Australia*. https://www.aph.gov.au/About_Parliament/House_of_Representatives/About_the_House_News/News/Parliament_Explained_Federation. (9 December, 2024).

Patrick, Peter L. 2008. Pidgins, Creoles, and Variation. In Silvia Kouwenberg & John V. Singler (eds.), *The Handbook of Pidgin and Creole Studies*, 461–88. Malden, MA: Wiley-Blackwell.

Pennington, Jeffrey, Richard Socher, & Christopher Manning. 2014. Glove: Global Vectors for Word Representation. In *Proceedings of the 2014 Conference on Empirical Methods in Natural Language Processing (EMNLP)*, 1532–43. Doha, Qatar: Association for Computational Linguistics. https://doi.org/10.3115/v1/D14-1162.

Perek, Florent. 2016. Using Distributional Semantics to Study Syntactic Productivity in Diachrony: A Case Study. *Linguistics* 54(1). 149–88. https://doi.org/10.1515/ling-2015-0043.

Perek, Florent. 2018. Recent Change in the Productivity and Schematicity of the *Way* -Construction: A Distributional Semantic Analysis. *Corpus Linguistics and Linguistic Theory* 14(1). 65–97. https://doi.org/10.1515/cllt-2016-0014.

Persson, Gunnar. 1990. *Meanings, Models and Metaphors: A Study in Lexical Semantics in English*. Stockholm: Almqvist and Wiksell.

Peters, Matthew, Mark Neumann, Mohit Iyyer, Matt Gardner, Christopher Clark, Kenton Lee, & Luke Zettlemoyer. 2018. Deep Contextualized Word Representations. In *Proceedings of the 2018 Conference of the North American Chapter of the Association for Computational Linguistics: Human Language Technologies, Volume 1 (Long Papers)*, 2227–37. New Orleans, Louisiana: Association for Computational Linguistics. https://doi.org/10.18653/v1/N18-1202.

Philippine Statistics Authoriry. 2023. Population and Housing | Ethnicity in the Philippines (2020 Census of Population and Housing). https://psa.gov.ph/statistics/population-and-housing/node/1684059978. (August 1, 2024).

Phoocharoensil, Supakorn. 2020. English Get-Passives: Reassessing the Frequencies across Genres. *GEMA Online® Journal of Language Studies* 20(3). 123–35. https://doi.org/10.17576/gema-2020-2003-08.

Pinker, Steven, David S. Lebeaux, & Loren Ann Frost. 1987. Productivity and Constraints in the Acquisition of the Passive. *Cognition* 26(3). 195–267. https://doi.org/10.1016/S0010-0277(87)80001-X.

Polinsky, Maria. 2020. *Heritage Languages and Their Speakers*. Cambridge: Cambridge University.

Polyglot Wiki. 2023. Sinhala Grammar → Unit 5: Advanced Grammar → Passive Voice. https://polyglotclub.com/wiki/Language/Sinhala/Grammar/Passive-Voice. (August 1, 2024).

Poplack, Shana. 1980. The Notion of the Plural in Puerto Rican English: Competing Constraints on (s) Deletion. In William Labov (ed.), *Locating Language in Time and Space* (Quantitative Analyses of Linguistic Structure 1), 55–68. New York: Academic Press.

Posit PBC. 2023. Quarto. https://quarto.org/.

Posit Team. 2023. RStudio: Integrated Development Environment for R. Boston, MA: Posit Software, PBC. http://www.posit.co/.

Powell, George. 1693. A Very Good Wife. Theater play. London, ms.

Princeton University. 2010. About WordNet. Princeton University. https://wordnet.princeton.edu/.

Pullum, Geoffrey. 2014. Fear and Loathing of the English Passive. *Language & Communication* 37. 60–74.

Puschmann, Cornelius, Hevin Karakurt, Carolin Amlinger, Nicola Gess, & Oliver Nachtwey. 2022. RPC-Lex: A Dictionary to Measure German Right-Wing Populist Conspiracy Discourse Online. *Convergence: The International Journal of Research into New Media Technologies* 28(4). 1144–71. https://doi.org/10.1177/13548565221109440.

Quinn, Jacob. 2015. JuliaData Contributors, & Julia Computing/CSV.jl. Julia. JuliaData. https://github.com/JuliaData/CSV.jl (accessed September 26, 2024).

Quirk, Randolph, Sidney Greenbaum, Geoffrey Leech, & Jan Svartvik. 1985. *A Comprehensive Grammar of the English Language*. London: Longman.

R Core Team. 2023. *R: A Language and Environment for Statistical Computing*. Vienna: R Foundation for Statistical Computing. http://www.r-project.org/index.html.

Ragini, J. Rexiline, P.M. Rubesh Anand, & Vidhyacharan Bhaskar. 2018. Big Data Analytics for Disaster Response and Recovery through Sentiment Analysis. *International Journal of Information Management* 42. 13–24. https://doi.org/10.1016/j.ijinfomgt.2018.05.004.

Rahim, Hajar A., & Shakila A. Manan. 2014. Postcolonial Malaysian English: Realities and Prospects. In Hajar A. Rahim & Shakila A. Manan (eds.), *English in Malaysia*, 9–34. Bern: Peter Lang.

Rahman, Tariq. 2020. Pakistani English. In Kingsley Bolton, Werner Botha, & Andy Kirkpatrick (eds.), *The Handbook of Asian Englishes*, 279–96. Hoboken, NJ: Wiley Blackwell.

Rauh, Christian. 2018. Validating a Sentiment Dictionary for German Political Language: A Workbench Note. *Journal of Information Technology & Politics* 15(4). 319–43. https://doi.org/10.1080/19331681.2018.1485608.

Reed, Lisa A. 2011. Get-Passives. *The Linguistic Review* 28(1). https://doi.org/10.1515/tlir.2011.002.

Řehůřek, Radim, & Petr Sojka. 2010. Software Framework for Topic Modelling with Large Corpora. In *Workshop on New Challenges for NLP Framework*, 46–50. Malta: University of Malta. https://doi.org/10.13140/2.1.2393.1847.

Rice, Wallace. 1932. Get and Got. *American Speech* 7(4). 280–96. https://doi.org/10.2307/451908.

Rohdenburg, Günter. 2003. Cognitive Complexity and Horror Aequi as Factors Determining the Use of Interrogative Clause Linkers in English. In Günter Rohdenburg & Britta Mondorf (eds.), *Determinants of Grammatical Variation in English* (Topics in English Linguistics 43), 205–49. Berlin: Mouton de Gruyter.

Roller, Stephen, & Katrin Erk. 2016. Relations such as Hypernymy: Identifying and Exploiting Hearst Patterns in Distributional Vectors for Lexical Entailment. arXiv. https://doi.org/10.48550/ARXIV.1605.05433.

Rosenfeld, Alex Bryant. 2019. Computational Models of Changes in Language Use. The University of Texas at Austin. https://doi.org/10.26153/TSW/12537.

Rosenfeld, Alex, & Lars Hinrichs. 2023. Capturing Fine-Grained Regional Differences in Language Use through Voting Precinct Embeddings. *Computational Linguistics* 49(4). 883–942. https://doi.org/10.1162/coli_a_00487.

Rossum, Guido van, & Fred L. Drake. 2009. *Python 3 Reference Manual.* Scotts Valley, CA: CreateSpace. https://www.python.org.

Rühlemann, Christoph. 2007. Lexical Grammar: The GET-Passive as a Case in Point. *ICAME Journal* 31. 111–27.

Sagi, Eyal, Stefan Kaufmann, & Brady Clark. 2011. Tracing Semantic Change with Latent Semantic Analysis. In Kathryn Allan & Justyna A. Robinson (eds.), *Current Methods in Historical Semantics*, 161–83. Berlin: De Gruyter. https://doi.org/10.1515/9783110252903.

Sand, Andrea. 2013. Jamaican English. In Bernd Kortmann & Kerstin Lunkenheimer (eds.), *The Mouton World Atlas of Variation in English*, 210–21. Berlin: De Gruyter. https://doi.org/10.1515/9783110280128.210.

Sankoff, David, & Suzanne Laberge. 1978. Statistical Dependence among Successive Occurrences of a Variable in Discourse. In *Linguistic Variation: Methods and Models*, 119–26. New York: Academic Press.

Schachter, Paul. 1975. The Subject in Philippine Languages: Topic, Actor, Actor-Topic, or None of the Above. In Charles Li (ed.), *Subject and Topic*, 491–518. New York: Academic Press.

Schachter, Paul, & Fé T. Otanes. 1972. *Tagalog Reference Grammar.* Berkeley: University of California Press.

Scherre, Maria Marta Pereira, & Anthony J. Naro. 1991. Marking in Discourse: "Birds of a Feather." *Language Variation and Change* 3(1). 23–32. https://doi.org/10.1017/S0954394500000430.

Schmied, Josef. 2013. Tanzanian English. In Bernd Kortmann & Kerstin Lunkenheimer (eds.), *The Mouton World Atlas of Variation in English*, 454–65. Berlin: De Gruyter Mouton.

Schneider, Edgar W. 2007. *Postcolonial English: Varieties around the World.* 1st edn. Cambridge: Cambridge University Press. https://doi.org/10.1017/CBO9780511618901.

Schneider, Edgar W. 2011. *English around the World: An Introduction*. 1st ed. Cambridge: Cambridge University Press. https://doi.org/10.1017/CBO9780511781711.

Schwarz, Gideon. 1978. Estimating the Dimension of a Model. *Annals of Statistics* 6(2). 461–4. https://doi.org/10.1214/aos/1176344136.

Schwarz, Sarah. 2015. Passive Voice in American Soap Opera Dialogue. *Studia Neophilologica* 87(2). 152–70. https://doi.org/10.1080/00393274.2015.1049831.

Schwarz, Sarah. 2017. "Like Getting Nibbled to Death by a Duck": Grammaticalization of the Get-Passive in the TIME Magazine Corpus. *English World-Wide* 38(3). 305–35. https://doi.org/10.1075/eww.38.3.03sch.

Schwarz, Sarah. 2018. *Passive Voices: Be-, Get- and Prepositional Passives in Recent American English*. Uppsala: Uppsala University PhD thesis.

Schweinberger, Martin. 2019. A Sociolinguistic Analysis of Emotives. *Corpus Pragmatics* 3. 327–61. https://doi.org/10.1007/s41701-019-00062-z.

Scrucca, Luca, Chris Fraley, T. Brendan Murphy, & Raftery Adrian E. 2023. *Model-Based Clustering, Classification, and Density Estimation Using mclust in R*. 1st ed. Boca Raton: Chapman and Hall/CRC. https://doi.org/10.1201/9781003277965.

Sharef, Nurfadhlina Mohd, Harnani Mat Zin, & Samaneh Nadali. 2016. Overview and Future Opportunities of Sentiment Analysis Approaches for Big Data. *Journal of Computer Sciences* 12. 153–68.

Shastri, S.V. 1988. The Kolhapur Corpus of Indian English and Work Done on Its Basis So Far. *ICAME Journal* 12. 15–26.

Sinclair, John. 2000. Lexical Grammar. *Naujoji Metodologija* 24. 191–203.

Smith, Adam, & Pam Peters. 2023. Australian Corpus of English (ACE). Macquarie University. https://doi.org/10.25949/24629712.V1.

Smith, Nicholas, & Paul Rayson. 2007. Recent Change and Variation in the British English Use of the Progressive Passive. *ICAME Journal* 31. 129–59.

Sneller, Betsy, & Sabriya Fisher. 2015. When Get Got Noticed: The Emerging Salience of Get-Passives. *University of Pennsylvania Working Papers in Linguistics* 21(1). 1–9.

Statista. 2024. Total Population of South Africa in 2022, by Ethnic Groups. *South Africa: Population, by Ethnic Groups 2022*. https://www.statista.com/statistics/1116076/total-population-of-south-africa-by-population-group/. (December 9, 2024).

Statistics Canada. 2022. Mother Tongue by Geography, 2021 Census. https://www12.statcan.gc.ca/census-recensement/2021/dp-pd/dv-vd/language-langue/index-en.html. (July 30, 2024).

Statistics South Africa. 2024. Statistics South Africa. Census Dissemination. https://census.statssa.gov.za/#/statsbytheme. (August 1, 2024).

Stein, Gabriele. 1979. *Studies in the Function of the Passive*. Tübingen: Gunter Narr Verlag.

Strelluf, Christopher, & Thomas Hills. 2021. Examining Emotionally Negative Affect in Syntactically Positive-Anymore through Sentiment Analysis of Tweets. Presentation at New Ways of Analyzing Variation (NWAV) 49. Austin, TX.

Sussex, Roland. 1982. A Note on the *Get*-Passive Construction. *Australian Journal of Linguistics* 2(1). 83–95. https://doi.org/10.1080/07268608208599283.

Svartvik, Jan. 1966. *On Voice in the English Verb*. The Hague: Mouton.

Svartvik, Jan, & Randolph Quirk. 1959. *The London-Lund Corpus of Spoken English (LLC)*. https://varieng.helsinki.fi/CoRD/corpora/LLC/.

Szmrecsanyi, Benedikt. 2006. *Morphosyntactic Persistence in Spoken English: A Corpus Study at the Intersection of Variationist Sociolinguistics, Psycholinguistics, and Discourse Analysis*. Berlin: Mouton de Gruyter.

Szmrecsanyi, Benedikt, Jason Grafmiller, Benedikt Heller, & Melanie Röthlisberger. 2016. Around the World in Three Alternations: Modeling Syntactic Variation in Global Varieties of English. *English World-Wide* 37(2). 109–37. https://doi.org/10.1075/eww.37.2.01szm.

Tagliamonte, Sali. 2011. *Variationist Sociolinguistics: Change, Observation, Interpretation* (Language in Society 40). Malden, MA: Wiley-Blackwell.

Tamminga, Meredith. 2016. Persistence in Phonological and Morphological Variation. *Language Variation and Change* 28(3). 335–56. https://doi.org/10.1017/S0954394516000119.

Terassa, Laura. 2017. *Morphological Simplification in Asian Englishes: Frequency, Substratum Transfer, and Institutionalization*. Freiburg: FreiDok plus. https://freidok.uni-freiburg.de/data/17386.

The World Factbook. 2024. Sri Lanka. *The World Factbook*. Central Intelligence Agency. https://www.cia.gov/the-world-factbook/countries/sri-lanka/. (August 1, 2024).

Tinker, Hugh Russel, & Syed Sajjad Husain. 2024. Bangladesh. History, Capital, Map, Flag, Population, & Facts. *Britannica*. https://www.britannica.com/place/Bangladesh. (February 27, 2024).

Tolstaya, Natalya. 1981. *The Panjabi Language: A Descriptive Grammar* (Languages of Asia and Africa 2). English ed., translated from Russian by G. L. Campbell. London: Routledge.

Toyota, Junichi. 2007. An Adversative Passive in English: In Search of Origins. In Nicole Delbecque & Bert Cornillie (eds.), *On Interpreting Construction Schemas: From Action and Motion to Transitivity and Causality* (Trends in Linguistics 198), 143–70. Berlin: De Gruyter Mouton.

Toyota, Junichi. 2008. *Diachronic Change in the English Passive* (Palgrave Studies in Language History and Language Change). Basingstoke: Palgrave Macmillan.

Toyota, Junichi. 2009. Fossilisation of Passive in English: Analysis of Passive Verbs. *English Studies* 90(4). 476–97. https://doi.org/10.1080/00138380902990283.

Traugott, Elizabeth Closs, & Graeme Trousdale. 2013. *Constructionalization and Constructional Changes* (Oxford Studies in Diachronic and Historical Linguistics). Oxford: Oxford University Press.

Turney, P. D., & P. Pantel. 2010. From Frequency to Meaning: Vector Space Models of Semantics. *Journal of Artificial Intelligence Research* 37. 141–88. https://doi.org/10.1613/jair.2934.

University of Cambridge Language Centre Resources. Zulu. https://www.langcen.cam.ac.uk/resources/langz/zulu.html. (August 1, 2024).

US Census Bureau. 2024. QuickFacts. https://www.census.gov/quickfacts/fact/table/US/RHI225223#RHI225223. (July 30, 2024).

Vanrespaille, Mia. 1991. A Semantic Analysis of the English Get-Passive. *Journal of Applied Linguistics* 5 (2). 95–112.

Vendler, Zeno. 1957. Verbs and Times. *Philosophical Review* 66(2). 143. https://doi.org/10.2307/2182371.

Viola, Lorella. 2023. On the Use of Sentiment Analysis for Linguistics Research. Observations on Sentiment Polarity and the Use of the Progressive in Italian. *Frontiers in Artificial Intelligence*. 1–9. https://doi.org/10.3389/frai.2023.1101364.

Wagner, Susanne. 2017. Totally New and Pretty Awesome: Amplifier–Adjective Bigrams in GloWbE. *Lingua* 200. 63–83.

Wang, Li. 1982. *Hanyu yufa gangyao [An Outline of Chinese Grammar]*. Shanghai: Shanghai Education Press.

Wankhade, Mayur, Annavarapu Chandra Sekhara Rao, & Chaitanya Kulkarni. 2022. A Survey on Sentiment Analysis Methods, Applications, and Challenges. *Artificial Intelligence Review* 55(7). 5731–80. https://doi.org/10.1007/s10462-022-10144-1.

Wanner, Anja. 2009. *Deconstructing the English Passive*. Berlin: Walter de Gruyter.

Wanner, Anja. 2013. The Get-Passive at the Intersection of Get and the Passive. In Artemis Alexiadou & Florian Schäfer (eds.), *Non-Canonical Passives*, 43–62. John Benjamins. https://doi.org/10.1075/la.205.

Ward, Joe H. 1963. Hierarchical Grouping to Optimize an Objective Function. *Journal of the American Statistical Association* 58(301). 236–44. https://doi.org/10.1080/01621459.1963.10500845.

Wasow, Thomas. 1977. Transformations and the Lexicon. In P. W. Culicover, Thomas Wasow, & A. Akmajian (eds.), *Formal Syntax*, 327–60. New York: Academic Press.

Wei, Hang, Yanping Dong, Julie E. Boland, & Fang Yuan. 2016. Structural Priming and Frequency Effects Interact in Chinese Sentence Comprehension. *Frontiers in Psychology* 7. 1–9. https://doi.org/10.3389/fpsyg.2016.00045.

Weiner, Judith E., & William Labov. 1983. Constraints on the Agentless Passive. *Journal of Linguistics* 19(1). 29–58.

Wickham, Hadley, Mara Averick, Jennifer Bryan, Winston Chang, Lucy McGowan, Romain François, Garrett Grolemund, Alex Hayes, Lionel Henry, Jim Hester, Max Kuhn, Thomas Lin Pedersen, Evan Miller, Stephan Milton Bache, Kirill Müller, Jeroen Ooms, David Robinson, Dana Paige Seidel, Vitalie Spinu, Kohske Takahashi, Davis Vaughan, Claus Wilke, Kara Woo, and Hiroaki Yutani. 2019. Welcome to the Tidyverse. *Journal of Open Source Software* 4(43). 1686. https://doi.org/10.21105/joss.01686.

Wijayawardhana, G. D., Daya Wickramasinghe & Theodora Bynon. 1995. Passive-Related Constructions in Sinhala. In David Bennett, Theodora Bynon, & George

Hewitt (eds.), *Subject, Voice and Ergativity: Selected Essays*, 105–41. London: School of Oriental and African Studies.

Wiktionary. 2024. Kena. *Wiktionary, the Free Dictionary*. https://en.wiktionary.org/w/index.php?title=kena&oldid=79357461. (August 1, 2024).

Winford, Donald. 1993. *Predication in Caribbean English Creoles* (Creole Language Library 10). Amsterdam: John Benjamins.

Winter, Bodo. 2019. *Statistics for Linguists: An Introduction Using R*. New York: Routledge.

Xiao, Richard Z., Tony McEnery, & Yufang Qian. 2006. Passive Constructions in English and Chinese: A Corpus-Based Contrastive Study. *Languages in Contrast* 6(1). 109–49. https://doi.org/10.1075/lic.6.1.05xia.

Yamamoto, Mutsumi. 1999. *Animacy and Reference: A Cognitive Approach to Corpus Linguistics* (Studies in Language Companion Series 46). Amsterdam: John Benjamins.

Zaenen, Annie, Jean Carletta, Gregory Garretson, Joan Bresnan, Andrew Koontz-Garboden, Tatiana Nikitina, M. Catherine O'Connor, & Tom Wasow. 2004. Animacy Encoding in English: Why and How. In *Proceedings of the Workshop on Discourse Annotation*, 118–25. Barcelona: Association for Computational Linguistics.

Zhu, Hao, Thomas Travison, Timothy Tsai, Will Beasley, Yihui Xie, GuangChuang Yu, Stéphane Laurent, Rob Shepherd, Yoni Sidi, Brian Salzer, George Gui, Yeliang Fan, Duncan Murdoch, Vincent Arel-Bundock, and Bill Evans. 2021. kableExtra: Construct Complex Table with "kable" and Pipe Syntax. R (≥ 3.1.0). https://cran.r-project.org/web/packages/kableExtra/index.html (accessed September 26, 2024).

Zhu, Yongping, & Chu-Ren Huang. 2023. *A Student Grammar of Chinese*. Cambridge: Cambridge University Press. https://doi.org/10.1017/9781009233507.

Zimmermann, Richard. 2019. Studying Semantic Chain Shifts with Word2Vec: FOOD>MEAT>FLESH. In *Proceedings of the 1st International Workshop on Computational Approaches to Historical Language Change*, 23–8. Florence, Italy: Association for Computational Linguistics. https://doi.org/10.18653/v1/W19-4703.

Zong, Jie, Jeanne Batalova, & Jeffrey Hallock. 2018. Frequently Requested Statistics on Immigrants and Immigration in the United States. The Online Journal of the Migration Policy Institute. *Migration Information Source*. https://www.migrationpolicy.org/article/frequently-requested-statistics-immigrants-and-immigration-united-states-7. (January 25, 2019).

Index

www.ingramcontent.com/pod-product-compliance
Ingram Content Group UK Ltd.
Pitfield, Milton Keynes, MK11 3LW, UK
UKHW020250290926
15470UKWH00002B/836